Prevent-Teach-Reinforce for Young Children

Prevent-Teach-Reinforce for Young Children
The Early Childhood Model of Individualized Positive Behavior Support

by

Glen Dunlap, Ph.D.
University of South Florida
University of Nevada, Reno

Kelly Wilson
Bal Swan Children's Center and
Colorado Department of Education

Phillip Strain, Ph.D.
University of Colorado Denver

and

Janice K. Lee, M.Ed.
University of Nevada, Reno

·P·A·U·L·H·
BROOKES
PUBLISHING CO.®

Baltimore • London • Sydney

Paul H. Brookes Publishing Co.
Post Office Box 10624
Baltimore, Maryland 21285-0624

www.brookespublishing.com

Typeset by Integrated Publishing Solutions
Manufactured in the United States of America by
Versa Press, Inc., East Peoria, Illinois.

Individuals in this book are composites based on the authors' experiences. In all instances, identifying details have been changed to protect confidentiality.

Library of Congress Cataloging-in-Publication Data

Prevent-teach-reinforce for young children : the early childhood model of individualized positive behavior
  support / by Glen Dunlap ... [et al.].
    p.   cm.
  Includes bibliographical references and index.
  ISBN-13: 978-1-59857-250-6 (pbk.)
  ISBN-10: 1-59857-250-4 (pbk.)
  1. Social skills—Study and teaching (Early childhood)   2. Behavior disorders in children—Prevention.
  3. Early childhood education.   4. Child development.   I. Dunlap, Glen.
  LB1139.S6 P74
  303.3'24—dc23   2012031591

British Library Cataloguing in Publication data are available from the British Library.

2022 2021 2020 2019

10   9   8   7   6

Contents

Contents of the Accompanying CD-ROM

About the Authors

Glen Dunlap, Ph.D., is a research professor at the University of South Florida in Tampa and the University of Nevada, Reno, where he works on research, training, and demonstration projects in the areas of positive behavior support, child protection, early intervention, developmental disabilities, and family support. He has been involved with individuals with disabilities for more than 40 years and has served as a teacher, administrator, researcher, and university faculty member. He has directed numerous research and training projects and has been awarded dozens of federal and state grants to pursue this work. He has authored more than 220 articles and book chapters, co-edited 4 books, and served on 15 editorial boards. Dr. Dunlap was a founding editor of the *Journal of Positive Behavior Interventions* and is the current editor of *Topics in Early Childhood Special Education.*

Kelly Wilson, B.S., works on two projects that utilize the principles of implementation science to directly support systems change and implementation of evidence-based practices to a level of fidelity that affects common practice and child outcomes. In addition to supporting systems change, she also provides training and focused support to staff, teachers, and families in the Pyramid Model and challenging behaviors using the Prevent-Teach-Reinforce (PTR) process. Previously, Ms. Wilson worked for the University of Colorado Denver for 13 years as a research assistant. She spent 5 years working on PTR research by supporting staff, teachers, and families with children with severe and persistent challenging behavior. She also worked as a consultant for Learning Experiences: An Alternative Program for Preschoolers and Parents (LEAP) Outreach Project, providing consultation in early childhood to preschools and elementary schools serving children with autism and challenging behaviors. Ms. Wilson has been involved in almost every aspect of early intervention and general and special education, with a special emphasis on children with challenging behaviors. She is the mother of four extraordinary children who all have fragile X syndrome and has experience with challenging behavior at a personal as well as a professional level. She has extensive experience as a trainer, coach, and mentor, and she specializes in challenging behavior and inclusive education.

Phillip Strain, Ph.D., is Professor of Educational Psychology and Director of the Positive Early Learning Experiences Center in the School of Education and Human Development at the University of Colorado Denver. Dr. Strain is the author of more than 300 professional papers that have focused on young children with autism, prevention of challenging behavior, and inclusion practices. In his 4 decades in the field, he has been a teacher, early intervention program administrator, and university professor. Dr. Strain's research on challenging behavior and autism has received more than 50 million dollars in grant support, and this work has garnered multiple career achievement awards.

Janice K. Lee, M.Ed., is a member of the research faculty at the University of Nevada, Reno, where she is the research coordinator for the randomized control trial of PTR-YC in Northern Nevada. In her role with Positive Behavior Support–Nevada, she is the coordinator for the statewide initiative to bring programwide Pyramid Model implementation and information to all early care and education settings throughout the state. Her experience and interests include early childhood, challenging behavior, positive behavior support, social and emotional development, autism, and working with families. She has a master's degree in early childhood special education. Since 1995, she has worked with children, families, practitioners, and professionals at the local, state, and national level as a consultant, coach, trainer, and technical assistance provider.

Foreword

In my first week as a student teacher, I was leading a large group activity when Lucy raised her hand. With a smile on her face, she said, "Ms. ML, I'm tired of this sh**." Having been trained to ignore such behavior, I continued the activity and pretended that I had not heard her. However, it was only a matter of seconds before she yelled, at the top of her lungs, a name that I cannot repeat here. Lucy's challenging behaviors were frequent, intense, disruptive, and often dangerous, and no one seemed to know what to do with her. I thought I knew about behavior management, but I didn't know where to start with Lucy. Anyone who has worked with young children has had a "Lucy" in their classroom. Working with children like Lucy is frustrating and challenging to even the most experienced teachers. Teachers report that dealing with children with challenging behavior is a primary training need and a factor that affects their job satisfaction (Burke, Greenglass, & Schwarzer, 1996; Hemmeter, Corso, & Cheatham, 2006).

Several years ago, a group of colleagues and I developed The Pyramid Model for Promoting Social Emotional Competence in Young Children (Fox, Dunlap, Hemmeter, Joseph, & Strain, 2003). The Pyramid Model is a tiered model that includes universal strategies for promoting the social-emotional competence of all young children; secondary strategies for children who are at-risk for or have some level of social, emotional, or behavioral issue; and tertiary interventions for children with ongoing, persistent problem behavior. The concurrent implementation of all levels of practice is necessary for addressing the needs of all children in a preschool classroom. Since 2000, we have conducted research on the Pyramid Model, trained thousands of early childhood professionals to use the practices associated with the Pyramid Model, and worked with states and programs to build systems to support the implementation of the model across early childhood service delivery systems. Across these efforts, we have found that one of the most challenging aspects of implementing the Pyramid Model is developing and delivering tertiary interventions for children with the most persistent and ongoing challenging behavior. Although many early childhood educators have received training on prevention and promotion practices, relatively few have received training on the type of intervention approach that is needed for young children with ongoing and persistent challenging behavior.

The book before you now, *Prevent-Teach-Reinforce for Young Children* (PTR-YC), was developed in response to the need for materials to support early childhood educators in designing and implementing tertiary supports for children with the most severe challenging behavior. Compared with the resources available on individualized behavior support planning for older children, there are relatively few resources available that clearly articulate the process for developing individualized behavior support plans for preschool-age children. PTR-YC is based on many years of research on designing and implementing tertiary supports for children with ongoing and persistent challenging behavior (e.g., Dunlap & Fox, 2011; Sailor, Dunlap, Sugai, & Horner, 2009). This research has resulted in a clearly defined process for developing and delivering individualized behavior support that is effective when implemented in a range of settings (e.g., preschool, elementary, and high school classrooms; homes; child care) by a range of people (e.g., teachers, family members). Although the major components of individualized behavior support planning (e.g., teaming, functional assessment, intervention planning) are similar across age ranges, the procedures and strategies must be tailored to the developmental needs of young children and the unique characteristics of early childhood settings (Fox & Hemmeter, 2009).

To ensure that PTR-YC reflects the unique needs of young children and the characteristics of early childhood settings, the authors identified a set of guiding assumptions about young children and social-emotional development in the early childhood years. These guiding assumptions, which are consistent with developmentally appropriate practice guidelines (Copple & Bredekamp, 2009), are reflected throughout the PTR-YC process:

1. *Healthy social-emotional development* is a primary emphasis in the early childhood years and is the context in which children learn.

2. Social behaviors are learned in social contexts, so it is important for children with challenging behaviors to be *included* in settings where they can learn from more skilled peers.

3. Many challenging behaviors and the magnitude of challenging behavior can be *prevented* through the use of effective universal promotion and prevention strategies.

4. *Comprehensive* approaches will be needed to resolve some children's challenging behavior.

5. *Including and supporting families* should be an integral component of developing behavior support plans for individual children.

Central to PTR-YC is a focus on the implementation of universal classroom practices that serve to prevent challenging behavior and promote social-emotional competence. The authors describe five universal classroom practices that should be in place prior to implementing individualized plans. Universal practices are less time consuming than individualized plans, support all children, and reduce the need for more intensive interventions for some children. Furthermore, the implementation of high-quality, universal practices provides a critical context for implementing individualized behavior supports. The authors recommend use of a broad validated approach for promoting healthy social-emotional development and preventing the emergence of challenging behavior as a context for implementing PTR-YC. Within a tiered model of behavior support, PTR-YC is a process for developing tertiary interventions.

The goal of the PTR-YC process is to develop an individualized behavior support plan based on an understanding of a child's challenging behavior and how that behavior is influenced by events that occur in the child's environment. The process is based on three principles of behavior: 1) challenging behaviors are communicative, 2) challenging behaviors are maintained by their consequences, and 3) challenging behaviors occur in context. These principles guide the assessment process that is used to identify strategies for each of the three components of a behavior support plan (i.e., *Prevent* strategies, *Teach* strategies, *Reinforce* strategies). Understanding how a child's behavior occurs in context leads to environmental or antecedent arrangements that serve to promote appropriate behavior and *prevent* challenging behavior. Understanding how a child's challenging behavior is communicative leads to strategies for *teaching* children more appropriate ways to communicate. Finally, understanding how a child's behavior is maintained by social responses from adults and peers leads to strategies that involve modifying consequences such as *reinforcement*. By connecting principles of behavior to the components of the behavior support plan, the authors have provided a context for understanding why all components of a behavior support plan are needed and why the process is likely to be effective in reducing problem behavior.

This manual includes a comprehensive list of strategies for each component of the behavior support plan: *Prevent, Teach, Reinforce.* For each strategy, the authors provide a description of the strategy, a rationale for the strategy, examples of how the strategy could be used, steps for implementation, special considerations, and supporting evidence. The list and description of the strategies is comprehensive and user friendly, and these strategies alone would be an invaluable resource for early childhood educators. Although they were developed for use in individualized behavior support plans, the strategies can be used to support all children.

The PTR-YC process is implemented using five steps: 1) establishing a team and goal setting, 2) data collection, 3) PTR-YC assessment (functional behavioral assessment), 4) PTR-YC intervention (developing a behavior support plan), and 5) using data and next steps. For each step, there is a self-evaluation checklist that teams can use to ensure that they are completing all necessary activities. Four case studies are included to provide examples of how each step is implemented. The case studies include a range of children, family situations, contexts, and professionals. Finally, there is a thorough description of how to plan for and evaluate the implementation of the plan. This will be a critical step in ensuring that plans are implemented with fidelity.

The authors acknowledge that PTR-YC requires a commitment of time and resources that may be challenging for some early childhood programs. They spend a great deal of time throughout the manual focusing on prevention as one way to reduce the need for the PTR-YC process, while emphasizing that there are some children whose behavior will require more intensive supports even when promotion and prevention practices are in place. The authors strike a nice balance between ensuring the process is implemented with fidelity and making the process feasible for implementation in classroom settings.

PTR-YC represents an important step in supporting the implementation of behavior support planning in early childhood settings. The authors have developed and described a process of behavior support that reflects a commitment to both evidenced-based practice and implementation in "real-world" settings.

The collective experience of the authors is evident throughout this manual. Across the group of authors, they have many years of experience as parents of children with challenging behavior, teachers, administrators, trainers, and researchers. This experience is evident in the care with which they describe the process, the wide range of examples they use, the inclusion of forms and materials that guide the team toward implementation fidelity, and the honesty with which they consider the benefits and limitations of the process. Furthermore, they have created a process that is not only effective and feasible, but which will be acceptable to the early childhood community. They did not merely "pull down" an approach that worked with older children, but they carefully considered the needs of young children, the context of early childhood programs, and the beliefs and commitment of early childhood educators. They clarified terminology that might be unfamiliar to early childhood educators (e.g., applied behavior analysis, positive behavior support) and addressed issues that might be philosophically challenging (e.g., time-out, praise). The authors have provided our field with an incredibly valuable tool. Now, the challenge for the early childhood field is to design systems for training and supporting professionals to implement this process in all programs serving young children and their families.

Mary Louise Hemmeter, Ph.D.
Associate Professor of Special Education and
Faculty Director, Susan Gray School
Vanderbilt University
Nashville, Tennessee

REFERENCES

Burke, R.J., Greenglass, E.R., & Schwarzer, R. (1996). Predicting teacher burnout over time: Effects of work stress, social support, and self-doubts on burnout and its consequences. *Anxiety, Stress, & Coping, 9,* 261–275.

Copple, C., & Bredekamp, S. (2009). *Developmentally appropriate practice in early childhood programs serving children from birth through age 8* (3rd ed.). Washington, DC: National Association for the Education of Young Children.

Dunlap, G., & Fox, L. (2011). Function-based interventions for children with challenging behavior. *Journal of Early Intervention, 33,* 333–343.

Fox, L., Dunlap, G., Hemmeter, M.L., Joseph, G.E., & Strain, P.S. (2003). The Teaching Pyramid: A model for supporting social competence and preventing challenging behavior in young children. *Young Children, 58,* 48–52.

Fox, L., & Hemmeter, M.L. (2009). A program-wide model for supporting social emotional development and addressing challenging behavior in early childhood settings. In W. Sailor, G. Dunlap, G. Sugai, & R. Horner (Eds.), *Handbook of positive behavior support* (pp. 177–202). New York, NY: Springer.

Hemmeter, M.L., Corso, R., & Cheatham, G. (2006, February). *A national survey of early childhood educators: Training needs and strategies.* Paper presented at the Conference on Research Innovations in Early Intervention, San Diego, CA.

Sailor, W., Dunlap, G., Sugai, G., & Horner, R.H. (Eds.). (2009). *Handbook of positive behavior support.* New York, NY: Springer.

Acknowledgments

This book has a predecessor, *Prevent-Teach-Reinforce: The School-Based Model of Individualized Positive Behavior Support* (Paul H. Brookes Publishing Co., 2010). The Prevent-Teach-Reinforce (PTR) model was based on extensive fieldwork and experimental research in kindergartens, elementary schools, and middle schools. The book attracted considerable attention from educators involved with children across the age span, and it piqued the interest of early childhood professionals working with young children whose development was hampered by challenging behaviors. However, it was readily apparent to these early childhood professionals, as it was to us, that the existing PTR model was an imperfect fit for early childhood and preschool settings.

The authors of the current book have spent decades working with young children, early childhood professionals, and a variety of preschool programs. Over the past years, we have worked to implement the steps of the PTR model in early childhood settings to help preschool-age children improve their behaviors. As with other early childhood professionals, it was clear to us that many aspects of the PTR model would need to be modified for the model to be effective in preschool classrooms. Although the basic structure of the PTR process was applicable, the examples, the interventions, the team composition, and the assessment forms and tools needed to be changed. Therefore, the current book is a new manual, explicitly and comprehensively designed for early childhood settings.

The current book would not have been possible without the earlier work conducted on the PTR model. We are indebted to our colleagues who worked with us as developers and authors of the PTR products (including Rose Iovannone, Donald Kincaid, Kathy Christiansen, and Carie English) and to the many children, teachers, parents, and school district personnel who tested and implemented the model and gave us helpful feedback. We are also very grateful to the early childhood professionals who gave us input regarding modifications that would be needed for preschool settings and who encouraged us to take on the work that is represented in the following pages.

Finally, we wish to acknowledge the primary funder of research that was conducted on the PTR model—the Institute of Education Sciences (IES) (Grant No. H324P04003). IES is also funding current research on implementation of the PTR-YC approach for young children (Grant No. H324A120097). However, the contents of this book do not necessarily represent the policy of IES or the US Department of Education, and no endorsement by the federal government should be assumed.

Introduction to PTR-YC

This book describes a model for resolving serious challenging behaviors of toddlers and preschool-age children: Prevent-Teach-Reinforce for Young Children (PTR-YC). In writing this book, we had two goals: 1) to provide a complete description of the model and 2) to develop a user's manual for implementing the model. The first goal will be achieved by presenting the rationale, background, and procedural steps of PTR-YC. The second goal will be achieved by laying out in operational detail everything that is needed for early childhood professionals to implement each step of the model with the fidelity required to effectively resolve even the most intensive and persistent challenging behaviors.

PTR-YC is a research-based strategy designed to reduce challenging behaviors of young children in preschool, early education, and child care settings. The model is intended to help young children whose behaviors are serious enough that they interfere with the child's ability to engage in positive relationships, form friendships, play with others, and learn expected skills.

When we use the term *challenging behaviors*, we are referring to any actions or behavior patterns that cause this type of interference. The most common kinds of behaviors referred to as "challenging" are excessive and inappropriate crying, violent tantrums, throwing objects, kicking, hitting, pushing, spitting, yelling, running, and repetitive or perseverative actions that occur for extended and unreasonable periods of time. *Challenging behavior patterns* can also be defined by excessive lack of cooperation (or noncompliance) and a marked failure to respond or interact with others.

Early childhood professionals are familiar with these kinds of behaviors because the behaviors are seen from time to time in virtually every preschool or child care setting. However, PTR-YC is not intended as a strategy for every instance of challenging behaviors. Rather, PTR-YC is an approach that is used when an individual child repeatedly engages in challenging behaviors over a period of weeks and when those behaviors are unresponsive to the regular guidance, redirection, and instructional strategies used within the classroom. PTR-YC requires a deliberate commitment by program staff and leadership to develop and implement a systematic strategy of intervention and, to be effective, it requires an effort to implement the strategy with care and consistency. Therefore, PTR-YC is used only when it is very clear that an individual child needs some extra help and carefully designed assistance to overcome his or her patterns of challenging behavior and begin to adopt more positive ways of interacting with peers and adults.

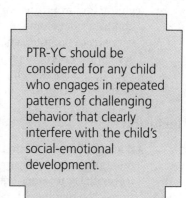

PTR-YC should be considered for any child who engages in repeated patterns of challenging behavior that clearly interfere with the child's social-emotional development.

So, who are the children for whom PTR-YC should be considered? The simple answer is any child who engages in repeated patterns of challenging behavior that clearly interfere with the child's social-emotional development. The model was developed for toddlers and preschoolers from 30 months old to kindergarten entry. It is applicable for children who have challenging behavior but otherwise have typical patterns of development, and it is applicable for children who are identified as having developmental disabilities or who are at risk for disabilities. PTR-YC can be used with children who have autism, intellectual disabilities, or an emotional disorder, and it can be used with children who have not been identified with any disability. PTR-YC can also be used in preschool programs, Head Start classrooms, child care centers, or any other program of early care and education.

PTR-YC is used by teams of individuals within a program (or classroom) who are concerned with and responsible for the child with challenging behaviors. The teams can vary in size, but they almost always include a lead teacher or provider and a family member. They often include a program director, a classroom aide, a behavior specialist, a mental health coordinator, or related services personnel. Teams may also include extended family members, friends, and volunteers if they are closely connected to the child. It is good to include any person who is directly involved with providing guidance, care, or education for the child, and it is important to have at least one or two people on the team who serve as facilitators or leaders and whose role is to be most familiar with the procedures and content of PTR-YC. We expect that it will be these leaders and facilitators who will offer guidance for the other team members. This book is for these leaders and facilitators.

GUIDING BELIEFS AND PRINCIPLES

As a group, we (the authors of this book) have worked for dozens of years with young children in public and private preschool programs, Head Start centers, child care, and infant and toddler programs. We have worked as teachers, directors, behavior specialists, researchers, and consultants, and we have developed and implemented model programs in classroom and home settings. In all of these roles, we have been convinced of the importance of certain assumptions or beliefs about young children and social-emotional development in early childhood. The PTR-YC model is based on these foundational principles, which are briefly described in the following paragraphs.

Healthy Social Development as an Essential Foundation

Learning of all sorts is fundamentally a social phenomenon, and the greatest pleasures, accomplishments, and satisfactions that people experience throughout their childhood and adult lives come from their relationships and their interactions with others. Therefore, it is vitally important for early care and education programs to place the greatest emphasis on children's development of social interaction skills, friendships, and healthy emotional responses to complex social situations. We believe it is good practice for early educators to screen for potential problems in social-emotional development, maintain practices that encourage prosocial behaviors, and implement additional supports for those children who may be experiencing difficulties.

Inclusion

Social behaviors are learned in social contexts, so it is important for children with developmental delays or disruptions—including challenging behaviors—to have rich opportunities to regularly interact with peers who have already developed patterns of positive interactions. The readiness model in which children with disabilities are educated in self-contained programs has not been shown to yield long-term benefits. Instead, considerable research has shown that inclusive programs, with appropriate supports, can be most beneficial in helping all children improve in their social-emotional and relationship abilities. We understand that inclusive programs are not always available for children with disabilities, so we appreciate that fully inclusive experiences may need to be arranged through supplemental services. Nevertheless, we emphasize the importance of providing many opportunities for successful, social participation by young children and especially for children with delays and difficulties in social interactions.

Prevention

As a general rule, efforts are more beneficial and cost efficient if they serve to prevent, rather than repair, social and emotional distress and challenging behaviors. There is much that can be done in the realm of universal strategies that can promote resilience and prevent the emergence of social and emotional difficulties. The topic of prevention is treated more thoroughly later in this chapter and throughout the book.

Comprehensiveness

All aspects of child and family functioning need to be appreciated and incorporated into the design and implementation of services for young children. This book focuses on procedures for resolving challenging behavior, but those procedures constitute only one aspect of the full array and continuum of services.

Family Centeredness

The social and emotional needs of children may reflect the needs of the family, and the most crucial resources available to children are often those of the family. All recommendations and assistance efforts must involve the family, and individual support efforts must be driven by the family's input and the family's goals. Respect for diversity among families is necessary. Family centeredness and sensitivity to and respect for the individuality of family perspectives also implies a need to be responsive to the cultural and linguistic characteristics that each family and child bring to the program.

PREVENTION

Although every effort has been made to make the procedures in this book as practical, effective, and feasible as possible, implementing PTR-YC requires some time, some effort, and a distinct commitment. Furthermore, considering PTR-YC means that at least one child has already developed patterns of serious challenging behaviors. Clearly, it would be preferable if the challenging behaviors had never emerged in the first place. That is, it would have been better if the development of challenging behaviors had somehow been prevented.

It is not possible to prevent all challenging behaviors. Some children have so many risk factors (including severe disabilities) that the emergence of some challenging behaviors may be inevitable. For these children, when challenging behaviors have become a detectable problem, then individualized intervention, such as with PTR-YC, is a necessary element of the child's service plan.

It is clear, however, that many, and perhaps most, challenging behaviors can be prevented from ever developing, even with children who are born with developmental and intellectual disabilities. Because prevention is preferable to intervention, we turn now to a brief discussion of reasonable approaches for helping to prevent the emergence of challenging behaviors.

A broad, validated approach for promoting healthy social-emotional development and preventing the occurrence of challenging behaviors is to establish and implement high-quality environments. Such environments are characterized by clarity, safety, structure, predictability, the presence of interesting and stimulating materials and activities, and clear expectations for how children should behave. The implementation of high-quality environments includes considerations related not only to the physical setting but also to the manner with which adult–child interactions are conducted. The National Association for the Education of Young Children published pertinent guidelines regarding developmentally appropriate practice (Bredekamp & Copple, 1997). More specific to the needs of children with developmental challenges, the Division for Early Childhood (DEC) of the Council for Exceptional Children has published detailed guidelines regarding recommended practices for children with multiple risk factors and/or disabilities (Hemmeter, Smith, Sandall, & Askew, 2005; Sandall, Hemmeter, Smith, & McLean, 2005). These practices are derived from the literature and have been validated in numerous ways. Adherence to these guidelines will serve to promote positive social development and prevent many, if not most, challenging behaviors.

In addition to the DEC recommended practices, frameworks have been established for organizing evidence-based strategies in a hierarchical system for promoting healthy social-emotional development, preventing the emergence of challenging behaviors, and intervening with challenging behaviors when they occur. Such frameworks are known as tiered or multitiered approaches. One well-known framework that pertains to social-emotional behaviors is the Pyramid Model (Fox, Dunlap, Hemmeter, Joseph, & Strain, 2003). Like many multitiered approaches, the Pyramid Model includes three levels, with each level being associated with evidence-based strategies.

The universal level, the base of the pyramid, consists of strategies that are applicable for all young children within a program, regardless of their developmental status. The universal level includes strategies relating to building positive, responsive relationships between children and caregiving adults as well as relationships with peers. The universal level also provides strategies for providing high-quality environments. For children who have risk factors or who show some potential problems with social interactions, the Pyramid Model describes secondary strategies. These strategies involve additional individualization and intensity with respect to the provision of guidance and support, the specificity of instruction, the degree of family involvement, and the collection of assessment and progress monitoring data. For some children who require secondary interventions, specialized curricula regarding social skills, problem solving, or emotional literacy may be recommended (Joseph & Strain, 2003). When children do not adequately respond to secondary interventions and when patterns of challenging behavior become evident, then more intensive and more individualized interventions may be needed. The top of the pyramid consists of tertiary interventions, which may also be known as individualized positive behavior support. This book describes a way to develop and implement tertiary interventions. In other words, PTR-YC is a tertiary intervention strategy.

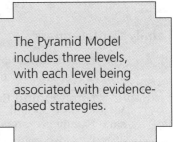

The Pyramid Model includes three levels, with each level being associated with evidence-based strategies.

The Pyramid Model is being implemented in many programs around the country, and it has been described in many publications. Research has documented the effectiveness of the model (e.g., Branson & Demchak, 2011; Snyder, Crowe, Miller, Hemmeter, & Fox, 2011), and systematic guidelines for Pyramid Model implementation have been described (e.g., Fox & Hemmeter, 2009; Hemmeter, Ostrosky, & Fox, 2006). Although a description of the specific practices is well beyond the scope of this book, we recommend that universal and secondary strategies of the Pyramid Model be implemented in programs prior to implementing tertiary practices. Implementing universal and secondary practices is likely to prevent some challenging behaviors from developing, and their presence is likely to make tertiary interventions for challenging behaviors that already exist more effective and efficient. The best location to obtain detailed information about the Pyramid Model and its processes and practices is at http://www.challengingbehavior.org.

Although a full presentation of the Pyramid Model is beyond the scope of this book, the PTR-YC model does include strategies for assessing and implementing a number of core practices that are pertinent for implementation within early childhood settings and applicable for all of the children within the program. Implementing these practices is useful for promoting desirable social behavior and for preventing many challenging behaviors. It is reasonable to expect that faithfully implementing these practices could completely resolve the challenging behaviors of some children, making the use of PTR-YC unnecessary.

UNDERSTANDING CHALLENGING BEHAVIOR

When challenging behaviors occur to the degree that a team determines that intervention is required, it is extremely helpful if members of the team have knowledge regarding the natural laws that explain how the environment influences behavior. This is the case because effective behavioral interventions are based on the principles that define the relationships between events in the environment and occurrences of a child's behavior. PTR-YC has its foundation in these natural laws, and all of our behavior is subject to their operations. In this section, we briefly describe the key principles that help us to understand how, when, and why challenging behaviors occur. As we understand how, when, and why challenging behaviors occur, we gain insight into how challenging behaviors can be resolved.

> Most challenging behaviors serve the same purpose as other forms of communication, such as speech, nonverbal gestures, and facial expressions.

Principle 1: Challenging Behaviors Are Communicative

This basic principle simply means that most challenging behaviors serve the same purpose as other forms of communication, such as speech, nonverbal gestures, and facial expressions. In this sense, challenging behaviors may often be the same as requests or demands. For instance, the loud tantrum of a 4-year-old boy may be communicating a request for food. Or, the crying of a 3-year-old girl may be communicating a request to stay longer at the sand table instead of moving to circle time. The hitting and kicking of a boy in the preschool playground may be indicating that he wants to grab a peer's toy truck to play with himself. Sometimes challenging behavior is used to communicate a desire for attention; sometimes challenging behavior is used to communicate a desire to get out of an activity; sometimes challenging behavior is used to communicate a request for a food item or a toy. The point is that challenging behaviors are often used because they work to act on the social environment in much the same way that other forms of communication act on the environment. For this reason, we usually see more challenging behaviors exhibited by young children whose speech (or other communication) is not well developed or by young children whose speech has not been as effective as their challenging behaviors.

There are a few things that are important to note about this principle. First, even though the challenging behavior may be communicative in nature, this does not mean that the behavior represents a conscious or deliberate act. To understand a challenging behavior in terms of its communicative properties does not mean that the behavior is cognitively determined or premeditated. Second, the form of the behavior (what it looks or sounds like) does not represent a specific communicative intent. For example, if a child spits at a teacher when he or she is being escorted to an art activity, then the form of the behavior may be spitting, but the intent (or function) of the behavior may be to escape from the art activity. Understanding the particular meaning of the communication involves an assessment that is different from identifying the form. The process for understanding the communicative purpose (or function) of the child's challenging behavior is an important element of PTR-YC and is described in Chapter 4. Finally, it is important to appreciate that a child's challenging behavior may look (or sound) the same in different situations, but the communicative purpose might be different. For example, a tantrum may have one meaning in the context of one routine, but it might have a different meaning in a different routine or circumstance.

Principle 2: Challenging Behaviors Are Maintained by Their Consequences

The law of reinforcement is perhaps the most basic law of behavioral science. It states that a behavior will be maintained if it is followed by a positive reinforcer. For our purposes, a positive reinforcer can be considered a reward. For challenging behavior that is communicative in nature, the reward would likely be the object or action that is being requested. If a child is using tantrums to communicate a desire for attention, then the reward would be when the teacher attends to the child. If a child is hitting a peer in order to obtain the peer's toy truck, then the reward would occur when the child actually obtained the truck. If a child is crying to extend her time at the sand table, then the reward would be the removal of the teacher's request to move to circle time. There are many kinds of consequences. One way to look at it is to say that consequences involve either getting something (e.g., attention, food, a toy) or getting rid of something (e.g., a demand, an unpleasant activity, a disliked peer). The big point is that consequences are important. Challenging behaviors will not continue if they are not somehow followed by consequences that serve as rewards. And by the same principle, desirable behaviors will not develop or occur if they are not followed by consequences that work as rewards.

Principle 3: Challenging Behaviors Occur in Context

Challenging behaviors occur at different rates or intensities in different contextual or environmental circumstances. For example, one child's screaming may occur frequently when he or she is being asked to participate in fine motor tasks, but the same child might never scream during snack or outdoor play. A different child might never have a tantrum during fine motor tasks but might cry and fuss a great deal during snack time. A third child might run around and appear out of control when he or she is expected to be in Ms. Prine's area but is always calm and productively en-

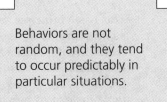

Behaviors are not random, and they tend to occur predictably in particular situations.

gaged when he or she is with Ms. Johnnie, the classroom aide. The observation that behaviors are not random and they tend to occur predictably in particular situations is a principle that can be useful in efforts to resolve children's challenging behavior.

The previous three principles are basic to the way in which we seek to understand how a child's challenging behavior is influenced by events that occur in his or her environment. As we describe in the remaining chapters of this book, this process of understanding is essential to the development of an intervention strategy that will be effective, efficient, and respectful of each child's individuality. The way that we go about understanding each child's challenging behaviors is through a straightforward process known as *functional assessment*, which is described in Chapter 5. Understanding how a child's behavior occurs in context leads to strategies of environmental or antecedent arrangements that we categorize as "prevent" because they serve to promote desirable behaviors and discourage challenging behaviors before they occur. Understanding how a child's challenging behaviors serve as communication leads to strategies involving teaching the child to communicate in more desirable ways; thus, we use the category of "teach." Understanding how consequences are maintaining challenging behaviors leads to strategies involving modifications of consequences, especially positive reinforcers; thus, we use the category "reinforce." And this is why we refer to the model as "Prevent-Teach-Reinforce."

THE PROCESS OF PTR-YC

The process of PTR-YC is similar to the well-documented, step-by-step process of individualized positive behavior support described in hundreds of articles, books, and web sites. The difference is in how the steps are implemented. In PTR-YC, the procedures are tailored for use with young children in early childhood settings, and the descriptions of the implementation strategies at each step of the process are designed to be as practical as possible, with the emphasis always on helping the team implement the steps with enough accuracy and consistency that desirable child outcomes are as likely as possible. The details of the steps are described in subsequent chapters, and the basic process is described next.

Step 1: Teaming and Goal Setting

The first step in the process involves the establishment of a classroom-based team, an agreement on how the team will function, and the specification of initial, short-term goals. Teams vary in size, but they must include the individual who will be responsible for implementation of the intervention plan, usually the lead teacher or care provider. Teams should also include a parent or other family member, an individual who can facilitate access to resources (e.g., director, administrator), and a classroom assistant. Other members may include a psychologist, speech-language therapist, counselor, or social worker. It is useful to have at least one member who is knowledgeable and experienced with behavioral theory, applied behavior analysis, functional assessment, and intervention planning and implementation. At least one member of the team is identified as a leader or facilitator, and he or she must be familiar with the content and the tools described in this book. Teams hold several meetings over the course of the PTR-YC process and are responsible for implementing the entire process as faithfully as possible.

The first responsibility of the team is to establish clear goals for the PTR-YC process. Goal setting includes two specific objectives: 1) identifying and defining an initial challenging behavior to be resolved and 2) selecting and defining a desirable behavior, which is usually a social-communicative behavior, that will be increased or taught and that will help serve as a replacement for the child's challenging behavior.

Step 2: Data Collection

The team must design a practical system of data collection for measuring the levels at which the challenging behavior and the desirable behavior are occurring. This measurement must start before intervention is begun because it is the way we determine whether our intervention is being successful or if it needs to be revised. There are many possible methods for measuring behavior and monitoring progress; however, we limit our recommendations to those strategies that are highly practical for use by teachers and other classroom personnel who have additional ongoing responsibilities. The strategy we recommend most often is the use of a 5-point behavior rating scale (Dunlap, Iovannone, Kincaid, et al., 2010; Kohler & Strain, 1992). The procedures for using the PTR-YC Behavior Rating Scale are described in detail in Chapter 4. The Behavior Rating Scale is designed to be user friendly, and we have found that classroom personnel can use the system with an expenditure of surprisingly little time or effort.

Step 3: PTR-YC Assessment (Functional Behavioral Assessment)

This step involves obtaining and organizing the information needed to understand how the challenging behavior is influenced by the environment, which is the key to developing intervention plans that will be effective and efficient. The PTR-YC assessment is a form of functional behavioral assessment in which questions are answered in a checklist format in three categories relating to antecedent variables (prevent), function and replacement variables (teach), and consequence variables (reinforce). The available response options are all commonly encountered in preschool and early care programs, and an open-ended response option is always provided. The assessment questionnaires are completed by each team member as well as other people who are involved with the child, and the responses are discussed and summarized in a team meeting, which provides for consideration and integration of team members' different perceptions of environmental events related to the target behaviors. The objective of the PTR-YC assessment is to arrive at a team consensus regarding 1) the antecedent events that are associated with a high probability of the challenging behavior occurring, as well as a low probability, 2) the purpose or function of the challenging behavior, and 3) the typical events that have followed the occurrence of the challenging behaviors and potential objects or events (rewards) that might be used as positive reinforcers during intervention. The results of the PTR-YC assessment are used to develop an intervention plan.

Step 4: PTR-YC Intervention

When the assessment is completed and the team has developed an understanding about how the challenging behavior is related to and influenced by the environment, then a team meeting is devoted to developing an intervention plan. Chapter 6 describes the process for selecting intervention procedures from each of the three categories and explains how to match assessment data with intervention strategies. Descriptions of evidence-based strategies for each of the three categories, along with information about how to implement the strategies, are presented in the appendixes at the end of the book. Chapter 6 also describes clear procedures for organizing the selected intervention strategies into a behavior intervention plan and specifies how, when, and by whom the strategies will actually be carried out. Finally, this step includes procedures that may need to be included to prepare classroom personnel to implement the strategies.

Step 5: Using Data and Next Steps

This step begins with (ongoing) examination of the progress monitoring data (usually the PTR-YC Behavior Rating Scale data) to determine if progress has occurred as anticipated or if the progress is unsatisfactory. If desirable progress has occurred, then the next steps involve doing what is necessary to make sure that the progress will be maintained and that continued progress will occur. If progress has been less than satisfactory, then there are a number of options to consider (see Chapter 7).

In addition to the five steps previously outlined, it has become apparent that a number of challenging behaviors that appear as if they would require individualized and assessment-based interventions can actually be resolved by implementing high-quality classroom practices that are applicable for all children. Therefore, we have incorporated additional material in Steps 3 and 4 (assessment and intervention) that is pertinent to the operation of the entire classroom. The practices described in Chapters 5 and 6 will be enough to resolve the challenging behaviors in some cases to the point that an individualized behavior plan is unnecessary.

The PTR-YC process usually occurs over a 2- to 4-month period with an average of three to four team meetings scheduled for planning and coordinating the multicomponent interventions. Key features of the PTR-YC package are explicitly intended to heighten the teams' fidelity in implementing the five-step process and the individualized interventions. These features include 1) team-based, rather than expert-driven, assessments and decision making; 2) a simple strategy of functional behavioral assessment that incorporates the observations of all team members; 3) menu-driven intervention planning with multiple evidence-based options for each of the PTR components; 4) self-evaluations to determine if each step was successfully completed; and 5) a requirement that reliable, but practical, progress monitoring data be obtained and summarized on an ongoing basis. In addition, we offer a PTR-YC Team Implementation Guide (TIG) as a supplement to the chapter-specific self-evaluations. It provides a concise overview and checklist of the entire process. The TIG is presented in Figure 7.6 at the end of Chapter 7. Team leaders and facilitators may wish to review the TIG prior to initiating the PTR-YC process.

Our purpose in writing this book is to describe the steps of the PTR-YC process in clear language and provide guidance and tools that will enable you and your team to effectively use the procedures. The following chapters describe all steps of the process. Chapter 2 begins with a discussion of families and how they can be involved in the PTR-YC process. Chapter 3 describes the development of a team and the procedures for setting clear goals and target behaviors. Chapter 4 describes strategies for beginning data collection. Chapter 5 is about the PTR-YC assessment process, and Chapter 6 describes the development of the behavior intervention plan. Chapter 7 is about using the data to take the next steps in the process. If these steps are implemented with care and consistency, then we believe that the majority of challenging behaviors will be resolved and that the child who is being supported will benefit from a healthier trajectory of social-emotional development. We believe this strongly because of our own experiences and the research we have conducted and because the entire process is based on a substantial foundation of multifaceted, applied research.

RESEARCH FOUNDATIONS

The procedures of PTR-YC are derived from well-established principles of behavior as well as extensive, practical research on strategies of intervention for challenging behavior. Intervention research that is the foundation of PTR-YC emanates primarily from two closely related approaches: applied behavior analysis (ABA) and positive behavior support (PBS).

ABA is a broad discipline in which principles of learning are applied to produce socially meaningful changes in a person's behavior. It is a discipline that has influenced and contributed to a number of fields including education, social work, psychology, child development, and business. Research conducted since the 1960s has clearly demonstrated the validity and numerous contributions of ABA. It is important to understand that ABA can be manifested in many ways and, therefore, the term can be misunderstood. For example, some people refer to ABA as a single, highly structured curriculum for treating children with autism. But ABA is a much broader approach than could ever be captured in a particular program, and it is relevant for virtually all populations in virtually all contexts. Programs that are strongly rooted in ABA may appear to be different when, in fact, they are based on the same conceptual and philosophical foundations (Cooper, Heron, & Heward, 2007).

PBS is also a broad approach, and it is derived in part from ABA. PBS is an approach for organizing environmental, social, educational, and systems strategies in order to improve the competence and quality of life for individuals with problems of behavioral adaptation. PBS seeks to reduce the occurrence of behavior problems because they interfere with learning and with the ability to pursue preferred lifestyles and positive relationships with adults and peers. PBS is a positive approach because it avoids harsh and stigmatizing punishments and emphasizes instruction and environmental arrangements to achieve desired outcomes. PBS emerged as a useful approach in the mid-1980s and has become an increasingly popular strategy for addressing difficult behaviors and promoting quality of life (Bambara & Kern, 2005; Carr et al., 2002; Dunlap, 2006; Dunlap, Carr, Horner, Zarcone, & Schwartz, 2008; Sailor, Dunlap, Sugai, & Horner, 2009).

The PTR-YC model is rightfully considered to be a PBS approach, and it is also derived from the principles and procedures of ABA. We raise this issue of the model's background because some early childhood professionals may be confronted with questions about the distinctions between PTR-YC, PBS, and ABA. In brief, some answers include the following:

1) PTR-YC is a specific model designed for young children that is entirely consistent with the PBS approach; 2) PBS is derived from the foundations of ABA, though it is different enough to warrant its own label (Dunlap et al., 2008); and 3) ABA is a broad term that refers to a widespread discipline that can accommodate many practices and programs.

Regardless of terminology, PBS and ABA have produced a tremendous amount of research on procedures for addressing behavior problems. The accumulating evidence has yielded a number of important points.

- Challenging behaviors can be interpreted as communication, and gaining an understanding of a child's communicative intent can lead to effective interventions.

- Functional assessment procedures can produce information that is useful for intervention, and the outcomes are more favorable when interventions are based on functional assessments than when interventions are not informed by such assessments.

- There is strong evidence that demonstrates that specific antecedent manipulations (prevent), assessment-based instructional strategies (teach), and consequence-based interventions (reinforce) can produce significant improvements in challenging behaviors and desirable alternatives.

- There is also evidence that multicomponent interventions produce more immediate and more durable effects than single-component interventions (Carr et al., 1999; Dunlap & Carr, 2007).

Interventions for Young Children's Challenging Behavior

The majority of research on challenging behaviors was conducted with children older than the age of 5. Since the 1990s, however, there has been an increase in research with younger children, and it has become possible to produce syntheses and general conclusions. One analysis of the literature with participants between the ages of 2 and 5 years rendered essentially the same general findings as the literature with older children (Conroy, Dunlap, Clarke, & Alter, 2005). That is, there is ample evidence that functional assessments and the use of assessment-based interventions can be effective for young children in a variety of child care, Head Start, prekindergarten, and home environments (Blair, Umbreit, & Bos, 1999; Blair, Umbreit, Dunlap, & Jung, 2007; Conroy, Davis, Fox, & Brown, 2002; Duda, Dunlap, Fox, Lentini, & Clarke, 2004; Dunlap & Fox, 2009, 2011). Furthermore, there are a number of individual studies that have demonstrated the feasibility and the efficacy of using instruction-based interventions with young children (e.g., Dunlap, Ester, Langhans, & Fox, 2006; Reeve & Carr, 2000). Other data have found positive effects from antecedent manipulations and consequence-based interventions (e.g., Asmus et al., 1999; Conroy et al., 2005). This congruence is not surprising given the universality of the basic principles of learning.

Although effective interventions may have common elements and a shared assessment-to-intervention process, important distinctions must be considered when challenging behaviors are exhibited by younger children. For example, the early developmental status of young children means that many of the intervention practices that are effective with older children may be unsuitable with toddlers and preschoolers. Similarly, the settings and contexts in which interventions are to be implemented differ in meaningful ways. Play is a much more important activity context, and home environments are even more essential for younger children than for older children. Therefore, functional behavioral assessments need to consider the characteristics of these settings and contexts; and family involvement, which is important for all ages, is more vital when children have not yet begun kindergarten. The PTR-YC model takes these important differences into account.

Prevent-Teach-Reinforce

PTR-YC is a model that is based on many elements of a previous intervention, Prevent-Teach-Reinforce (PTR; Dunlap, Iovannone, Kincaid, et al., 2010), that has been rigorously evaluated using a randomized group design (Iovannone et al., 2009). The 2009 study included 247 participating students between kindergarten and eighth grade in five school districts in Florida and Colorado. The students were from diverse cultural and economic backgrounds, and the study included children in general and special education, including children with a variety of disabilities. Results showed statistically significant differences in problem behavior and social skills as well as academic engaged time, with all results favoring the children who were randomly assigned to the PTR condition as opposed to the business-as-usual condition. In addition, scores on a measure of fidelity for the PTR teachers were high, as were scores on a social validity treatment acceptability scale (Iovannone et al., 2009).

The PTR intervention for school-age children has also been evaluated with single-case experimental and quasi-experimental designs (Dunlap, Iovannone, Wilson, Kincaid, & Strain, 2010; Strain, Wilson, & Dunlap, 2011). A multiple baseline across participants design was used in the study by Strain and colleagues to examine the effects of PTR in comparison with a baseline condition. The participants were three students with autism (5, 8, and 9 years of age) who were in general education placements. The results showed clear and consistent reductions in challenging behaviors and improvements in academic engagement when the PTR intervention was implemented. In other words, the PTR approach is supported by strong evidence of effectiveness when used in real school situations with children who have a variety of characteristics.

FACTORS THAT PROMOTE EFFECTIVENESS OF PTR-YC

There are a number of factors that influence the effectiveness of PTR-YC. The more these factors are optimized, the more effective PTR-YC will be in addressing challenging behaviors.

Prevention

We have previously discussed prevention, but it warrants repeated emphasis. The more that a program or classroom incorporates features of high-quality environments and recommended adult–child interactions, the greater the likelihood that serious challenging behaviors will be prevented. Just as important, more children will be likely to learn desirable behaviors for getting along with their peers and adults when these preventive practices are in place. In addition, even when challenging behaviors do emerge, implementing PTR-YC will be easier and more effective, and improvements in the levels of challenging behaviors will be easier to maintain when the classroom is characterized by high-quality environments and positive adult–child interactions.

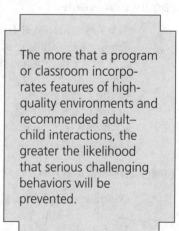

The more that a program or classroom incorporates features of high-quality environments and recommended adult–child interactions, the greater the likelihood that serious challenging behaviors will be prevented.

Commitment to Successful Outcomes for Children

The ability to effectively implement PTR-YC is inevitably related to the level of explicit commitment that a program has to the success of all of its children, including children who have disabilities or who exhibit troubling patterns of behavior. Sometimes it may seem easier for a program to say that children who are different belong somewhere else and to address challenges by expelling the child or asking the parents to find another setting for the child's care and education. The programs in which PTR-YC will be most effective are those that have adopted clear policies pertaining to the delivery of supports for all children and the director and key staff have demonstrated a willingness to take extra steps to enable all children to succeed.

Fidelity of Implementation

The greater the extent to which the intervention team (e.g., teachers) is able to implement PTR-YC as intended, the more effective it will be in addressing challenging behaviors. Although PTR-YC is designed to be robust enough that perfect fidelity is unnecessary (and unrealistic), it is likely that interventions that are infrequently and inconsistently implemented will not produce the intended outcomes for children. If the team is implementing with very high fidelity and the plan is still not as effective as anticipated, then it is time to reevaluate the plan and consider revisions to the intervention strategies.

Capacity of the Team

There are two characteristics of a team that influence the degree to which PTR-YC will be effective. The first is the commitment of the team members to make the plan work. Frankly, we believe that this may be the most important factor of all. If the team is unified in its vision and its commitment to seeing that the child succeeds, then the child will usually prosper. If some members (or even one) fail to embrace the commitment, then there is a greater chance that the effort will fail. The second characteristic involves the knowledge and experience that team members have with respect to functional assessment, problem-solving strategies, activity-based instruction, and implementation of behavior intervention plans. Although relatively inexperienced personnel can often do an excellent job, a general rule is that experience with assessment-based interventions is helpful in identifying problems and resolving them early in the process.

Family Involvement

The more involved family members are in the process, the better the overall outcomes. Even though the focus of the PTR-YC intervention may be on classroom behavior, parents and other family members may have useful tips and results of previous interventions to contribute. Furthermore, if a family is involved with the development and implementation of the classroom intervention, then there is a chance that parts of the plan may be carried out at home, thereby promoting transfer and generalization. If family members are unable to attend team meetings, then they can still be informed of the discussions, decisions, and actions related to the PTR-YC process.

LIMITATIONS AND ACCOMMODATIONS

We believe that PTR-YC will be effective most of the time, and the more that the previous factors are addressed, the more effective it will be in addressing challenging behaviors. However, the model cannot be effective in every situation. First, some factors may contribute to behavior problems that are beyond the capacity of PTR-YC to address. For instance, some children experience neurological and/or medical conditions that are not amenable to the educational and behavior intervention strategies that make up PTR-YC. Uncontrolled seizures, chronic illness, or neurological syndromes can contribute to the presence of challenging behaviors, and it would be inappropriate to attempt to resolve such problems with strictly educational-behavioral procedures. When neurological or medical issues are involved, it is necessary to obtain appropriate medical, neurological, and psychiatric services.

Some children may experience major disruptions in their home environments, and these disruptions may result in problems in a student's emotional and behavioral functioning. The PTR-YC approach is not designed to address serious problems that occur beyond the school setting. Although PTR-YC may be helpful for classroom behavior, additional services will be required in these circumstances before the full source of the problem can be resolved. Furthermore, PTR-YC will not be effective if a child has excessive absences.

There are also times when the PTR-YC approach does not produce fully adequate behavior change, despite the best efforts of the classroom-based team. For example, the child's behavior may be so difficult to observe (e.g., hurting animals, setting fires, injuring others) and so infrequent or unobservable that it is impossible to complete an adequate classroom-based functional behavioral assessment. Staff may be at a loss to determine the function of problem behavior and, therefore, cannot implement an individualized intervention. It may be necessary to call in outside help to monitor the child for serious problem behaviors that rarely occur and/or occur when adults may not typically be present. Such monitoring should have the completion of a reliable functional behavioral assessment as its end goal. In addition, programs may want to solicit a diagnostic evaluation by a licensed child psychologist or psychiatrist for behaviors that have a covert quality to them (e.g., the child seems to purposely engage in challenging behavior when adults are absent). The goal of this assistance should be to determine if other supports and/or professionals need to be involved in this child's life.

In other situations, the team may have designed an individualized intervention plan and implemented the plan with fidelity but the child's behavior has not improved over a period of several weeks. We first recommend checking to see if the reinforcers are sufficiently powerful and then repeating the functional behavioral assessment to confirm the communicative message of the problem behavior. It is not uncommon for a behavior to be found originally to serve one function and then subsequently found to serve different and/or multiple functions. If this step does not yield satisfactory results, then it may be appropriate to call on a consultant who is more experienced in functional behavioral assessment. This individual may decide to 1) use alternative observation procedures to analyze behavior, 2) more thoroughly explore the possible role of events external to the classroom, or 3) ask staff to briefly try interventions that are consistent with several functions. It is vital that staff become trained to implement the methods used by the consultant. Circumstances such as these are more thoroughly addressed in Chapter 7.

SUMMARY

PTR-YC is a specific model of intervention planning and implementation for young children with serious challenging behaviors. It is applicable for preschool children from 30 months old to kindergarten entry and for children with a broad range of developmental and intellectual characteristics. An extensive base of research documents the effectiveness of PTR-YC's components as well as the process as a whole.

This book is intended to be used as a manual by classroom-based teams in preschool, Head Start, child care, and other early care and education programs. The chapters in the book describe steps in the process of PTR-YC implementation. The chapters include descriptions of the steps, objectives, tools, and recommendations. Each chapter also includes implementation tips, family involvement tips, and case examples. The content of the chapters is designed to be specific enough for teams to follow the process without difficulty. If the steps are carefully followed with precision, then evidence indicates that the child's behavior will likely improve in meaningful ways.

APPENDIX

Key Terms

The following list describes some terms that may not be familiar to all readers. These terms are described with the meaning that is intended in the book.

antecedents (antecedent variables)   Events, actions, items, and circumstances that are present in the environment and have an influence on the occurrence of a child's behavior. Antecedents can serve as triggers for challenging behavior or for desirable behavior, or they can act to make a behavior more likely to occur. Almost anything can potentially serve as an antecedent variable; however, common antecedents for challenging behavior are requests for a child to do something that the child does not want to do.

applied behavior analysis (ABA)   A scientific discipline that includes practical approaches for assessing and modifying behavior. ABA uses principles of learning theory to develop intervention strategies. ABA is a broad approach that has been demonstrated to be useful for helping many populations of children and adults to develop improved behavior.

baseline   The period of time before the PTR-YC intervention is implemented. It is a period during which data are collected (see Chapter 4) and during which classroom personnel are using their regular procedures for dealing with challenging behaviors.

challenging behavior   A term used to describe any repeated pattern of behavior that interferes with optimal learning or engagement in prosocial interactions with peers and adults. This book refers to challenging behavior as persistent behaviors that appear to be unresponsive to normative guidance strategies, with common topographies being prolonged tantrums, physical and verbal aggression, disruptive vocal and motor responding (e.g., screaming, stereotypy), property destruction, self-injury, noncompliance, and withdrawal (Smith & Fox, 2003).

data   A word meaning facts or information. *Data* in PTR-YC usually refers to observations made about a child's behavior. Data obtained for purposes of conducting a functional assessment (see Chapter 5), monitoring progress (see Chapter 4), and assessing fidelity of implementation (see Chapters 6 and 7) are especially important in the PTR-YC model.

desirable behavior   A broad term used in PTR-YC to mean a child's behaviors that the team would like to establish or increase. Desirable behaviors include positive social and communicative behaviors and can also include cooperative or parallel play, attending, independent responding, self-care, and self-regulation.

fidelity   Refers to the extent that an intervention strategy in PTR-YC is accurately implemented as intended. The term is often stated as fidelity of implementation or integrity of implementation.

function   The purpose or motivation of the child's challenging behavior. There are many possible functions, but they usually can be categorized as to get something (e.g., a toy, someone's attention) or to get rid of something (e.g., a demand, the presence of an irritating peer). The function of challenging behavior can almost always be understood as an attempt to communicate.

functional assessment (functional behavioral assessment; FBA)   A process that involves collecting information (data) to develop an understanding of how a challenging behavior is influenced, or controlled, by events in the environment. There are many methods for conducting an FBA. In PTR-YC, the FBA is conducted by having team members independently complete three checklists (for prevent, teach, and reinforce) and then synthesize the information on the PTR-YC Functional Behavioral Assessment Summary Table (see Chapter 5).

hypothesis (hypothesis statement)   A simple statement that summarizes the team's understanding of how a challenging behavior is influenced by the environment. The hypothesis has three elements—the antecedent conditions, a description of the behavior, and the consequences that appear to be maintaining the behavior. For some children, there may be more than one hypothesis statement.

operational definition   A definition or description of a behavior that is presented in terms that are fully observable and measurable. A good operational definition would mean that all team members would be able to agree at any moment in time on whether the behavior is occurring.

positive behavior support (PBS)   An approach for helping people (including children) to develop improved desirable behaviors and reduce challenging behaviors. It is an individualized approach that is based on information (data), results of an FBA, and a multi-element behavior intervention plan. PTR-YC is a PBS model that is designed for optimal practicality. It is worth noting that PBS can also be applied to larger units such as classrooms, entire programs, and schools. However, PTR-YC is a model of individualized PBS, and this book is focused on the needs of individual children with persistent challenging behaviors.

prevent   The first component of the PTR-YC approach. It refers to intervention strategies involving antecedent variables.

reinforce   The third component of the PTR-YC approach. It refers to intervention strategies involving changes in the delivery of consequences, especially positive reinforcers.

reinforcer (positive reinforcer)   A consequence provided to a child following a behavior that results in the behavior being increased or strengthened. Part of the PTR-YC approach involves using reinforcers to help increase desirable behaviors, as well as removing reinforcers that may be inadvertently maintaining the child's challenging behaviors.

target behavior   A term that is used to refer to a behavior that is identified by the team as being in need of change. Target behaviors can be challenging behaviors as well as desirable behaviors.

teach   The second component of the PTR-YC approach. It refers to intervention strategies involving the delivery of instruction of desirable behaviors.

Families

2

Family centeredness is one of the guiding principles for this book because families are a crucial resource for any young child. For our purposes, we use the broadest definition of *family* to include any adult who has primary caregiving responsibilities for a child (including parents), but it can also include those who have regular contact with and influence on a child, such as extended family members, baby sitters, and so forth. We use the term *family* throughout this book to include anyone who falls into this category.

When a child has challenging behaviors, the quality of life for the child and anyone else he or she interacts with is affected in a profound way. Challenging behaviors very often affect a family's ability to be active members of groups outside the immediate family unit, affecting their ability to go shopping, eat out, attend family and community activities, or find and keep a baby sitter. Understanding that a child's challenging behavior can affect the family as a whole is important to consider when including families as an important and valuable team member for the PTR-YC process. When children have social and emotional needs, this may reflect that family members have needs as well, and a family's needs should always be considered in every step of this process.

Families are the one constant in a child's life, which gives them a considerable and essential role in their child's development. Involving families as partners in the PTR-YC process not only allows families to contribute valuable information, but it can also help staff build more positive relationships with families. When a child's challenging behavior is significant enough to require the need for individualized interventions, communicating to families that everyone wants to help the child learn more socially appropriate skills is another way to improve relationships with families. Families often know many of the situations that contribute to a child's challenging behaviors, so involving families in meaningful ways can help improve the effectiveness of the PTR-YC process. Families often develop ways to cope with or avoid challenging behavior, and these types of interventions or preventative strategies can be informative when designing an effective intervention plan that can benefit everyone. When children engage in challenging behaviors in a store, families might prevent these challenging behaviors by not walking down certain aisles in the store, such as the candy aisle. When children want something that they cannot have, families may develop an intervention to provide other acceptable choices to divert the child's attention away from the unacceptable option, such as showing the child a favorite toy when he or she is trying to take everything out of mom's purse. There are so many examples, but the key is that families often have identified interventions and preventative strategies to manage challenging behavior. Utilizing this valuable information can greatly contribute to an effective intervention plan.

We readily acknowledge that it may not always be easy to involve families because they come with a variety

> Involving families as partners not only allows families to contribute valuable information, but it can also help staff build more positive relationships with families.

17

of experiences, either with their own child or with their own personal experiences as children. Some families may come with a variety of risk factors, may show a lack of interest in being involved at the school or center level, and may not agree that the challenging behavior exists or may believe it is only a problem at the school or center. The relationships that exist with families can influence how much a family participates, and it is important to acknowledge that each family has strengths as well as challenges.

Cultural and language differences can further affect how, when, and where families participate. We all have different perspectives on when children should walk, talk, use utensils, play independently, or sleep by themselves, and sometimes these differences can cause problems between families and staff. Understanding that we all grew up differently, regardless of culture or language, can help us avoid judging families for decisions they make and help develop strong partnerships with families in raising their children. It is our position that a recommended assumption for teams is that families are doing the best they can with their current knowledge and skills. This assumption will aid individuals in avoiding judgments, especially related to differences in families.

The PTR-YC process can still be completed without family involvement, but it may influence the effectiveness of the plan. It is likely that the inconsistency with how behaviors are handled between home and school or center will affect the amount and/or rapidness of behavior change that you will see. Our experience has shown, however, that we can affect behavior change even when it is limited to interventions implemented in the classroom setting.

ENGAGING FAMILIES IN THE PTR-YC PROCESS

The following section provides suggested ways to involve families in each step of PTR-YC. Families have individual needs, perspectives, and strengths, and these suggestions should be considered in terms of each family. It may be helpful to refer back to this section throughout the PTR-YC process for suggestions on involving families.

Step 1: Getting Ready—Families as Partners

All team members are important, but family members play a critical role in designing intervention plans for young children. Therefore, we put a strong emphasis on including and engaging families. We recognize that not all families will be involved in a meaningful way, and this should not hinder a team from moving forward with designing a PTR-YC intervention plan if a child exhibits significant challenging behaviors in the classroom. Nevertheless, families can be involved in a variety of ways and should be included to the extent that they are comfortable and it fits their needs. For example, families can provide relevant information if they cannot attend team meetings. Communicating to families about their importance and relevance as part of the team can occur over the telephone, with face-to-face conversations, in an e-mail, with a text message, with notes between home and school, or any other method that works for the family and the staff.

It is important to remember that parents are equal members of the team, they have valuable information to contribute, and their perspectives are valid and appreciated. Research supports that families provide valid and reliable information for functional behavioral assessments, can develop accurate hypotheses for challenging behaviors, and can implement effective interventions in reducing challenging behaviors (Arndorfer, Miltenberger, Woster, Rortvedt, & Gaffaney, 1994; Frea & Hepburn, 1999). When we treat families as equal members and empower them by giving them skills to reduce chal-

> Families can be included to the extent that they are comfortable and it fits their needs.

lenging behaviors and teach their child effective and desirable skills, there is a likelihood that this will result in long-term positive effects for the child and family.

When working with families, it is important to use language that everyone understands and avoid using jargon. Focus discussions on what the child can do well and what is already working (use a strength-based approach) and avoid complaining about what the child cannot do. Focus on the PTR-YC steps and the information collected throughout this process to avoid irrelevant discussions that tend to turn into complaining sessions. Meetings will be more efficient and effective if these rules are established and maintained for each meeting. An important consideration for this step is to check whether your school or center requires any consent forms, releases of information, or any other legal documents to proceed with this process.

Step 2: Goal Setting and Data Collection—Families as Consultants

Families have valuable contributions in identifying functional goals for their child. These can be communicated in a variety of ways (as in Step 1), but getting the information may take more than just asking a family member, "What do you think Charlie should be doing?" Sometimes a simple question is enough and a family will give you some ideas of what they would like the child to learn, such as participating in routines, following directions, or waiting his or her turn. Yet, there are many families who may say something such as, "I just want him to be like the other kids" or "I just wish she wouldn't cry all the time." Although these statements let us know that families think the challenging behavior needs to be addressed, it does not give any specific goals to work toward. As described in Chapter 4, goals need to be specific and should realistically be accomplished in about 2 months. These guidelines can help us consult with families and ask more specific questions to help guide the goal-setting process. For example, if a family wants their son to be "just like the other kids," then it is helpful to begin asking them what specific things the other kids do that they would like their son to do. If they are still struggling with identifying specific skills, then brainstorming some ideas with them could help get the conversation going. Family members are often not familiar with child development, so they are not sure what a child should be doing at a certain age. Brainstorming ideas and targeting a goal that provides benefits at home and at the school or center can improve the likelihood that interventions will be implemented in both environments and that behavior change will have a more meaningful affect on the child and his or her family.

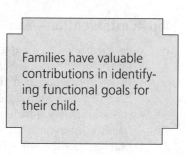

Families have valuable contributions in identifying functional goals for their child.

Step 3: PTR-YC Assessment—Families as Informants

Family members often know a lot of information that will be helpful in completing the functional behavioral assessment. It is generally pretty easy to determine the young child's function, or what he or she is trying to communicate, such as wanting a particular toy, wanting to play outside, not wanting to stop building with the blocks, or not wanting to share with his or her friends. It may seem like a waste of time to get information from the team members to find out what you might already know. This is a critical step in the teaming process, however, as each team member, including parents, gains investment in the process and in implementing strategies when they are actively involved

Family members often know a lot of information that will be helpful in completing the functional behavioral assessment.

in every step. In addition, when you take the time to think about all of the elements that can influence behavior, you may think of additional information that can be useful or identify details that you would not have if you did not participate in this part of the process. It is also important to discuss these elements as a team and get everyone to see the challenging behavior in a similar way. Furthermore, things may not be as obvious as they look, and sometimes what appears obvious may be more complicated than it originally seems. Taking the time to gather the assessment information is crucial to identifying effective intervention strategies, and identifying intervention strategies cannot be completed until there is an understanding of the function of the challenging behavior.

When gathering assessment information, it may take more than sending forms home and getting them returned. It may take a conversation or several conversations with the family to get all of the relevant information. These conversations can occur during drop-off and pickup times, in a telephone conversation, via e-mail, or whatever way is most convenient for the family. The assessment information does not need to be collected all at one time. If you are gathering the information through conversations, then it may take a few conversations to get all of the information that you need.

Step 4: Intervention—Families as Teachers

As discussed in Chapter 6, this step involves identifying intervention strategies and designing an intervention plan. Involving families in this step can include having them help decide which interventions to implement (based on the assessment information), getting feedback on identifying the intervention steps; scripting, modeling, and role playing how the steps will be taught; or simply sharing the plan with the family and asking for any input. Some families will want to implement the interventions at home and will want to know how to do so. Being transparent throughout all steps of the process is important when a family has not been actively involved, and it is equally important to maintain a positive and friendly tone in all communications regarding challenging behavior.

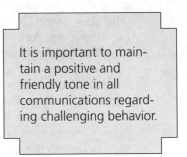

It is important to maintain a positive and friendly tone in all communications regarding challenging behavior.

Step 5: Using Data and Next Steps—Families as Collaborators

Sharing progress, especially successes, is a wonderful way to strengthen or reinforce relationships with families. It is important to share progress with families using data, including when small successes and progress has been achieved. If the frequency, intensity, or duration of a child's behavior begins to decrease, then that is a wonderful success to share with a family. If you have a child who is hitting others more than 10 times per day, then sharing with families that the hitting is down to 5 times per day is a great way to let families know that progress is being made. Although that is not the ultimate goal, sharing success is a way for families to stay connected and involved in what is happening in the classroom. Decreases in challenging behaviors typically allow opportunities for children to engage in more appropriate behaviors, and families should be informed of all of these improvements. When families are part of the process from the beginning (in a way that is meaningful for them), it is natural to share information about all parts of the process as you would for any other team member.

Even if a family has not been involved actively in prior PTR-YC steps, seeing improvement with the child in your setting may be a catalyst for greater involvement. When families do not respond in ways that we expect, we often assume that they are not pleased with the progress or think it is not important. It is important to consider each family's perspectives in how they handle public issues, which are heavily influenced by past experiences, cultural differences, or personal preferences. Some people are willing to share anything and everything about themselves openly, whereas others are more reserved and private about personal information.

SUMMARY

One of our guiding principles is that family centeredness is crucial when dealing with young children. Children and families are powerfully affected when everyone has the same goals and works together to handle challenging behaviors. Taking the time to engage families on an individual basis as much as you can throughout the PTR-YC process should be a priority. It is easy and natural to include families in all aspects related to their child when they are valued and appreciated.

APPENDIX

Case Examples

The following pages introduce you to four case examples—Hasani, Joel, Jessi, and Ethan. These cases describe four young children with challenging behaviors and the PTR-YC process used to improve their social adaptation and reduce their challenging behaviors. The cases are fictitious, but they are based on our real experiences. They are presented in order to illustrate how the PTR-YC process can occur in different contexts with children who have different behaviors, different families, and different strengths and needs.

The case examples are presented at the end of each chapter and are intended to demonstrate how each PTR-YC step is implemented. The use of the checklists and data forms is illustrated, and each case reveals some potential challenges that can occur as teachers and their preschool teams seek to implement the assessment and intervention strategies. We hope that these case examples help you to understand how the process can work most effectively.

HASANI, 2½ YEARS OLD

History

Family Background   Hasani is a 2½-year-old African American girl who lives with her mother, Amara, and father, Jerry, in a small town. Amara and Jerry have extended family members who live nearby and provide a lot of support and respite. Amara and Jerry are middle class, work full time, and are involved in Hasani's life and the services she receives as much as their work schedules will allow. Amara and Jerry both spend time helping in Hasani's classroom, attend most family activities and events held at the center, and communicate daily at drop-off, at pick-up, and through e-mail. In addition to attending a community college child care program on a full-time schedule, Hasani receives early intervention services (until she is 3 years old) and attends speech therapy twice per week, occupational therapy once per week, and a structured play group once per week.

Description of Child   Hasani is a beautiful girl who has a diagnosis of autism spectrum disorder. She has a beautiful smile, loves to play outside, and loves to eat anything sweet, especially cake. She enjoys finger painting, participating in art activities, looking at books, listening to music, tearing paper, and watching certain shows on television (e.g., *Sesame Street*). Hasani does not have any verbal language but does make some sounds. She usually lets others know that she wants something either by getting it herself or taking a person's hand and leading him or her to what she wants. She does not typically interact with others unless she wants something that she cannot get on her own. Looking at letters of the alphabet is one activity that she enjoys with others. She will point to the letters and wants the person to say the letter. She looks at the person during these types of interactions, and she will usually smile and sometimes laugh or squeal with excitement when the person responds appropriately by saying the letter. She rarely plays with toys, and when she does, she typically does not play with them appropriately.

Description of Behavior   Hasani's challenging behaviors include not responding to adults or peers, not following directions or classroom routines, not participating in classroom activities, tearing up classroom materials, leaving the classroom, and taking things from others. When adults or peers try to initiate play or conversation with Hasani, she will ignore them and continue with whatever she was doing without looking up or acknowledging their presence. If the peer or adult is persistent in trying to get Hasani to interact, Hasani will eventually walk away from the peer or adult. When Hasani is given a direction, she will ignore the direction and again walk away if the adult is persistent. During classroom activities, Hasani will often sit quietly for 2–3 minutes independently with little to no active engagement. She will begin to make squealing noises after a couple of minutes and eventually just get up and walk away from the activity. She often wanders into the book area or sits in the cozy corner. Teachers let her stay there as long as she wants. Hasani will follow the classroom routine when it is of high interest to her, such as outside time, snack, and painting activities. If it is not of high interest to her, then she will ignore directions and go sit in the cozy corner or book area. When teachers redirect Hasani back to the routine, she walks away. Sometimes, Hasani will tear materials and take things from her peers.

JOEL, 4 YEARS OLD

History

Family Background   Joel is a 4-year-old Caucasian boy who lives with his father, Gary, and two older siblings: Karen, who is 8 years old, and Eugene, who is 5 years old. Gary and his children live in a major city and do not have any extended family support nearby. Gary does have a neighbor, Joyce, in the apartment complex where he lives who helps him when she can. She is like a grandmother to the children but is not available all the time to help when Gary needs it. Gary works full time at a local factory, takes overtime when he can, and is not able to spend much time with the children. Joel attends a full-day Head Start program (where he has been for 1 year), Eugene attends full-day kindergarten, and Karen is in second grade. All the children ride the bus to school and home, so Gary does not see any school staff very often. Joel has challenging behaviors at home and at school, and Gary thinks that if Joel's teachers just yelled at him that Joel would behave much better because it works that way at home.

Description of Child   Joel is a busy and enthusiastic boy who has a speech delay. His speech delay was previously attributed to being the youngest child as well as a boy and that he would grow out of it. Now that he is 4 years old, there is greater concern about his language development. Joel loves to run and play outside. He enjoys building anything and then likes to have it all crash down. He likes to play with cars and trucks of any kind and is emphatic about anything to do with food (e.g., meals, snacks, cooking activities, parties). Although Joel has some language (uses two- to three-word sentences) and can usually say what he wants, he typically just takes what he wants or finds ways to get things he wants on his own. When Joel is interested in the activities in the classroom, he will participate, but he does not like being told what to do.

Description of Behavior   Joel's challenging behaviors include hitting others when he does not get his way or when he wants attention, taking toys from his peers, and telling teachers "no" all the time. Joel will also leave an activity that he is not interested in and go to other areas of the room. He will begin playing with other materials in a way that is loud enough to disrupt the class and his peers and get adult attention. When Joel is not motivated by an activity, he will not follow directions. He is often loud in the classroom, and he plays too rough with the toys.

JESSI, 3½ YEARS OLD

History

Family Background   Jessi is a 3½-year-old girl who lives with her foster mom, Lucy, foster dad, Kohachi "Kay," and their biological son, Doug, who is 8 years old. Jessi, who is half Hispanic and half Caucasian, lives in a metropolitan city. She has lived with Lucy and Kay for 7 months, and Lucy is regularly involved at her child care center. Lucy and Kay have some extended family support, and there are also services that are available to them through Child and Family Services. Jessi has attended a large community-based child care center that has 10 classrooms for 6 months. Because Doug attended the center as a young child, staff members were enthusiastic about having Jessi at their center, despite her multiple disabilities, and thought that they would be able to accommodate her needs on their own. After several months, they realized that they needed more help to meet Jessi's needs but did not want her to leave because they had grown so attached to her. Lucy and Kay are also realizing that they need to do more to help Jessi learn more appropriate skills. Many of her behaviors were cute as they were getting to know her, but now they are becoming increasingly harder to manage and are causing problems at home and at the center.

Description of Child   Jessi is a charming little girl with an infectious smile and laugh. She has multiple disabilities, which include vision impairment, seizures, intellectual disability, and multiple health issues. Jessi loves to be held; loves giving and getting hugs; loves listening to music; likes any toy that makes noise (the louder the better); enjoys swinging, rocking, and spinning around; and likes listening to stories while sitting in someone's lap. If she can sit in someone's lap, then she will do almost anything with their help. Jessi rarely does anything independently and will exhibit a variety of challenging behaviors to express herself. Jessi makes some verbal utterances but does not have any clear words, although she will try to make sounds on occasion. Overall, Jessi is very likeable, and many adults and children take to her and enjoy being around her. Her challenging behavior is becoming a barrier to making friends and participating in classroom routines and activities.

Description of Behavior   Jessi's challenging behaviors include screaming loudly, high-pitched squealing, hitting, kicking, hitting her head on the floor, throwing objects, pinching, hugging too tightly, taking things from others, and crying. Jessi loves being around adults and the adults enjoy her presence. Most of her challenging behaviors are directed toward other children in the classroom. Although Jessi has not seriously hurt another child, staff members do not want to see anyone get hurt and would like Jessi to stay at their school.

ETHAN, 5 YEARS OLD

History

Family Background   Ethan is a 5-year-old Native American boy who lives with his grandmother, Veronica, and his sister Elizabeth ("Liz"), who is 3 years old. They live in a rural town without proximity to extended family. Ethan has been at a small child care center (two classrooms) for the past 2 years, and Veronica is only involved on occasion because she works full time during the day. Liz attends the same center but is in the other classroom. Ethan has challenging behaviors at home and at school.

Description of Child   Ethan is a charismatic boy who does not have any identified delays or disabilities, but he does present with some social and emotional concerns. Ethan loves most of the classroom activities, enjoys being a classroom helper, likes playing with his friends, and does well most of the time. When Ethan does not get his way, his challenging behaviors become disruptive in the classroom.

Description of Behavior   Ethan's challenging behaviors include taking toys from his peers, yelling "no" to peers, tattling to teachers that his peers are not sharing, crying, pulling hair, destroying a peer's play when Ethan cannot join in play, and yelling profanities.

Getting Ready
Teaming and Goal Setting

This chapter describes the steps involved in getting ready to implement the assessment and intervention steps of the PTR-YC process. There are actually two important elements described in the chapter. The first is teaming, which involves establishing a team that will design and implement the PTR-YC process. As we will describe, the team is the central entity in the process and is responsible for carrying out all assessment and intervention strategies, so the membership and functioning of the team is a key element of success. The second major step described in this chapter is goal setting. Goal setting involves identifying and carefully defining the target behaviors in such a way that everybody on the team understands and agrees on the major short-term objectives.

TEAMING

The first step of PTR-YC is to develop a cohesive team committed to being involved in every step of the process for the purpose of helping the child with significant challenging behaviors. The step is usually initiated by one or two individuals (e.g., teacher, program director, psychologist, behavior specialist) who determine that a child's challenging behavior is so persistent and severe that a concerted and individualized effort is required. These individuals who initiate the process will typically serve as the facilitators or leaders of the team, and it is expected that they will be most familiar with the details of the PTR-YC process. However, we emphasize at this point that the facilitator does not make the decisions for the team. As discussed later in this chapter, it is important that the team members make joint decisions and work through the entire process by achieving consensus on all of the essential steps.

The team should include individuals who have direct experience and direct contact with the child and the child's challenging behavior. Any individuals who will be responsible for implementing the plan should also be part of the team. Team members include those individuals who work closely with the child, have intimate knowledge of the child and the child's behaviors, and have a vested interest in assisting the child with positive behavior change. The size of the team will be determined by the needs of the child, the classroom teacher or provider, available resources within the center or program, and the availability of other supports and resources from outside the center or program setting. The child's teacher must be a member of this team (by *teacher*, we are referring to any and all adults who have primary responsibilities for caring for children in early care and education settings), and we recommend including the classroom assistant and all other classroom staff when available. In addition, the child's parents or primary caregivers will be valuable team members. If the child's parents or caregivers cannot or do not choose to participate on the team, then the team still continues with the process. As mentioned in Chapter 2, we recommend offering ongoing opportunities for parents to become involved and sharing the intervention plan with parents and caregivers even when they are not able to participate actively.

Other team members may include special education staff, occupational therapists, speech therapists, nurse consultants, and other related services providers. Also, it is usually helpful to include an individual with knowledge of behavioral principles and practical experience with positive behavior support, applied behavior analysis, and functional behavioral assessment. Behavior analysts, school psychologists, and mental health consultants may bring these kinds of qualifications to the team. An individual who has knowledge of the context and resources available should be included on the team whenever possible (e.g., administrators, directors). Finally, it is essential that at least one member of the team be familiar with the content in this manual.

The primary responsibilities of all team members are to 1) attend and participate with team meetings; 2) contribute to the functional assessment and intervention planning; and 3) contribute to implementation of the intervention plan, data collection and data monitoring, and all decisions related to future steps in the process. Planning meetings are usually 60–90 minutes in duration and are scheduled at a place and time when core team members, including family members, are able to meet.

PLANNING MEETINGS

The planning meetings are scheduled as follows.

> *Meeting 1:* This meeting is to assemble the team, arrange roles within the team, agree on a unified long-term vision for the child, and develop short-term goals and carefully defined target behaviors.

> *Meeting 2:* The second meeting occurs shortly after the first meeting and is for the purpose of developing a system of data collection and determining how and by whom the data will be obtained and summarized. In cases when the team is already working together effectively, and when the objectives of Meeting 1 can be achieved quickly, then it may be possible to combine this meeting with the first meeting.

> Be sure to establish clear methods of communication during the first meeting. Effective communication is essential to effective teaming.

> *Meeting 3:* This meeting is to discuss information related to the functional behavioral assessment and summarize that information into hypothesis statements. The hypothesis statements comprise the foundation of the team's understanding of the child's challenging behavior and lead directly to the behavior intervention plan. The third meeting usually occurs within 1 week of the second meeting.

> *Meeting 4:* This meeting is devoted to the development of the behavior intervention plan, including the key strategies in the categories of prevent, teach, and reinforce. It also includes the specifics regarding who will implement the strategies and exactly how and when the strategies will be used. Further details of this meeting are described in Chapter 6.

PROGRESS MONITORING MEETINGS

Progress monitoring meetings begin approximately 2 weeks following the fourth meeting. The purpose is to review the data to determine whether anticipated progress is occurring and to modify the behavior intervention plan, if necessary. These meetings are usually briefer than most planning meetings.

Additional meetings are scheduled at the discretion of the team and are usually devoted to providing follow-up, refining the plan, troubleshooting when there are less than favorable outcomes, and adding target behaviors. Additional meetings might not be required in cases where good progress is evident.

TEAM PROCESSES

With team membership established, it is important for teams to take some time to establish a process for making decisions based on the data collected and to establish a method for reaching consensus. PTR-YC provides a sequential meeting structure that carefully guides teams in gathering and reviewing data and using that data to inform and guide decisions. The meetings themselves should also have a structure that guides team members in making decisions that are based on data. Following the initial planning meeting, this structure generally conforms to a format that includes

- Presenting and reviewing information that is relevant to the target behaviors and the PTR-YC process

- Brainstorming and organizing ideas based on the data

- Prioritizing ideas generated from the data and making decisions for the next step

- Reaching agreement and implementing the agreed-on next steps

Information related to target behaviors and functions of behavior is presented and discussed at each meeting. Teams need to bring all data and other information to all meetings. It is recommended to have a folder or binder for all meeting notes, data, and other information.

Brainstorming within meetings should involve a structured method that allows all team members to share thoughts and ideas. For example, teams could use a round robin format that engages team members to write down their ideas and to share at least one with the group. The ideas shared can be listed and discussed for clarification. Teams can then prioritize these ideas based on which ones 1) are derived from careful and repeated observation, 2) fit within the context of the classroom, and 3) would result in greater positive outcomes for the child. This can also be done with the use of a sticky wall in which ideas may be posted on the wall and moved during discussions to help the team see common themes. This process of brainstorming will be illustrated in the case studies in the appendix at the end of the chapter.

Reaching consensus is still necessary once the brainstorming process has occurred. Sometimes teams can readily identify priorities and reach consensus quickly; other times, it may require more effort. Many teams may consist of multiple members with a variety of experiences and differing perspectives. This diversity among team members contributes to comprehensive data and rich information throughout the process. Teams must also be able to come to consensus, in spite of differing opinions and perspectives. Accomplishing this requires teams to create and maintain effective communication with all members. Norms for communication are advisable and should include methods for communication (e.g., e-mail, conversation, notetaking) and guidelines for how to communicate (e.g., strength-based, factual information; positive language). Reaching team consensus means that all team members understand the information presented, have asked all pertinent questions, and are committed to following through with the next steps. PTR-YC requires all team members to be committed to creating an intervention plan and implementing the plan with the highest level of fidelity possible.

If conflicts arise, then teams are advised to reflect back to the data collected. Although differing opinions can exist, factual data provide a foundation for teams that can lead to a

> It can be useful to have the brainstorming discussion facilitated by the team member who has knowledge and experience with challenging behavior. It is necessary to focus on factual and observable information and the plan to achieve positive outcomes.

foundation of agreement. If consensus on what the data show cannot be reached, then teams may need to gather more data on that specific topic or area. Specific questions for gathering more information can be generated with a time frame for reviewing the additional data. The next meeting date to review the additional data should be set. For example, a team that is having trouble reaching agreement around which challenging behavior to target may need to get additional information about how often each behavior occurs (e.g., how often does hitting occur compared with how often spitting occurs). This additional information may help guide teams to reach agreement by targeting the challenging behavior that occurs most often. Sometimes teams may even consider using video as a means to gather more data.

Outside Services

Some children in early childhood settings who exhibit challenging behavior may receive additional services outside of the center, program, or preschool they attend, and these services and service providers may have little or no connection to the setting using the PTR-YC process. For example, some children might receive private speech therapy or occupational therapy, and some children might be provided with specialized interventions associated with applied behavior analysis. Although it is recommended that services and interventions be coordinated to the greatest extent possible, such coordination can be difficult to accomplish due to the limited availability of professionals to attend meetings or even to communicate with one another on a consistent basis. It is important to emphasize, however, that active coordination across multiple providers is not essential for the PTR-YC process. Teams are still encouraged to purposefully consider strategies at this stage that serve to promote communication and carryover of PTR-YC strategies across providers and other settings. There are two strategies that we recommend to enhance the success of PTR-YC across environments and with outside services: 1) have outside providers complete all questionnaires related to PTR-YC assessments (see Chapter 5), and 2) provide each outside service provider with a copy of the intervention plan (see Chapter 6).

GOAL SETTING

Optimal support for setting useful goals in the PTR-YC model involves a person-centered approach that encompasses the whole child. Teams using this approach discuss the child's strengths and what they want the child to learn or achieve over a period of years. It helps immeasurably to have input from the child's family members in order to understand family priorities and possible cultural influences that might affect such priorities. Long-term goals might be considered in the context of questions such as, "What skills would we like to have Karen learn before she enters kindergarten?" or "What kinds of social relationships should Thomas enjoy 3 years from now?" For some children, long-term goals would include abilities to communicate, make friends, engage independently in self-care and cleanliness routines, or play cooperatively with numerous peers. The point is that it is valuable to have team members agree on a vision for the child's development so that short-term goals are steps toward achieving longer-term outcomes. We encourage teams to devote time in their initial meeting to discussing this important "big picture" of the child's developmental trajectory.

Goal setting in PTR-YC, however, does not linger on this broad and long-term vision. Instead, PTR-YC focuses on specific target behaviors and develops goals that can be reasonably achieved in a period of 2–3 months, which is the purpose of PTR-YC. These short-term goals will focus on the child's challenging behavior that the team would like to decrease and the desirable behavior that the team would like to increase. Goals can include having positive peer relationships, sharing, turn taking, problem solving, expressing and regulating emotions, and communicating with others. The PTR-YC Goal Sheet described next will help teams identify target behaviors with which to begin the process. The PTR-YC Goal Sheet has two categories: 1) behaviors to decrease and 2) behaviors to increase. Teams will brainstorm what challenging behaviors exist, brainstorm desirable behaviors the team members would like to see the child exhibit, identify one behavior from each category to target and focus on for creating an intervention plan, and define each of the behaviors in operational terms so that the behaviors described are observable (can be seen or heard) and measurable (can be counted or timed).

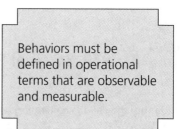

Behaviors must be defined in operational terms that are observable and measurable.

We have identified six steps for using the PTR-YC Goal Sheet (see Figure 3.1; blank fillable and printable versions can be found on the accompanying CD-ROM), and each team member should have an opportunity to contribute to all of the steps. If there are team members who cannot be present (e.g., family members, other service providers), then the facilitator(s) can gather ideas from all relevant team members prior to this meeting in order to include everyone's input. This PTR-YC Goal Sheet could be sent to those who cannot be present, and they could return it before the meeting. The information could be gathered by e-mail or over the telephone for those who cannot attend the meeting, or the PTR-YC Goal Sheet could be given to everyone prior to the meeting to come up with ideas to contribute to the discussion during the first meeting. If teams choose to gather information prior to the meeting, then it is important to instruct those who fill out this form or provide information to ignore or not worry about Steps 3 and 6. Operational definitions should be discussed and defined at the meeting with input from all team members. Including everyone's thoughts and ideas is the important component of this process, and the meeting is used to work out all the details (e.g., identifying the target behaviors, creating operational definitions). Use the PTR-YC Goal Sheet to record everyone's input and follow the steps, which are described next.

Step 1: Identify the Child's Challenging Behaviors to Decrease

This step is an opportunity for all team members to identify any and all challenging behaviors that the child exhibits that create barriers to participating in the classroom. This can include not following directions, not responding to peers or adults, always wanting to be by him- or herself, taking things from others, screaming, hitting, throwing things, and so forth. Some teams may only have to list one or two behaviors, and the brainstorming step will only take a few seconds. Other teams may have a lengthy list of challenging behaviors, and the brainstorming may take several minutes. When brainstorming ideas, do not worry about getting the terminology correct or including all the particulars; the key is to identify the challenging behaviors that create the most problems. It is important to note that it is not necessary to include every single challenging behavior either—it is okay for teams to only list the most important or most troublesome ones.

Step 2: Select One Challenging Behavior to Target

This step is an opportunity for team members to decide which challenging behavior to target for the PTR-YC process. There may be several behaviors that teams want to decrease right away, and we understand that need. In our experience, however, it is much easier to target one behavior at a time in order to increase the likelihood of success for the child as well as the adults who will be implementing the behavior intervention plan. If the behavior intervention plan is too complicated and has too many behaviors to address, then it is highly unlikely that it will be completely successful, and teams will continue to struggle with challenging behaviors. If there are any behaviors that are a threat to the child's safety or to another's safety (e.g., physical aggression toward self, physical aggression toward others,

FORM 1

PTR-YC Goal Sheet

1. Identify the child's challenging behaviors to decrease.
2. Select ONE challenging behavior to target.
3. Operationally define this target behavior—observable (seen or heard) and measurable (counted or timed).
4. Identify the child's desirable behaviors to increase.
5. Select ONE desirable behavior to increase.
6. Operationally define this target behavior—observable (seen or heard) and measurable (counted or timed).

Child: _____ Date: _____

1. Behavior(s) to decrease	
2. Target behavior	
3. Operational definition	
4. Behavior(s) to increase	
5. Target behavior	
6. Operational definition	

Figure 3.1. PTR-YC Goal Sheet. (*Note:* Blank fillable and printable versions can be found on the accompanying CD-ROM.)

throwing items, running away), then it is vital to begin with these types of behaviors, and, in general, these types of behaviors are what teams will typically identify as the most important. By targeting one challenging behavior to start with, teams have an opportunity to focus all of their efforts around effectively decreasing or eliminating the target challenging behavior and teaching the child more desirable behaviors. Chapter 7 has information about next steps when challenging behaviors have been decreased to a manageable level or have been eliminated.

The one challenging behavior selected may actually be a cluster of behaviors that may appear to be different in terms of their form but which actually tend to occur together (in clusters) and tend to serve the same purpose for the child. For example, some aggressive behaviors may cluster together and may be functionally the same. For instance, Jill is a 4-year-old girl in a Head Start classroom who reacts violently when she is asked to do something that she does not like to do. She may scream, hit, kick, or pull hair. But the behavior is essentially the same because it occurs under the same circumstances and appears to serve the same purpose. This cluster of violent disruption can be considered one behavior. The different forms (e.g., hitting, kicking) in Jill's case are interchangeable and will be treated the same in the assessment and intervention process.

> **Implementer's Tip**
>
> Sometimes a group of behaviors has a sequence of escalation. For example, first Jill screams, then she hits. When behaviors have a consistent pattern of escalation, a team may choose to target the first behavior in the sequence, such as Jill's screaming.

For some teams, it will be easy to identify a challenging behavior to target, and this process will not take any time. For other teams, it may be difficult to come to an agreement about which challenging behavior to target as a starting point. Teams may need to have further discussions to come to an agreement. Guiding questions for discussion can include the following.

- Is there a challenging behavior that is exhibited in a variety of contexts or across multiple activities such as transitions, large-group times, arrival, and dismissal?

- Is there a challenging behavior that is used with frequency to communicate wants and needs?

- Is there an aggressive behavior that needs to be immediately addressed?

- Are there any behaviors that begin mildly then escalate to more extreme or intense behaviors? (Meaning one behavior occurs initially and escalates to another behavior and possibly another when no intervention or interference occurs. For example, a child screams, then kicks, and eventually hits others as the behavior episode continues.)

These guiding questions can aid the team in deciding on a challenging behavior to target that is an agreed-on priority for the team. Teams should be cautious of choosing challenging behaviors largely based on personal feelings about the form of the behavior. For example, individuals who have strong emotional reactions to certain behaviors may gravitate toward targeting that behavior, even though it may not occur often or be a challenging behavior of concern to others. For instance, a teacher might be especially offended by a child's playful belching, even though it does not occur more than once per week and is not particularly disruptive to the classroom routines. The teacher might wish to target the belching, whereas other adults hardly notice the behavior and would prefer to focus on the more frequent problem in which the child throws materials in the block area. Here the potentially dangerous behavior of throwing blocks would be the challenging behavior that should be selected initially. Again, asking the previous questions will assist teams in focusing on the factual information and help avoid making emotion-driven decisions.

Table 3.1. Operational definitions of challenging behavior

Challenging behavior	Nonexample of definition	Example of definition
Aggression toward others	Hurting others	Kicking, biting peers/adults, pinching, scratching, falling to the floor, and/or picking up and throwing items toward peers/adults
Noncompliance/not following directions	Wants control (manipulates the situation)	When asked or told to do something that she does not want to do, will walk away from the adult or continue to engage in the activity that she was engaged with when the direction was given
Tantrum and destroying property	Throws a fit when he does not get his way	Falls to the floor, kicking his legs and flailing his arms while screaming, "I hate you!" or "That's not fair!"; runs around the room (may scream with or without words), pushes people, throws or "sweeps" items off surfaces in the classroom, and/or tears things off the walls
Withdrawal	Prefers to be by herself	During activities when she is free to be where she prefers, stays at least 3 feet away from other children

Step 3: Operationally Define This Target Behavior

This step is an opportunity for teams to describe the target behavior in terms that are observable (can be seen or heard) and measurable (can be counted or timed). It is important for teams to create these definitions so that whoever observes the behavior can agree that the target behavior is occurring, interventions are used in the appropriate situations and contexts that the team identifies, and the data that will be collected are valid (measure what they are supposed to measure) and reliable (that everyone can agree). One way to make sure that definitions are clear is to say them out loud and pretend you are describing the actual behaviors over the telephone to someone who cannot see what is happening. If a person who has never seen the child's challenging behavior before can create a mental picture of what you observe, then it is likely that you have a sufficient operational definition. See Table 3.1 for examples and nonexamples of operational definitions for challenging behaviors.

Step 4: Identify the Child's Desirable Behaviors to Increase

Now that the team has identified all the details about the challenging behavior to decrease, the team identifies any and all desirable behaviors that the team would like the child to exhibit to improve his or her participation in the classroom and to learn new skills. This is an opportunity for all team members to brainstorm ideas about what skills they would like the child to learn in order to participate in classroom routines and activities. Desirable behaviors can include communicating wants and needs verbally or nonverbally, taking turns, sharing, expressing emotions appropriately, entering a play situation appropriately, calming strategies, problem-solving strategies, and so forth. For some teams, this brainstorming may only take several seconds; for other teams, this brainstorming may take several minutes and result in a long and lengthy list. It is not important to get the terminology correct or to include every single skill team members would like the child to learn when brainstorming ideas. It is okay for teams to only list the most important or most desirable behaviors. It is important to identify behaviors that will help the child be an active participant in daily classroom routines and activities.

Step 5: Select One Desirable Behavior to Increase

This is an opportunity for team members to decide which desirable behavior to target for the PTR-YC process. It is likely that many teams will have several desirable behaviors that they want to see increase, but it is easier for those who are implementing strategies to be

Table 3.2. Operational definitions of desired behavior

Desired behavior	Nonexample of definition	Example of definition
Uses appropriate communication	Uses her words	When she wants something that another child has, will say, "My turn" and put her hand out
Follows directions	Is obedient	When asked to do something or given a direction (paired with a picture of what he is supposed to do), will do what he has been asked
Engages in positive social interactions with peers	Is nice with the other children	Initiates with or responds to peers by smiling and using words that convey cooperation or positive feelings

able to focus on one behavior or skill at a time. It is important to consider behaviors that improve the child's ability to interact and form relationships with peers and adults, communicate appropriately with others, and participate in classroom routines and activities.

Step 6: Operationally Define This Target Behavior

This step is an opportunity for teams to describe the desirable target behavior in terms that are observable (can be seen or heard) and measurable (can be counted or timed). It is important for teams to create this definition so that all team members can agree whether the desirable behavior is occurring, and it will be important when monitoring progress to see if the child is learning the new skill. Defining exactly what we want to see a child do can be difficult for teams to identify, so some teams may take a while for this step. See Table 3.2 for examples and nonexamples of operational definitions of desirable behaviors. In addition, the case examples in the following appendix will help illustrate how this process can occur.

FIGURE 3.2

Self-Evaluation Checklist for Teaming and Goal Setting

	Yes	No
1. Has a team been assembled that includes the people who are most involved with the child and who are most responsible for the child's behavior in the classroom?	☐	☐
2. Does the team include a member of the child's family?	☐	☐
3. Have outside services been considered in terms of the role that they might play in the development and implementation of the behavior intervention plan?	☐	☐
4. Has the team discussed a long-term vision for the child?	☐	☐
5. Does the team have a unified long-term vision for the child?	☐	☐
6. Have short-term goals been described for challenging behavior and desirable behavior?	☐	☐
7. Have specific target behaviors been operationally defined for both challenging behaviors and desirable behaviors?	☐	☐

If the answer to each of these questions is "yes," then the team should proceed to the next step.

Figure 3.2. Self-Evaluation Checklist for Teaming and Goal Setting.

When the steps described in this chapter are completed, the team should take a moment to review and fill out the Self-Evaluation Checklist for Teaming and Goal Setting in Figure 3.2. It is important that all steps are scored as "yes" before moving to the next chapter.

APPENDIX

Case Examples

MEETING 1: HASANI

Teaming and Goal Setting

Hasani's PTR-YC process was initiated by classroom staff and welcomed by her parents. The team included her parents, her grandparents, the lead teacher, the classroom assistant, the director of the center, and the assistant director. The team also received input from the private service providers (speech and occupational therapy). This was a large team with many active, contributing members.

The team was motivated and came together with common long-term visions for Hasani. All members on the team introduced themselves by stating their name and role with Hasani. They also shared one thing they love about Hasani and one thing they would like to teach Hasani. This was recorded on large sticky notes on the wall around the room. The team talked about how they would reach agreement regarding which goal to start with and the importance of starting with just one goal. People were identified to take roles in the meeting, and a recorder, facilitator, and time keeper were selected. Next, the team decided to move ahead into goal setting. They were all eager to get things started for Hasani.

Many goals were identified, and the challenge for this team was to prioritize and reach agreement regarding where to start. Figure 3.1A presents the goals identified by the team using the PTR-YC Goal Sheet.

The team facilitator decided to refer to the questions about goal setting to help guide the discussion in deciding which challenging behavior and which desirable behavior they should target. This kept the discussion factual and helped the team reach agreement. The questions and answers are as follows.

- Is there a challenging behavior that is exhibited in a variety of contexts or across multiple activities such as transitions, large-group times, arrival, and dismissal? (*Answer from data:* Not responding and walking away and grabbing and tearing items.)

- Is there a challenging behavior that is used with frequency to communicate wants and needs? (*Answer from data:* Walking away and leaving the classroom.)

- Is there an aggressive behavior that needs to be immediately addressed? (*Answer from data:* No, although there are safety concerns around leaving the classroom.)

- Are there any challenging behaviors that begin mildly then escalate to more extreme or intense behaviors? (*Answer from data:* Not responding and walking away.)

From the information generated on the PTR-YC Goal Sheet and the answers from the questions above, the team was able to reach consensus on the challenging behavior to target and the desirable behavior to teach. The team also decided that in order to follow directions, Hasani would first need to be able to respond to adults. Therefore, the team decided to focus on decreasing nonresponsive behavior (not responding, looking away) and increasing engagement as the target behavior and goal to start with.

This first meeting lasted for 1 hour. A team was developed, and a method for reaching agreement was established. This team identified a challenging behavior and a desirable behav-

---

FORM 1   **PTR-YC Goal Sheet**

1. Identify the child's challenging behaviors to decrease.
2. Select ONE challenging behavior to target.
3. Operationally define this target behavior—observable (seen or heard) and measurable (counted or timed).
4. Identify the child's desirable behaviors to increase.
5. Select ONE desirable behavior to increase.
6. Operationally define this target behavior—observable (seen or heard) and measurable (counted or timed).

Child: _Hasani_   Date: _September 6_

1. Behavior(s) to decrease	Not responding, looking away, and walking away when given directions Leaving the classroom Not responding to peers Not responding to adults Tearing materials Taking things from others Leaving classroom activities Walking away during transitions and other routines in which she does not want to participate
2. Target behavior	Not responding, looking away
3. Operational definition	When presented with a familiar request, does not respond within 5 seconds
4. Behavior(s) to increase	Engaging with adults Following directions Responding to adults when given directions—look at, interact, and respond Following classroom routines Participating in classroom activities Requesting wants and needs Using materials and toys appropriately Responding to peers and adults Interacting with peers Taking turns Sharing Playing with peers
5. Target behavior	Engagement
6. Operational definition	When spoken to, Hasani will engage by looking at, interacting, or responding to the request.

Figure 3.1A. Hasani's PTR-YC Goal Sheet. (*Note:* Blank fillable and printable versions can be found on the accompanying CD-ROM.)

ior to target for intervention and operationally defined these behaviors. After completing the Self-Evaluation Checklist for Teaming and Goal Setting (see Figure 3.2), the team scheduled the next meeting for later that week.

MEETING 1: JOEL

Teaming and Goal Setting

Joel's PTR-YC process was initiated by the Head Start staff. This team consisted of the preschool teacher, classroom assistant, and educational specialist. Although Joel's dad, Gary, supported this process, he also stated that he would most likely not be able to attend meetings due to his inflexible work schedule. He stated that he could participate by written correspondence and occasionally by telephone calls. Because Gary did not have consistent access to the Internet, the team decided that communication would be through handwritten letters that would be shared in Joel's back-and-forth book in his backpack. Gary agreed to check Joel's backpack daily for updates and information about the PTR-YC process. The team agreed to provide Gary with specific ways he could actively participate in the process. For example, the team would send home a PTR-YC Goal Sheet for Gary to complete, with instructions and examples of how to complete the forms. The team followed the same process with all steps related to PTR-YC. This communication agreement also included time lines that stated when each assignment would be due.

The team easily reached consensus on the target behavior to decrease. Team members felt that hitting others and taking toys from peers were the behaviors of most concern; however, they felt that hitting was of the most concern. Because hitting others seemed to be related to escaping from activities and getting attention, the team chose to teach Joel how to actively participate in activities and get attention in a more appropriate manner. There was a lot of discussion about how to increase the attention Joel receives when he is participating in activities appropriately; this concept of paying attention to Joel following the appropriate behavior will continue to be developed. Gary expressed concerns related to hitting through written correspondence, especially when told to follow routines such as going to bed and getting ready for preschool. Although both home routines were problematic, Gary decided that bedtime was of the most concern and would be willing to try something different if an intervention was working at school. The team decided to develop a school intervention and assist Gary in adapting this for the bedtime routine at home when he was ready. The team developed operational definitions of the target behaviors and sent the team's PTR-YC Goal Sheet home for Gary (see Figure 3.2A).

MEETING 1: JESSI

Teaming and Goal Setting

Jessi's PTR-YC process was initiated by the classroom staff and Jessi's family. The team included Lucy and Kay, Jessi's foster mother and father; Jessi's social worker; Jessi's biological parents; Elle, the classroom teacher; Lauren, the classroom assistant; and the center director. It was clear to everyone involved at that time that Jessi would need to be referred to the local school district, so the team was going to be expanding. The team decided to move along with PTR-YC to begin to address Jessi's behavioral issues. Because it sometimes took a while for school district services to begin, the team was not willing to wait to address Jessi's needs. Elle also wanted to keep Jessi in her classroom if possible and was willing to make accommodations to try to meet Jessi's needs given their resources at the time. Although Jessi's team included several members, the main participants for the PTR-YC process were Lucy, Elle, and Lauren. School district personnel were involved on a regular basis during future meetings and interventions.

Jessi's biological parents were not able to attend the first meeting, but their long-term vision was shared with the team. Every team member shared a long-term vision for Jessi, and

FORM
1

PTR-YC Goal Sheet

1. Identify the child's challenging behaviors to decrease.
2. Select ONE challenging behavior to target.
3. Operationally define this target behavior—observable (seen or heard) and measurable (counted or timed).
4. Identify the child's desirable behaviors to increase.
5. Select ONE desirable behavior to increase.
6. Operationally define this target behavior—observable (seen or heard) and measurable (counted or timed).

Child: _Joel_   Date: _September 23_

1. Behavior(s) to decrease	Hitting teachers Leaving activities Not responding to directions Telling teachers "no" Being loud in the classroom Playing too rough with toys Taking toys from peers Hitting peers
2. Target behavior	Hitting others
3. Operational definition	Joel will hit teachers and peers, usually with an open hand.
4. Behavior(s) to increase	Participating in classroom activities in which he may not be interested Following directions Using an inside voice Playing with toys appropriately Requesting what he wants or needs Asking for what he wants Sharing with peers Taking turns Asking or requesting from peers
5. Target behavior	Participate in classroom activities in which he may not be interested
6. Operational definition	When presented with a nonpreferred activity, Joel will actively participate in the activity for a minimum of 2 minutes.

Figure 3.2A. Joel's PTR-YC Goal Sheet. (*Note:* Blank fillable and printable versions can be found on the accompanying CD-ROM.)

the teacher wrote everyone's responses on a piece of paper that was kept as part of Jessi's behavior intervention plan and was also sent home to Jessi's biological parents. Because Lucy, Elle, and Lauren were the consistent members for the meetings, Elle agreed to keep track of all the forms and documents for PTR-YC, which she kept in a binder in her classroom. The assistant agreed to be the time keeper, and Lucy agreed to bring a snack or treat to each of their meetings.

FORM 1

PTR-YC Goal Sheet

1. Identify the child's challenging behaviors to decrease.
2. Select ONE challenging behavior to target.
3. Operationally define this target behavior—observable (seen or heard) and measurable (counted or timed).
4. Identify the child's desirable behaviors to increase.
5. Select ONE desirable behavior to increase.
6. Operationally define this target behavior—observable (seen or heard) and measurable (counted or timed).

Child: _Jessi_   Date: _January 10_

1. Behavior(s) to decrease	Hitting others (mostly children) Kicking others (mostly children) Hitting her head on the floor Throwing objects Pinching Hugging too tightly Crying
2. Target behavior	Physical aggression toward self or others
3. Operational definition	Hits/slaps others with an open hand (usually around the face or head); kicks her legs toward others while sitting on the floor (does not always make contact with the other person); pinches others (usually on the arm) with her thumb and first finger; throws objects toward others or object gets within 5 feet of another person; if on the floor, lays down on her back, lifts her head up, and then slams it back down to the floor; if sitting down, bends her body at the waist, leans forward, and hits her forehead on the ground
4. Behavior(s) to increase	Following directions Following the daily schedule Participating in class activities Making the transition to the appropriate area/activity in the classroom Not hurting others Being able to express herself appropriately
5. Target behavior	Follow the daily schedule
6. Operational definition	When directly told to go to a particular area or told that it is time for a specific activity, Jessi will walk to the appropriate area on her own (within 5 feet of the designated location).

Figure 3.3A.   Jessi's PTR-YC Goal Sheet. (*Note:* Blank fillable and printable versions can be found on the accompanying CD-ROM.)

Jessi's team identified many goals using the PTR-YC Goal Sheet and agreed that they did not need to list everything that they wanted to work on, so they reduced their list to priority goals identified by the team (see Figure 3.3A). The team agreed that all of the challenging behaviors would be good to target first and tried to figure out a way to decide which would be first. Although several team members expressed that only targeting one behavior is not enough, everyone eventually agreed that targeting one behavior to start with would be a good idea to see how the process works and to find effective ways to manage Jessi's challenging behaviors. During this discussion, it became evident that several of the behaviors often happened during the same behavior episode, or were clustered together. Once the team identified that Jessi's physical aggression toward herself or others was a priority (as well as a safety issue), the team quickly agreed that targeting physical aggression would be the place to start for addressing Jessi's challenging behaviors. Creating the operational definition was difficult for the team and took a long time because there were so many behaviors the team was trying to define. The team did not have a chance to identify any desirable behaviors because this part of the meeting took so long. Because several members would not be able to meet again to help identify desirable behaviors to target with Jessi, the center director suggested that everyone send her their ideas by e-mail by the end of the next day and she would compile a list of responses from team members. Elle, Lauren, and Lucy decided to meet again before school in 2 days to identify a desirable behavior to target from all of the responses that were compiled. They also decided that they would start the next step of the process (data collection) during this second meeting in order to continue to move forward with PTR-YC.

MEETING 1: ETHAN

Teaming and Goal Setting

Ethan's PTR-YC process was initiated by Joan, the center director who also serves as Ethan's classroom teacher, and Carol, the teaching assistant. Veronica, Ethan's grandmother, welcomed the process in order to help Ethan be more successful at the center. Ethan's team consisted of Joan, Carol, and Veronica. Veronica was not as involved as she would have liked because she worked full time and counted on the center's flexibility and willingness to help her as much as they could. Veronica was able to meet with Joan and Carol for an initial meeting, but subsequent meetings were between Joan and Carol, with input and feedback from Veronica via text and/or e-mail messages. Veronica was hopeful that the plan that was developed was successful and that she would be able to implement some of the strategies at home as well. Due to Veronica's limited availability, the team filled out the PTR-YC Goal Sheet prior to the first meeting in order to be more effective and efficient (see Figure 3.4A). When Joan approached Veronica to discuss the possibility of trying out the PTR-YC process with Ethan, there was discussion about a long-term vision, even though no one really thought of it in that way at the time.

When the team met to discuss goals for Ethan, Joan recalled that Veronica wanted Ethan to be an active member of the classroom in a positive way and that she wanted Ethan to be ready to go to kindergarten. The team immediately agreed that this was their long-term vision for Ethan—that he would be an active and positive member of any classroom and would be ready for whatever milestone was coming next. This led to the team discussing what barriers were keeping him from doing so, and each team member shared the challenging behaviors they had written on their PTR-YC Goal Sheet. Joan used a blank PTR-YC Goal Sheet to record all of their responses. The three members had almost all the same answers, so it was clear that they were all seeing Ethan's challenges in a similar way. As they began discussing which behavior they would like to target, Veronica thought that pulling hair or yelling profanities would be the best place to start because the pulling hair physically hurts the other child and she did not want the other children to be hearing profanities every day. Joan agreed that pulling hair was definitely something they wanted to target but that it did not necessarily occur every day.

FORM
1

PTR-YC Goal Sheet

1. Identify the child's challenging behaviors to decrease.
2. Select ONE challenging behavior to target.
3. Operationally define this target behavior—observable (seen or heard) and measurable (counted or timed).
4. Identify the child's desirable behaviors to increase.
5. Select ONE desirable behavior to increase.
6. Operationally define this target behavior—observable (seen or heard) and measurable (counted or timed).

Child: _Ethan_   Date: _March 9_

1. Behavior(s) to decrease	Taking toys from his peers Yelling "no" to peers Tattling to teachers that his peers are not sharing Crying Pulling hair Destroying a peer's play when Ethan cannot join in play Yelling profanities Impulsiveness—can be explosive Very emotional and intense
2. Target behavior	Disruptive behavior
3. Operational definition	Taking toys from peers without asking, yelling "no" to peers, tattling to teachers, crying, pulling a peer's hair, destroying a peer's play (kicking or knocking over a peer's structure, ripping up or crumpling a peer's work done on paper, or taking a play item that is a part of the peer's current play activity), and yelling profanities
4. Behavior(s) to increase	Accepting being told "no" Learning to negotiate with others Taking care of situations on his own in an appropriate way (problem solve) If told "no," being able to calmly and nicely ask again instead of getting so upset right away and immediately engaging in the disruptive behaviors Being able to express his anger without taking it out on others or yelling profanities
5. Target behavior	If told "no," being able to nicely ask again
6. Operational definition	When a peer tells Ethan he can't have something that he asked for or isn't allowed to join in another's play, Ethan will be able to ask the peer again using an inside voice, holding his open hand out to gesture that he would like something, and having a calm body.

Figure 3.4A. Ethan's PTR-YC Goal Sheet. (*Note:* Blank fillable and printable versions can be found on the accompanying CD-ROM.)

Joan shared with the group that she read the entire PTR-YC manual in order to understand the process and to find out if it was something that they would be able to do. She continued to share that there was a section that talked about clusters of behavior and that she distinctly remembered that because she immediately thought about Ethan. Joan and Carol noted that the behaviors they listed did not occur all the time, but Ethan would do some of them when things did not go his way. Joan and Carol shared a few examples with Veronica, and it helped her understand what they were talking about. It also helped the team to see the cluster of behaviors as options of what Ethan would do when he did not get his way, based on the situation (e.g., who was around, what the activity was, what he was trying to do). As the team decided that they would target all of the behaviors as a cluster, they decided to refer to the cluster as disruptive behavior. It was pretty easy to create an operational definition because they already created the list of all the things that contributed to disruptive behavior.

As the team created the operational definition, they named some skills that would be good for Ethan to be able to do, and Joan began recording them in the "increase" section on the PTR-YC Goal Sheet. Although each team member brought ideas to the meeting that they thought of before, the current discussion generated more relevant ideas in terms of what to teach Ethan based on what he was trying to accomplish with his current challenging behaviors. The team agreed that they had a good list of things but really struggled with what they wanted to start with because they felt that he needed to learn all of the skills they listed. As they were trying to make a decision, Joan wondered out loud if she and Carol should try some of the classroom practices that she read about and shared what the practices are from the manual. Veronica was excited about all the things that were discussed and wondered if they could still continue the process with Ethan while the classroom practices were implemented. Veronica felt that anything to help Ethan would be beneficial, and she did not want to wait too long. Joan and Carol agreed that they would go over the classroom practices together and figure out what they were going to implement. In the meantime, they would proceed with Ethan's individual plan for 15 minutes each morning before the children arrived and would keep Veronica updated on their progress. Once that was agreed on, the team went back to what desirable behavior they wanted to target. They finally agreed on getting Ethan to be able to calmly ask a peer for something a second time. They hoped that if he could ask a peer for something a second time in a calm and appropriate manner, then he would be able to accept being told "no" and try to problem solve. It was a little difficult for the team to create an operational definition for the desirable behavior, but once they did, it became clearer about what they wanted Ethan to be able to do for this particular skill.

As they wrapped up their meeting, Joan and Carol confirmed that Veronica would not be able to make any more meetings but wanted to participate as much as she could. Veronica said she trusted what Joan and Carol would come up with for the next step in the process—data collection. Joan said that she would e-mail a copy to Veronica in case she had any suggestions, questions, or comments.

Data Collection

The step that follows goal setting is designing and implementing a clear, simple, and valid system for collecting data. Now, we understand that most professionals do not like the idea of data collection. When we raise the topic in workshops, we almost always hear audible groans of protest. And there are many good reasons for this aversion. All too often teachers and other early childhood professionals are asked to collect data that are too effortful, too cumbersome, and essentially useless in the practice of early care and education. But data collection in PTR-YC is different. Really. It is different for two big reasons: 1) It is simple, and 2) it is valuable to you and your team. In this chapter, we describe why this is the case and the specifics of how data collection is implemented in PTR-YC.

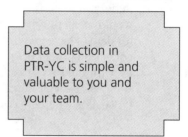

Data collection in PTR-YC is simple and valuable to you and your team.

IMPORTANCE OF DATA COLLECTION

Data in the PTR-YC model are primarily used to monitor progress, which is a necessary component of effective behavior interventions. Data help to inform the team about the effectiveness of the intervention strategies and help the team make decisions about changes that might be needed in the behavior intervention plan. Data can also help to inform others about the status of the child's behavior and about progress that has occurred. This can be extremely important for accountability purposes. Even in those instances when initial progress is not evident, the fact that data have been collected shows everybody that you are truly serious about doing everything that can be done to help.

It is not possible to collect accurate data on every challenging behavior that occurs in your program. That is not realistic. When a behavior is serious enough that a team has been assembled and a systematic intervention plan is going to be developed and implemented, however, then we are no longer talking about every challenging behavior. We are talking about behaviors that interfere with a specific child's healthy development, and we are talking about behaviors that will have negative consequences for the child's future if left untreated. The point is that if a challenging behavior is persistent enough or severe enough, then we have to do the best we can to resolve the problem as effectively and efficiently as possible. And this requires data collection. There are no two ways about it. If PTR-YC is going to be used, then data must be collected. The good news is that data collection does not need to be difficult, and in the PTR-YC model, it is reasonably simple.

There are many ways to collect data. The literature is packed with methods and procedures for collecting data in classrooms and other programs. You have undoubtedly heard of many of these methods, and you might have even used some of them. They include interval recording and time sampling and duration recording and event recording and on and on. But in our experience, most of these methods are not workable in preschool or Head Start classrooms or child care programs. They are too complicated and take up too much time for regular human beings to use—especially if those regular human beings also have responsibilities for teaching, classroom management, implementing a curriculum, meeting with parents, arranging materials, keeping classroom records, and doing the thousand other things that teachers and other classroom personnel do on a daily basis. But there are two methods of data collection that we believe are useful and simple enough to be used by classroom personnel on a daily basis.

Before we describe these methods, it is useful to consider some features of data collection that are essential if the data are to have value. First, the data must be reasonably accurate (i.e., the data that are collected should conform closely to what actually happened). For instance, if the data we collect indicate that Billy initiated interactions with his classmates on six separate occasions between arrival and mid-morning snack time, then we must assume that it was exactly or at least very close to the number of times that Billy actually initiated social contact with his peers. The data would not be helpful if Billy actually initiated interactions on 20 or more occasions because the magnitude of such an error would mean that we would not be able to trust the data. A second quality that is important for data to have is *reliability*. Reliability means that two or more people using the same data collection procedures to observe the same behavior over the same time period would end up with the same result, or at least a very similar result. If Billy's teacher recorded six instances of social initiation, and Billy's teaching assistant also recorded six instances, then those data would be considered to be very reliable. If the teaching assistant recorded seven instances, then the comparison would still be reasonably reliable. But if the teaching assistant recorded only two instances, then the reliability would be very poor, and we would be unable to trust the data. The problem causing such poor reliability could be an inadequate definition of *social initiation* (perhaps the assistant was looking for something different from what the teacher was looking for) or it could be that the assistant failed to observe during a crucial period when Billy was most active with his social initiations. Either way, the problem would have to be identified and corrected before the data could be trusted. This is important because data that are not trustworthy are not worth collecting.

There is another quality of data that is important to mention. This third quality is known as *face validity*, which simply means that the data that are being collected actually represent the behavior of greatest interest to the team. In Billy's case, the collection of data on the number of social initiations between arrival and mid-morning snack implies that this behavior is the genuine priority for the team. It also implies that the definition being used by the team captures exactly what the team is most interested in. Face validity is an important feature to consider whenever data collection systems are being developed and implemented.

Data Collection in PTR-YC

There are two types of data collection that we believe are feasible for typical program personnel to implement for purposes of progress monitoring. The most flexible, and the one we recommend most often, is the use of behavior rating scales. We expect that behavior rating scales will be used in about 80%–90% of the cases in which PTR-YC is applied. The other method is frequency counts, or tallying, in which instances of specific behaviors are counted as they occur. In both methods, teams should always make sure that the system, whatever it might be, will be accurate and reliable and have face validity.

FREQUENCY COUNTS

Although we recommend behavior rating scales most often, we will begin by describing frequency counts. Frequency counts are simply tallies of the actual number of times that a behavior occurs during a designated period of time. For instance, a 4-year-old girl named Erica had a challenging behavior of crying. She had been observed engaging in short episodes of crying several times during the morning of her daily pre-school session (8:00 a.m. to 11:30 a.m.). Crying had persisted despite the diligent use of universal and secondary prevention strategies. Erica's team had been counting the number of episodes of crying for several weeks and found that she averaged seven episodes per morning, with no indication that the number was declining. Because these counts were fairly simple for the team to obtain and they seemed accurate (nobody had any problem determining when Erica had a crying episode), the team decided to continue to use this method of frequency counts as their ongoing method of progress monitoring when they initiated the PTR-YC process. Erica's team had not been obtaining data on a desirable, replacement behavior, so the team members still had to identify a data collection method for this behavior. The desirable behavior that was chosen was "positive interactions with peers," and this turned out to be more difficult to measure with frequency counts. The team decided to use the behavior rating scales as data for this desirable behavior. The steps for using behavior rating scales are described following the description of steps for using frequency counts.

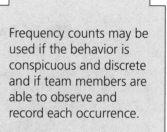

Frequency counts may be used if the behavior is conspicuous and discrete and if team members are able to observe and record each occurrence.

Frequency counts should be used for ongoing data collection in the following instances:

- The behavior is conspicuous so that each instance is easy to observe.

- The behavior is discrete, meaning that each instance is relatively brief and separate from other instances. If a behavior tends to occur for long periods of time (e.g., 20-minute tantrums) or in rapid bursts so that one instance is hard to distinguish from another (e.g., a series of loud screeches), then frequency counts are probably not the best method for data collection.

- Team members in the classroom are able and willing to record a tally each time the behavior occurs.

If these criteria are met, then we encourage the teams to use frequency counts for the identified target behaviors. If teams are already using frequency counts and the data are accurate and reliable, then of course it is reasonable for the teams to continue this method of data collection.

Steps for Using Frequency Counts

The steps for using frequency counts are simple but important. If each step is implemented correctly, then frequency counts can provide useful data for progress monitoring.

Step 1: Define the target behavior in terms that are observable and clearly indicate when the behavior is occurring and when it is not. The definition should be precise enough that everybody on the team agrees when the behavior is present.

Step 2: Determine the period of time in the day during which the behavior will be counted. This period of time should remain the same throughout all of the days of data collection, from baseline throughout intervention. The period of time can be all day or just the activities or time periods when the behavior is of greatest concern, but it should remain the same throughout data collection.

Step 3: Determine how the behavior will be counted and who will do the counting. Because frequency data should be recorded when the behavior occurs (it is not a good idea to rely on memory for this kind of data), there should be a means of recording the count that is easy to use. For instance, the person doing the counting could keep

FORM 3

PTR-YC Daily Log

	Session date	Number of occurrences
Baseline	September 25	3
	September 26	10
	September 27	9
	September 28	4
	October 1	8
	October 2	8
	October 3	10
	October 4	5
	October 5	7
Intervention	October 8	3
	October 9	1
	October 10	0
	October 11	2
	October 12	0
	October 15	1
	October 16	1
	October 17	0

Figure 4.1. PTR-YC Daily Log for Erica's crying. (*Note:* Blank fillable and printable versions of this form can be found on the accompanying CD-ROM.)

an index card in his or her pocket to make tally marks on or use a golf counter or some other device that is comfortable and accurate. The person doing the counting should be someone in the classroom who will always be in a position to notice when the behavior occurs.

Step 4: Determine where the permanent records will be maintained and establish a method for graphing the data. The location where data will be maintained should be a central but private area, such as a drawer in a desk or a daily file log for the child

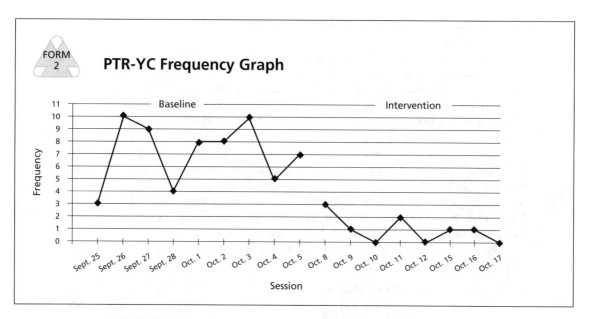

Figure 4.2. PTR-YC Frequency Graph of Erica's crying. (*Note:* Blank fillable and printable versions of this form can be found on the accompanying CD-ROM.)

whose behavior is being observed. As soon as the observational period is concluded, the total number of occurrences for that day should be entered into the log. When the data are entered into the log, they should also be entered on a simple line graph.

A graph is developed with the date of observation on the horizontal axis and the number of occurrences on the vertical axis. The scale on the vertical axis is determined by noting zero occurrences at the bottom of the vertical line, and the maximum number of occurrences on the child's most difficult day (for challenging behavior) at the top of the vertical line. Figures 4.1 and 4.2 show an example PTR-YC Daily Log and an example PTR-YC Frequency Graph for challenging behavior. (*Note:* Blank fillable and printable versions of these forms can be found on the accompanying CD-ROM.)

BEHAVIOR RATING SCALE

The PTR-YC Behavior Rating Scale is the data collection procedure that we recommend most of the time. It is a perceptual scale, which means that it relies on observers' perceptions or estimates of the magnitude of a behavior during the specified observation period. The PTR-YC Behavior Rating Scale has a number of advantages. The main advantage is that it is completed only once at the end of every observation period and, therefore, it is much less demanding than other data collection strategies that require ongoing data recording. Studies have also shown that the behavior rating scales can be sufficiently accurate and reliable for typical purposes of progress monitoring (e.g., Chafouleas, Riley-Tillman, & Sugai, 2007; Iovannone, Greenbaum, Wang, Kincaid, & Dunlap, in press). The feasibility of the PTR-YC Behavior Rating Scale for use by typical preschool personnel is the most important reason for our recommendation. If used correctly, the PTR-YC Behavior Rating Scale can provide all of the data

> If used correctly, the PTR-YC Behavior Rating Scale can provide all of the data that are needed to track progress and make informed decisions regarding the effects of the PTR-YC intervention.

that are needed to track progress and make informed decisions regarding the effects of the PTR-YC intervention.

The PTR-YC Behavior Rating Scale can be used to collect data on a child's challenging behavior and on a child's desirable behavior. A separate scale is used for each behavior. The key issue in effectively using the PTR-YC Behavior Rating Scale is to spend a little time creating the individualized rating scale and making sure that the data collectors can use it in a manner that is valid and reliable. The steps for developing an individualized rating scale for a particular child are described next.

Step 1: Define the target behavior in terms that are observable and correspond to the goals established by the team. The challenging behavior is the first target behavior to be defined. You should use the definition developed by your team. The desirable behavior is the second target behavior to be defined. For simplicity, the following description of steps focuses on the challenging behavior. The same process should be used to develop an individualized rating scale for desirable behaviors.

Step 2: Determine the most important dimension of the behavior that should be measured. Dimensions include the following:

- *Frequency:* The number of times a behavior occurs during the period of observation. For instance, frequency is a good dimension for measuring the number of times Ahmad screams (or engages in an episode of screaming) during a morning session.

- *Duration:* The overall amount of time that the behavior lasts. Duration is a reasonable dimension for behaviors that occur for long periods of time and may include some tantrums or crying episodes.

- *Intensity:* Refers to the forcefulness or loudness of the behavior. For example, a highly intense instance of hitting might produce pain or result in injury, but a mildly intense instance of hitting might barely be noticed. Similarly, an ear-piercing scream that breaks windows would be scored as highly intense, but a gentle scream might be scored as having low intensity.

- *Percentage of time:* The percentage of actual time in which the behavior is present over a total observation period. A good example of this dimension is engagement, in which the behavior of interest is the child's active involvement with the classroom's designated activities.

- *Percentage of opportunities:* How often the behavior occurs in relation to the available opportunities. For instance, if the team is concerned with a child's responsiveness to spoken requests, then the measure of interest might be the percentage of verbal requests or questions to which to child makes a response.

Each dimension represents a different way of assessing magnitude, or how much of the behavior is exhibited, but different behaviors are measured best with different dimensions. The dimension is important because it determines how the scale on the behavior rating scale will be constructed, so the team must decide which dimension is most important.

Step 3: Determine when the behavior will be observed. The team decides the time period during which the behavior will be measured. The time could be all day, all morning, or during specifically targeted routines. This time period should be the one that is most important and is often the time when the problem is most conspicuous.

Step 4: Develop anchors for the rating scale. The PTR-YC Behavior Rating Scale is based on a rating scale of 1–5. Each number in this rating scale is considered an anchor. These numbers are used to measure behavior. The day with the highest magnitude of the challenging behavior would be rated a 5, and the very best day would be a 1. For example, consider a 3½-year-old boy named Teddy who had a serious problem of hitting his peers during his 4-hour daily preschool session. The team agreed that Teddy's most difficult days were those with 10 or more episodes of hitting. Therefore, a score of 5 on the PTR-YC Behavior Rating Scale was recorded if there were 10 or more episodes in the morning's observations. An ideal day would be no instances of hitting, so that day would be scored as a 1. The team then needed to specify anchors for the intermediate instances of hitting. The team decided that a score of 4 would mean 6–9 instances, a score of 3 would mean 3–5 instances, and a score of 2 would be recorded if there were 1 or 2 occurrences of hitting. These anchors are then written on the bottom portion of the PTR-YC Behavior Rating Scale.

Anchors are also developed for desirable behaviors. Teddy's team decided that he should learn how to get peers' attention by tapping them on the shoulder and saying their name. The dimension for measurement was decided to be the percentage of times when it was clear that Teddy wanted to interact with a peer. Although this is a dimension that might be difficult to determine with great precision, it was agreed that team members could make good enough estimates and that they could agree on general percentages. Therefore, it was decided that a great day would be when Teddy used the tapping and naming on 80% or more opportunities. This level became the anchor point for a score of 5. A day without any instances of Teddy using the desired strategy was scored as a 1. Intermediate anchors were defined as 4 = *about 51%–79%*, 3 = *about 21%–50%*, and 2 = *about 20% or less*. Again, it was not expected that observers would calculate precise percentages. The scores represented observers' perceptions of the percentage of opportunities that Teddy used the desired strategy for obtaining peers' attention. It is worthwhile to note that high scores for desirable behavior (e.g., 5) are positive, and the team will wish for a child's behavior to move toward these high scores, whereas high scores for challenging behavior represent difficult days, and the team will wish for challenging behavior ratings to descend in the direction of 1.

Step 5: Determine who will be responsible for recording the PTR-YC Behavior Rating Scale score at the end of the observation period each day. This person can be any member of the classroom team who is in a position to make accurate judgments. That is, it is a person who will be in a good position to observe Teddy's behavior. The person might be the lead teacher or caregiver, but it also might be the assistant teacher or other staff member. From time to time it is a good idea to have more than one person complete the PTR-YC Behavior Rating Scale independently so that the scores can be compared for agreement. This is a good and important strategy for making sure that the rating scale is well calibrated. If there are large differences in the scores, then the team should figure out the reasons and provide some correction. It might be that the definition of the behavior needs to be reviewed or one of the observers missed some crucial part of the observation. It is important for the team to keep alert to possible problems with the accuracy of the data.

Step 6: Determine where the permanent records will be maintained and establish a system for graphing the data. The location where data will be maintained should be a central but private area, such as a drawer in a desk or a daily file log for the child whose behavior is being observed. As soon as the observational period is concluded, the behavior rating scale score should be entered into the log or directly on the PTR-YC Behavior Rating Scale. The PTR-YC Frequency Graph provides a simple template for producing a graph of the scores, showing trends of progress over time. The graph is created by simply charting the points on the PTR-YC Behavior Rating Scale or the numbers collected on the PTR-YC Daily Log (see Figures 4.3 and 4.4).

Once the individualized rating scale is developed, you should begin data collection as you begin the next step in the PTR-YC process.

SUMMARY

This chapter described and illustrated the process of developing and implementing a data collection system. We recommend using the PTR-YC Behavior Rating Scale for the majority of behaviors, although frequency counts can be used under certain circumstances. Teams

FORM 3

PTR-YC Daily Log

Date	Ratings number
November 4	4
November 5	3
November 6	5
November 7	4
November 8	4
November 11	4
November 12	5
November 13	3
November 14	3
November 15	2
November 18	1
November 19	2
November 20	1

Ratings
5 = 10 or more occurrences
4 = 6–9 occurrences
3 = 3–5 occurrences
2 = 1–2 occurrences
1 = 0 occurrences

Figure 4.3. PTR-YC Daily Log for Teddy's hitting. (*Note:* Blank fillable and printable versions of this form can be found on the accompanying CD-ROM.)

have been established, goals have been developed, and the data collection system has been created at this point in the PTR-YC process, and implementation of the data collection should be initiated. The next step in the PTR-YC model is functional behavioral assessment. It is important that data collection on the identified target behaviors be conducted while the functional behavioral assessment is being completed. The data collection invariably helps in the assessment process, and it is useful to establish a record of baseline levels (levels that occur before PTR-YC intervention) of the target behaviors.

The case examples in the following appendix help illustrate how the process of establishing a data collection system can occur.

PTR-YC Behavior Rating Scale

Child: Teddy   Rater: J.L.   Observation period: Morning   Month: November

Date/time

	4	5	6	7	8	11	12	13	14	15	18	19	20	21	22					
Desirable behavior Tap peer on shoulder, say name	5	5	5	5	5	5	5	5	5	5	5	5	5	5	5	5	5	5	5	5
	4	4	4	4	4	4	4	4	4	4	4	4	4	(4)	4	4	4	4	4	4
	3	(3)	3	3	3	3	3	3	3	(3)	3	(3)	(3)	3	(3)	3	3	3	3	3
	2	2	2	2	2	2	2	2	(2)	2	(2)	2	2	2	2	2	2	2	2	2
	(1)	1	(1)	(1)	(1)	(1)	(1)	(1)	1	1	1	1	1	1	1	1	1	1	1	1
Challenging behavior Hitting peers	5	5	(5)	5	5	5	(5)	5	5	5	5	5	5	5	5	5	5	5	5	5
	(4)	4	4	(4)	(4)	(4)	4	4	4	4	4	4	4	4	4	4	4	4	4	4
	3	(3)	3	3	3	3	3	(3)	(3)	3	3	3	3	3	3	3	3	3	3	3
	2	2	2	2	2	2	2	2	2	(2)	2	(2)	2	2	2	2	2	2	2	2
	1	1	1	1	1	1	1	1	1	1	(1)	1	(1)	(1)	(1)	1	1	1	1	1

<— Baseline —>   <— Intervention —>

Desirable behavior: Tap peer on shoulder, say name
5 = 80% or more of opportunities
4 = about 51%-74%
3 = about 21%-50%
2 = 20% or less
1 = no instances

Challenging behavior: Hitting peers
5 = 10 or more occurrences
4 = 6-9 occurrences
3 = 3-5 occurrences
2 = 1-2 occurrences
1 = 0 occurrences

Figure 4.4. PTR-YC Behavior Rating Scale for Teddy's hitting. (*Note:* Blank fillable and printable versions of this form can be found on the accompanying CD-ROM.)

FIGURE 4.5

Self-Evaluation Checklist for Data Collection

	Yes	No
1. Has the team carefully defined the target behaviors in observable terms?	☐	☐
2. Did the team determine the dimension (e.g., frequency, duration, percentage of time) that will be used to measure behavior?	☐	☐
3. Did the team decide whether to use the PTR-YC Behavior Rating Scale or frequency counts for the target challenging behavior and the desirable behavior?	☐	☐
4. Have the observation period and the primary data collectors been specified?	☐	☐
5. Have the anchors been carefully defined and written on the PTR-YC Behavior Rating Scale?	☐	☐
6. Has the procedure for keeping the frequency count during the observation period been specified (if applicable)?	☐	☐
7. Has the location of the permanent data logs and graphs been indicated, and has it been determined who will be responsible for maintaining the logs and graphs?	☐	☐

If the answer to each of these questions is "yes," then the team should proceed to the next step.

Figure 4.5. Self-Evaluation Checklist for Data Collection.

When the steps described in this chapter are completed, the team should take a moment to review and fill out the Self-Evaluation Checklist for Data Collection (see Figure 4.5). It is important that all steps are scored as "yes" before moving to the next chapter.

APPENDIX

Case Examples

MEETING 2: HASANI

Data Collection

Hasani's team listed the challenging behavior and the desirable behavior on sticky notes during their data collection meeting. The team discussed the dimension of the behavior to be measured. The team decided it was important to track the percentage of time Hasani engaged in the challenging behavior—does not respond. They developed a definition for each number, or anchor, on the behavior rating scale for collecting data. The team decided to track the development of the desirable behavior through the levels of prompting necessary for Hasani to be independently engaged.

These definitions were noted on the PTR-YC Behavior Rating Scale, and data collection began on Monday. The team decided the teacher and assistant would complete one PTR-YC

Behavior Rating Scale, and a separate PTR-YC Behavior Rating Scale would be completed by the family. The data would be reviewed every 2 weeks by the team. Hasani's behavior would be scored once per day at the end of the day. The data would be shared once weekly with the private providers (see Figure 4.1A).

Once the data collection system was established, the team reviewed and completed the Self-Evaluation Checklist for Data Collection (see Figure 4.5) and proceeded to the PTR-YC assessment. The challenging behavior—does not respond—was listed on the top of the PTR-YC Functional Behavioral Assessment Checklists (see Figures 5.3–5.5), and each team member was instructed to independently complete a copy of the checklists for the next meeting. (See Chapter 5 for more information about these checklists.)

MEETING 2: JOEL

Data Collection

Joel's school team sent home requests for information from Gary, Joel's father, but had not received a response prior to the next scheduled meeting. The team would be deciding in this meeting what dimension of the behavior was to be measured and how to measure this on the behavior rating scale. The team proceeded with this meeting and would continue to offer opportunities for Gary to participate and would send all information home for Gary to review and provide input when he was able.

The team had no trouble deciding to measure the frequency of hitting episodes. They also decided to count every time Joel hit, regardless of whether he was hitting a teacher or a peer. The team discussed what the worst day looked like with regard to the number of times Joel hit others. They determined that it was more than 10 times. The team chose to make this a 5 on the scale. The team also decided that the best day would be no hitting, so that became a 1 on the scale. The team decided to keep daily tally marks for the number of times Joel hit others to get an accurate reading on how frequently this behavior was occurring.

The bigger challenge for Joel's team was how to measure the desirable behavior. As the team continued to discuss the desirable behavior, the conversation often revolved around Joel actively participating in activities in appropriate ways instead of allowing him to get out of participating. The teacher and assistant were not comfortable with allowing Joel to do what he wanted because they felt that if Joel was allowed to "get away with it," then the other children would start to do so as well. The team had a long discussion about what children are expected to do at various activities and realized this discussion aided in their own clarity of what the expectations were. With some routines and behavior expectations defined, the team decided to focus on classroom practices and how to implement them. The team would record data on the challenging behavior and desirable behavior for a baseline of where to start with Joel. Because hitting was a safety issue for Joel and others, it was important for the team to continue with the individualized process and focus on decreasing Joel's hitting (see Figure 4.2A).

MEETING 2: JESSI

Goal Setting (Continued) and Data Collection

The second meeting of Jessi's team consisted of Lucy, Jessi's foster mother; Elle, the classroom teacher; and Lauren, the classroom assistant. Their task was to finish setting goals, choose a desirable behavior, and decide what data to begin collecting. They reviewed the list of desirable behaviors that the director received from other team members as well as their own responses. After the experience they had 2 days prior in identifying a challenging behavior and operationally defining it, they were anxious to identify a desirable behavior fairly quickly. Once the desirable behavior was decided on and defined, the team began discussing how they were going to collect data.

Figure 4.1A. Hasani's PTR-YC Behavior Rating Scale with blank areas to be completed by the teacher and assistant or the family. (*Note:* Blank fillable and printable versions of this form can be found on the accompanying CD-ROM.)

FORM 4

PTR-YC Behavior Rating Scale

Child: _Hasani_   Rater: _____   Observation period: _All day_   Month: _September_

Date/time

Desirable behavior Engagement	5	5	5	5	5	5	5	5	5	5	5	5	5	5	5	5
	4	4	4	4	4	4	4	4	4	4	4	4	4	4	4	4
	3	3	3	3	3	3	3	3	3	3	3	3	3	3	3	3
	2	2	2	2	2	2	2	2	2	2	2	2	2	2	2	2
	1	1	1	1	1	1	1	1	1	1	1	1	1	1	1	1
Challenging behavior Does not respond	5	5	5	5	5	5	5	5	5	5	5	5	5	5	5	5
	4	4	4	4	4	4	4	4	4	4	4	4	4	4	4	4
	3	3	3	3	3	3	3	3	3	3	3	3	3	3	3	3
	2	2	2	2	2	2	2	2	2	2	2	2	2	2	2	2
	1	1	1	1	1	1	1	1	1	1	1	1	1	1	1	1

Desirable behavior: _Engagement_
5 = _Looks independently_
4 = _Looks with a prompt or reminder_
3 = _Looks with physical assistance_
2 = _Does not look or answer_
1 = _Walks away_

Challenging behavior: _Does not respond_
5 = _Does not respond at all_
4 = _Does not respond 75% of the time_
3 = _Does not respond 50% of the time_
2 = _Does not respond 25% of the time_
1 = _Responds to adults and peers_

54

PTR-YC Behavior Rating Scale

Child: _Joel_   Rater: _____   Observation period: _Arrival_   Month: _October_

Date/time													
Desirable behavior Participates in activities	5	5	5	5	5	5	5	5	5	5	5	5	5
	4	4	4	4	4	4	4	4	4	4	4	4	4
	3	3	3	3	3	3	3	3	3	3	3	3	3
	2	2	2	2	2	2	2	2	2	2	2	2	2
	1	1	1	1	1	1	1	1	1	1	1	1	1
Challenging behavior Hitting others	5	5	5	5	5	5	5	5	5	5	5	5	5
	4	4	4	4	4	4	4	4	4	4	4	4	4
	3	3	3	3	3	3	3	3	3	3	3	3	3
	2	2	2	2	2	2	2	2	2	2	2	2	2
	1	1	1	1	1	1	1	1	1	1	1	1	1

Desirable behavior: _Participates in activities_

5 = _Independently participates in activities_

4 = _Participates with visual prompts for 2 minutes_

3 = _Participates with partial assistance for 2 minutes_

2 = _Participates with full assistance for 2 minutes_

1 = _Hits adults or peers or leaves activity_

Challenging behavior: _Hitting others_

5 = _Hits 10 or more times_

4 = _Hits 7–9 times_

3 = _Hits 4–6 times_

2 = _Hits 1–3 times_

1 = _Hits 0 times_

Figure 4.2A. Joel's PTR-YC Behavior Rating Scale with blank areas to be completed by Joel's school team. (*Note:* Blank fillable and printable versions of this form can be found on the accompanying CD-ROM.)

The team decided that it would be important to know how often Jessi's challenging behavior—physical aggression toward self or others—occurred each day, and they decided to measure its frequency. For the desirable behavior, the team decided that it would be important to keep track of how much help Jessi needed to follow the daily schedule. The teacher and assistant felt that they spent a lot of time trying to make sure Jessi was where she was supposed to be, and that if she could follow the schedule on her own, they would have more time to spend with her actually trying to get her engaged in activities if she could follow the schedule on her own. Once the team decided on what they were going to measure, they decided that they would use the PTR-YC Behavior Rating Scale to begin taking data. Although they had a general sense for how often Jessi engaged in her challenging behavior, they never kept track of it in any formal way. The teacher took out the PTR-YC Behavior Rating Scale and identified what each number stands for (developed the anchors), decided that they would rate Jessi's behavior for the whole day, and noted that the teacher and assistant would agree on a number at the end of the day to record on the PTR-YC Behavior Rating Scale (see Figure 4.3A). They completed the Self-Evaluation Checklist for Data Collection (see Figure 4.5). Then, the teacher made copies of the PTR-YC Functional Behavioral Assessment Checklists (see Figures 5.3–5.5) for all the team members to fill out and return to her. She decided to begin collecting data the following day. Lucy took one copy of the three checklists for her family and took a second copy of the checklists to give to Jessi's biological parents. The teacher and assistant agreed to each fill one copy of the checklists out and would give one copy to the center director to fill out. The teacher requested that the checklists be returned to her by Wednesday because the team would meet on Thursday morning to go over the completed checklists. Once the behavior intervention plan is implemented, Lucy, Elle, and Lauren will meet every Friday after school to briefly review the data.

MEETING 2: ETHAN

Data Collection

Ethan's second team meeting included only Joan, the center director and classroom teacher, and Carol, the teaching assistant, and occurred after school on the same day that they met with Veronica, Ethan's grandmother. They had both previously looked at the PTR-YC Behavior Rating Scale and considered using it but thought that a frequency count would be easier for them to do right away. Because Ethan's disruptive behaviors occurred in clusters, they did not have a good idea of how often the behaviors really occurred. They realized that most of the disruptive behaviors occurred during choice time because the children were able to choose what they wanted to play with or what center they wanted to play in, which was mostly unstructured. Joan and Carol decided that they would keep a piece of tape on one leg during choice time and make a tally mark for each time the disruptive behavior occurred. They also decided to take turns each day staying close to Ethan so that they could keep track of how many times the disruptive behavior actually happened. Whoever kept the tallies was responsible for recording the number on the PTR-YC Frequency Graph for that day. They also realized that Ethan never demonstrated the desirable behavior that they identified (i.e., being an active and positive member of the classroom and being ready for the next milestone), so they did not think that they would have any tally marks for the desirable behavior, but Joan and Carol agreed to keep track of that, too. Because it was Friday, they agreed to begin on Monday, and Joan volunteered to try it out first. They also agreed to meet on Tuesday morning to begin the next step. Joan sent Veronica a text message to let her know they were going to be keeping track of how many times the disruptive behavior occurred and that they were sending home the PTR-YC Functional Behavioral Assessment Checklists (see Figures 5.3–5.5) for Veronica to fill out over the weekend and return on Monday. Veronica agreed to fill out a copy of the checklists and thought the frequency count was a good idea.

PTR-YC Behavior Rating Scale

Child: _Jessi_   Rater: _Elle and Lauren_   Observation period: _All day_   Month: _January_

Date/time

Desirable behavior _Follow the daily schedule_	5	5	5	5	5	5	5	5	5	5	5	5	5	5	5	5	5
	4	4	4	4	4	4	4	4	4	4	4	4	4	4	4	4	4
	3	3	3	3	3	3	3	3	3	3	3	3	3	3	3	3	3
	2	2	2	2	2	2	2	2	2	2	2	2	2	2	2	2	2
	1	1	1	1	1	1	1	1	1	1	1	1	1	1	1	1	1
Challenging behavior _Physical aggression toward self/others_	5	5	5	5	5	5	5	5	5	5	5	5	5	5	5	5	5
	4	4	4	4	4	4	4	4	4	4	4	4	4	4	4	4	4
	3	3	3	3	3	3	3	3	3	3	3	3	3	3	3	3	3
	2	2	2	2	2	2	2	2	2	2	2	2	2	2	2	2	2
	1	1	1	1	1	1	1	1	1	1	1	1	1	1	1	1	1

Desirable behavior: _Follow the daily schedule_

5 = _Teacher points to activity/area_
4 = _Teacher provides initial physical guidance_
3 = _Teacher provides physical guidance part of the way_
2 = _Teacher provides physical guidance most of the way_
1 = _Teacher physically guides to activity/area_

Challenging behavior: _Physical aggression toward self/others_

5 = _8 or more times per day_
4 = _6 or 7 times per day_
3 = _4 or 5 times per day_
2 = _2 or 3 times per day_
1 = _0 or 1 time per day_

Figure 4.3A. Jessi's PTR-YC Behavior Rating Scale with blank areas to be completed by the classroom teacher and assistant. (*Note:* Blank fillable and printable versions of this form can be found on the accompanying CD-ROM.)

PTR-YC Assessment (Functional Behavioral Assessment)

The preceding chapters, Chapters 3 and 4, described the preparation for developing an individualized, assessment-based intervention, PTR-YC. The present chapter focuses on assessment. The general purpose is to obtain an understanding of a child's challenging behaviors that is necessary to develop and implement an intervention that will be optimally effective, sensitive to the individual child's characteristics, and as efficient as possible. The majority of the chapter addresses specific steps for conducting a functional behavioral assessment, or FBA. The information gathered through the FBA process will help your team to understand the 1) purpose or function of the child's challenging behavior, 2) the antecedent and environmental conditions that are associated with the child's challenging behavior as well as the child's desirable behavior, and 3) the consequences that may be maintaining both challenging and desirable behavior. This understanding is summarized in what we call *hypothesis statements*, which are simple ways of describing how the behavior is influenced by the environment, and these statements then lead directly to the child's individualized behavior intervention plan.

In the past, the FBA process comprised the entirety of our assessment strategies when children were in need of specific interventions for challenging behavior. We have learned in our work with hundreds of preschool classrooms and child care centers, however, that many challenging behaviors are, in part, related to more basic classroom practices. These are the practices that are used with all of the children in the program to provide guidance and encouragement in their social-emotional development. We now know that there are certain classroom practices that can prevent the emergence and escalation of challenging behaviors if they are implemented consistently and in a high-quality manner. For this reason, we have added consideration of these classroom practices to our assessment protocols, and we have also added the practices to our intervention strategies.

This chapter has two major sections. The first concerns classroom practices. The assessment strategy for this section is a simple, team-based exercise for considering the manner with which a number of classroom practices are being implemented. The second section concerns the individualized FBA.

CLASSROOMWIDE PRACTICES

Challenging behaviors are at times a direct product of the presence or absence of some very basic classroom-level or universal practices. It is essential to the success of PTR-YC to understand when the challenging behavior of an individual child or, more likely, a group of children is directly related to whole-class practices or their absence. As a beginning step to understanding where your class or team may be functioning in this regard, please complete the brief profile in Figure 5.1 as a team. Answer each item with the whole class in mind, not a particular child.

If you answer "yes" to two or more items, then it is likely that classroom practices in general are unwittingly contributing to the challenging behaviors of individual children. As a next step to understanding where your team needs to begin with specific classroom

<table>
<tr><td>FIGURE 5.1</td><td colspan="3">Classroom Profile of Challenging Behavior</td></tr>
</table>

1. Does challenging behavior occur across most or all classroom routines?	Yes	No
2. Are more than two or three children engaging in persistent challenging behavior?	Yes	No
3. Have you reduced the time allotted for large-group activities because of challenging behavior?	Yes	No
4. Have you eliminated any routine activities because of challenging behavior?	Yes	No
5. Have one or more children been permanently removed from class because of challenging behavior during a year's period of time?	Yes	No
6. Are children often removed from an activity because of challenging behavior?	Yes	No
7. Are the problem behaviors of specific children being imitated by peers?	Yes	No
8. Have challenging behaviors gotten worse over the course of the year?	Yes	No
9. Are specific personnel assigned to children with challenging behaviors because of their challenging behaviors?	Yes	No
10. Has the composition of adult providers changed in the course of the year because of challenging behavior (e.g., staff quitting, more staff added)?	Yes	No

Figure 5.1. Classroom Profile of Challenging Behavior.

practices, please complete the brief assessment in Figure 5.2 as a team.

If the team answered "no" or cannot give a confident "yes" to the five questions, then our invitation is to immediately begin implementing the relevant strategy (see Chapter 6). Indeed, we strongly recommend that such implementation begin as soon as possible, and we emphasize that there is no need to wait until the individualized behavior intervention plan is developed. We believe that, in many cases, implementing high-quality classroom practices may be necessary to ensure PTR-YC success. In addition, when classroom practices are sufficiently enhanced, there will be occasions when the challenging behavior of some children may be successfully altered without the necessity of the full, individualized PTR-YC process. The positive impact of using high-quality classroom practices occurs with surprising regularity, even when individual children are singled out for their severe challenging behavior.

> When classroom practices are enhanced sufficiently, there will be occasions when the challenging behavior of some children may be successfully altered without the necessity of the full, individualized PTR-YC process.

INDIVIDUALIZED FUNCTIONAL BEHAVIORAL ASSESSMENT

This section provides the background and describes the steps for implementing the individualized FBA. The FBA is the heart of the PTR-YC process because it results in an understanding of how the challenging behavior is influenced by the environment and it guides the development of the behavior intervention plan.

The field is replete with manuals, articles, and books that spell out procedures and offer forms for completing an FBA. Many of these are very good, offering strategies that we can readily endorse. Many of them, however, are also complicated, and many require dedicated observations that can involve more resources than many early childhood programs have available. Our strategy is different because it depends solely on the familiarity with the child's behavior that team members have accumulated over weeks or months of observing the child's behavior in many classroom and nonclassroom contexts. Although our process may be less precise than more effortful procedures, we believe (and our experience indicates) that the strategies are more practical and quite sufficient for the vast majority of preschool-age children with challenging behaviors.

The FBA process in PTR-YC involves three checklists that are independently completed by all team members as well as any outside professionals who may be involved with the child. The checklists pertain to the three components of the model—prevent, teach, and reinforce. The questions on the checklists are designed to help complete the major objectives of the FBA: 1) to identify the antecedents and environmental influences that are associated with (and trigger) challenging behavior (prevent); 2) to determine the function or purpose of the challenging behavior (teach); and 3) to identify the events, items, people, and activities that serve as reinforcers for the child's challenging behavior (and desirable behavior) (reinforce).

In the remainder of this chapter we describe the three components of the PTR-YC process and the three checklists that correspond to the components. We then describe how the checklists are completed, how they are summarized, and how the summaries are presented in hypothesis statements. Finally, we provide examples of how both sections of the assessment process (classroom practices and the FBA) are completed and how they are used to develop a practical understanding of the child's behavior and the environment.

> Use the functional behavioral assessment to identify antecedents and environmental influences, determine function, and identify effective reinforcers for challenging and desirable behaviors.

PREVENT

Prevent is the first component of the PTR-YC model and refers to antecedent events and circumstances that are associated with challenging behaviors. If such events and circumstances can be identified, then it should be possible to make changes in those events and circumstances so that challenging behavior will no longer occur. Antecedent variables include a broad array of events or circumstances that occur in the environment prior to the occurrence of challenging behavior. There are two categories of antecedent events that we are concerned with—those that make the challenging behavior more likely to occur and those that make desirable behavior more likely to occur. The prevent component involves identifying what those antecedent events are for a particular child's behavior and then changing those events so that challenging behavior is less likely and desirable behavior is more likely (see Chapter 6).

Relevant antecedent variables can be a broad array of events that occur in the environment or that somehow affect the child's likelihood of engaging in a particular behavior. For example, some events may serve as triggers, which are usually discrete events or stimuli that occur just before the challenging behavior and may be seen to set off the behavior or to cause the behavior to occur. Common triggers are teachers' requests to perform a task or to make a transition from a preferred activity. Other triggers can be when a peer interferes

FIGURE
5.2

Classroomwide Practices Assessment

1. Where are you giving your time and attention? It is easy to fall into a pattern of giving time and attention to challenging behavior and to largely ignore children who have persistent challenging behavior when they are behaving appropriately. It is critical to be spending the vast majority of time with every child when he or she is behaving well. Ask yourselves this question:

   - Are we providing positive feedback to children with persistent challenging behavior   Yes   No
     at five times or more the rate that we are giving corrective feedback for challenging
     behavior?

2. Where are you at in providing children with a level of predictability in the daily schedule that prevents challenging behavior? Most every early childhood setting has a schedule of activities in place. Many of these settings, however, do not have a level of predictability to the schedule that provides children with the certainty necessary to act as a prevention to challenging behavior. Schedules that become interrupted or altered by challenging behavior, different adults in the class, or a whim to do something different are not prevention schedules. Likewise, schedules that are not taught directly to children, reviewed with children on a regular basis, or discussed beforehand with children when a necessary modification needs to be made (e.g., a field trip day) are not prevention schedules. Ask yourselves this question:

   - Are we using schedules in a way that is likely to prevent challenging behavior?   Yes   No

3. Looking more deeply into the question of schedules, are there predictable routines within routines within routines as a planned part of your classroom? For example, circle time is often a routine that occurs on a regular basis (every day). Simply having that general routine as a predictable event, however, will not function to prevent challenging behavior. There must be a consistent routine within the circle time. For example, Ms. Alexa's class does circle time as the first activity every day, and the first routine within her circle time is a greeting song. Simply having a greeting song within your routine, however, is not sufficient for many children with challenging behavior. They need yet another level of predictability. Ms. Alexa has a routine within the child choice song routine such that every day the sequence of events is for a child to pass out props to accompany the song, the song is then sung, and then another child picks up the props. Ask yourselves this question:

   - Do we have routines within routines within routines across the preschool day?   Yes   No

4. Are we explicitly teaching the behavioral expectations for each classroom routine? Many early childhood settings have classroom rules for general deportment (e.g., use walking feet, share toys and materials, use inside voice, keep our friends safe). Having these rules is worthwhile, but, in many cases, they simply occupy a space on the classroom wall, are only reviewed early in the preschool year, or are never translated into their application for specific, multiple routines. Early childhood providers may make the colossal mistake in many circumstances of assuming that children know how to behave appropriately and that their misbehavior is simply noncompliance. Sometimes this is the case, but the only way to be certain is to have explicitly taught the specific expectations in the first place. Ask yourselves this question:

   - Have we taught children the specific behaviors we want to see for each classroom   Yes   No
     routine?

5. Are we explicitly teaching peer-related social skills on a classroomwide basis to prevent challenging behavior? A certain fraction of all challenging behavior in any group care setting for young children will derive from peer conflicts over toys, materials, and the attention of adults. Peer-related social skills such as sharing, taking turns, and following another child's play idea can function to prevent challenging behavior. Unfortunately, up to 20% of all typically developing young children show signs of peer-related skill deficits (Asher, 1995), and an overwhelming number of young children with special needs show similar deficits. Acquiring peer-related social skills is not a simple task. Social behavior is complex, subtle at times, and requires a lot of practice to reach what we might consider mastery. Not only do peer-related social skills need to be directly taught, but many children will need explicit instruction across the entire school day to yield good outcomes. Ask yourselves this question:

   - Are we providing explicit peer-related social skill instruction on skills such as sharing,   Yes   No
     taking turns, and following another child's lead throughout the day?

Figure 5.2. Classroomwide Practices Assessment.

with a play activity or when somebody says, "No!" Although there are some events that are common triggers, it is important to appreciate that triggers are idiosyncratic and that every challenging behavior has its own triggers that are individually developed over time. It is also important to remember that triggers do not necessarily always work the same way. If a child is in a good mood and is well rested, then triggers that had previously set off a challenging behavior might be inactive. And this brings us to another type of antecedent events.

Setting events are the second type of antecedent variables. Setting events do not act as immediate triggers but, instead, tend to make triggers more likely to set off a challenging behavior. Setting events are conditions that are separate from the challenging behavior in time and space, but, nevertheless, have effects on the child. For instance, common setting events are physiological circumstances such as illness, pain, exhaustion, hunger, and anxiety. If a child experiences any of these conditions, then it is understandable that a trigger would be more likely to lead to problems than if the child is in a good place physiologically and emotionally. For instance, if 4-year-old Darius had little sleep the night before, then he might be more likely to engage in a tantrum when asked to leave his favorite activity at the sand table. Similarly, if Karen is upset because her parents were having a big fight in the morning before school, then her distress could increase the chances of her challenging behaviors occurring. Setting events are individualized phenomena. Again, setting events do not cause behavior in the same way that triggers do, but they are, nevertheless, important elements of the antecedent circumstances and need to be considered in the assessment and intervention steps of the prevent component.

Before proceeding, we should emphasize that the notion of antecedent influences is firmly established in the science of learning and behavior and that the practical implications are also clearly documented. In the scientific literature, the technical terms for antecedent influences include "discriminative stimuli," "establishing operations," and other jargon that is unnecessary for our current purposes. We can mention here that this is also true for the other components of PTR-YC—teach and reinforce (i.e., the information and guidance we are providing on assessment and intervention is all grounded strongly in scientific knowledge). PTR-YC is a model that uses scientific knowledge to provide an effective and feasible process for addressing challenging behaviors. We recommend texts in the areas of learning theory, applied behavior analysis, and positive behavior support (e.g., Bambara & Kern, 2005; Cooper et al., 1987) for readers who are interested in basic principles and the process of applying these principles into practical strategies.

The PTR-YC Functional Behavioral Assessment Checklist: Prevent in Figure 5.3 is intended to help identify the antecedent conditions that influence challenging behavior and desirable behaviors. (*Note:* Blank fillable and printable versions of this form can be found on the accompanying CD-ROM.) The checklist (along with the teach and reinforce checklists) is to be independently completed by each team member and then summarized in a group team meeting.

> The three checklists should be independently completed by each team member in order to obtain each member's perception and experience with the child and the challenging behavior. This information can be supplemented by team discussions.

TEACH

Teach is the second component of PTR-YC and refers to what is done in intervention. Teaching a skill (or multiple skills) to the child that will make challenging behavior unnecessary and less likely to occur is one of the core strategies of an intervention plan. But that is intervention, and this chapter is about assessment. So what do we assess? The answer is that we use the FBA process to understand why the challenging behavior is occurring. We are seeking to understand what the function or purpose of the challenging behavior is from the child's perspective. In what way does the challenging behavior serve the interests of the child? How does the challenging behavior act on the environment to get something (e.g., attention, a toy)? How does the challenging behavior act on the environment to escape, avoid, or get rid of something (e.g., a teacher's demand, the need to make a transition, a peer's pestering)?

The way that a challenging behavior acts on the environment is referred to as the function of the child's challenging behavior, and, more important, when we understand the function, we should be able to identify other behaviors that could serve the same function. In other words, there are desirable behaviors that can also act on the environment in order to get something, and there are desirable behaviors that can act on the environment in order to get rid of something as well. It should be obvious at this point that communication is the primary type of desirable behavior that acts on the environment in the same way as challenging behavior. A specific communicative behavior that will actually serve as a replacement for the challenging behavior is the best type of behavior to teach as a central part of an intervention plan. See Figure 5.4 for the PTR-YC Functional Behavioral Assessment Checklist: Teach. (*Note:* Blank fillable and printable versions of this form can be found on the accompanying CD-ROM.)

Before we know exactly what we should be teaching, we need to understand the function of the child's challenging behavior. And that is what the next assessment checklist is primarily about.

REINFORCE

Reinforce is the third component of PTR-YC and has to do with consequences that occur for challenging behavior and for other behaviors. It is well known that consequences have a great influence over the frequency of behavior. If favorable consequences (reinforcers) follow a behavior, then it is likely that the behavior will be strengthened and will occur more often and perhaps with greater magnitude. If reinforcers do not follow a behavior, then that behavior will be weakened and will occur less frequently. This law of positive reinforcement is the most basic and most important principle of behavior.

Just because a principle is well known, however, does not mean that it is simple or that it is effectively applied in practice. There are a number of reasons that reinforcement can be complicated. A first source of complexity is that it is not always easy to identify the reinforcer for challenging behavior because the reinforcer is almost always inadvertent. Nobody intentionally sets out to reinforce a child's challenging behavior. Nevertheless, reinforcement in one form or another occurs. If challenging behavior has developed to the point that it is persistent and severe, then it is somehow being reinforced. Sometimes the reinforcement is in the form of adult or peer attention, and sometimes it is in the form of escape or avoidance of nonpreferred activities. But, one way or another, it is being reinforced.

> It is not always easy to identify the reinforcer for challenging behavior (or desirable behavior). It may help to observe the child when challenging behavior is not occurring to determine what items or activities are most attractive to the child.

Another complication is that for reinforcement to be effective, it does not have to occur with every instance of the behavior. In fact, sometimes the reinforcer is more effective if it follows the behavior only some of the time (this is referred to as a partial or intermittent schedule of reinforcement). This can make the reinforcer more difficult to observe.

Third, reinforcers are individualized, meaning that a reinforcer for one child will not necessarily be a reinforcer for another child. Although it is true that most children

FORM 5

PTR-YC Functional Behavioral Assessment Checklist: Prevent

Challenging behavior: _____ Person responding: _____ Child: _____

1. Are there times of the day when challenging behavior is most likely to occur? If yes, what are they?

___ Morning ___ Afternoon	___ Before meals ___ Evening	___ During meals ___ Naptime	___ After meals	___ Preparing meals

Other: _____

2. Are there times of the day when challenging behavior is least likely to occur? If yes, what are they?

___ Morning ___ Afternoon	___ Before meals ___ Evening	___ During meals ___ Naptime	___ After meals	___ Preparing meals

Other: _____

3. Are there specific activities when challenging behavior is very likely to occur? If yes, what are they?

___ Arrival ___ Dismissal ___ Large-group times ___ Small-group times	___ Naptime ___ Toileting/diapering ___ Special event (specify) _____	___ Peer interactions ___ Centers/free play ___ Meals	___ Snack ___ Transitions (specify) _____

Other: _____

4. Are there specific activities when challenging behavior is least likely to occur? What are they?

___ Arrival ___ Dismissal ___ Large-group times ___ Small-group times	___ Naptime ___ Toileting/diapering ___ Special event (specify) _____	___ Peer interactions ___ Centers/free play ___ Meals	___ Snack ___ Transitions (specify) _____

Other: _____

5. Are there other children or adults whose proximity is associated with a high likelihood of challenging behavior? If so, who are they?

___ Siblings ___ Family member(s) ___ Care provider(s) ___ Other adults	Specify:_____ Specify: _____ Specify: _____ Specify: _____	___ Teacher ___ Parent ___ Other children (specify) _____

Other: _____

6. Are there other children or adults whose proximity is associated with a low likelihood of challenging behavior? If so, who are they?

___ Siblings ___ Family member(s) ___ Care provider(s) ___ Other adults	Specify:_____ Specify: _____ Specify: _____ Specify: _____	___ Teacher ___ Parent ___ Other children (specify) _____

Other: _____

Prevent-Teach-Reinforce for Young Children: The Early Childhood Model of Individualized Positive Behavior Support
by Glen Dunlap, Kelly Wilson, Phillip Strain, and Janice K. Lee.
Copyright © 2013 Paul H. Brookes Publishing Co., Inc. All rights reserved.

(page 1 of 2)

(continued)

Figure 5.3. PTR-YC Functional Behavioral Assessment Checklist: Prevent. (*Note:* Blank fillable and printable versions can be found on the accompanying CD-ROM.)

Figure 5.3. (*continued*)

FORM 5   **PTR-YC Functional Behavioral Assessment Checklist: Prevent** (*continued*)

7. Are there specific circumstances that are associated with a high likelihood of challenging behavior?

___ Asked to do something	___ Seated for meal	___ Transition	___ Structured time
___ Given a direction	___ Playing with others	___ End of preferred activity	___ Unstructured time
___ Reprimand or correction	___ Sharing	___ Removal of preferred item	___ Down time (no task specified)
___ Being told "no"	___ Taking turns	___ Beginning of non-preferred activity	___ Teacher is attending to someone else
___ Sitting near specific peer	___ Playing by self	___ Activity becomes too long	___ During a non-preferred activity
___ Change in schedule	___ Novel/new task		
___ Getting peer/adult attention	___ One-to-one time with adult		

Other: _____

8. Are there conditions in the physical environment that are associated with a high likelihood of challenging behavior (e.g., too warm, too cold, too crowded, too much noise, too chaotic, weather conditions)?

___ Yes (specify) _____

___ No

9. Are there circumstances that occur on some days and not other days that may make challenging behavior more likely?

___ Illness	___ No medication	___ Change in caregiver	___ Home conflict
___ Allergies	___ Change in medication	___ Fatigue	___ Sleep deprivation
___ Physical condition	___ Hunger	___ Change in routine	___ Stayed with noncustodial parent
___ Change in diet	___ Parties or social event	___ Parent not home	

Other: _____

Additional comments not addressed:

<table>
<tr><td>

FORM 6

PTR-YC Functional Behavioral Assessment Checklist: Teach

</td></tr>
</table>

Challenging behavior: _____ Person responding: _____ Child: _____

1. Does the challenging behavior seem to be exhibited in order to gain attention from other children?
___ Yes (specify peers) _____ ___ No
2. Does the challenging behavior seem to be exhibited in order to gain attention from adults? If so, are there particular adults whose attention is solicited?
___ Yes (specify adults) _____ ___ No
3. Does the challenging behavior seem to be exhibited in order to obtain objects (e.g., toys, games, materials, food) from other children or adults?
___ Yes (specify objects) _____ ___ No
4. Does the challenging behavior seem to be exhibited in order to delay a transition from a preferred activity to a nonpreferred activity?
___ Yes (specify transitions) _____ ___ No
5. Does the challenging behavior seem to be exhibited in order to terminate or delay a nonpreferred (e.g., difficult, boring, repetitive) task or activity?
___ Yes (specify nonpreferred tasks or activities) _____ ___ No
6. Does the challenging behavior seem to be exhibited in order to get away from a nonpreferred child or adult?
___ Yes (specify peers or adults) _____ ___ No

7. What social skills(s) could the child learn in order to reduce the likelihood of the challenging behavior occurring in the future?

___ Getting attention appropriately ___ Sharing—giving a toy ___ Sharing—asking for a toy ___ Taking turns ___ Beginning interactions with peers and adults ___ Responding or answering peers and adults	___ Engaging in interactions (staying on topic with peers and adults in a back-and-forth exchange) ___ Giving a play idea ("You be the mommy") ___ Playing appropriately with toys and materials with peers	___ Accepting positive comments and praise ___ Making positive comments ___ Giving praise to peers ___ Waiting for acknowledgment or reinforcement ___ Skills to develop friendships

Other: _____

(continued)

Figure 5.4. PTR-YC Functional Behavioral Assessment Checklist: Teach. (*Note:* Blank fillable and printable versions can be found on the accompanying CD-ROM.)

Figure 5.4. *(continued)*

FORM 6   PTR-YC Functional Behavioral Assessment Checklist: Teach *(continued)*

8. What problem-solving skill(s) could the child learn in order to reduce the likelihood of the challenging behavior occurring in the future?

___ Controlling anger ___ Controlling impulsive behavior ___ Strategies for calming down ___ Asking for help ___ Using visuals to support independent play	___ Self-management ___ Playing independently ___ Playing cooperatively ___ Following directions ___ Following schedules and routines ___ Accepting "no" ___ Managing emotions	___ Getting engaged in an activity ___ Staying engaged in activities ___ Choosing appropriate solutions ___ Making choices from appropriate options ___ Following through with choices

Other: _____

9. What communication skill(s) could the child learn in order to reduce the likelihood of the challenging behavior occurring in the future?

___ Asking for a break ___ Asking for help ___ Responding to others ___ Requesting wants and needs	___ Communicating effectively with words ___ Communicating effectively with pictures ___ Communicating effectively with sign language	___ Expressing emotions (e.g., frustration, anger, hurt) appropriately ___ Saying, "No" or "Stop"

Other: _____

Additional comments not addressed:

enjoy positive attention (e.g., praise, favorable acknowledgment), the form that such attention takes may affect children in different ways. Some children respond well to a smile and a thumbs-up gesture; others may respond better to a pat on the back or a hug. It is possible in some cases that a child will be reinforced by negative attention (e.g., a scolding, a reprimand). A concrete reinforcer such as a sticker may be a powerful reinforcer for some children, but a sticker might have little or no meaning for other children. It is important to know which stimuli or events are actually effective as reinforcers for a particular child if they are to be included in a behavior intervention plan.

A behavior intervention plan in PTR-YC must always include some kind of adjustment to the way that reinforcers are delivered. For some children, this might involve using more reinforcers. It might involve being sure that reinforcers for challenging behavior are withheld. It will be important to be sure that certain kinds of desirable behavior are reinforced for some children, and it might mean that the specific kinds of consequences (reinforcers) need to be changed for other children. See Figure 5.5 for the PTR-YC: Functional Behavioral Assessment Checklist: Reinforce. (*Note:* Blank fillable and printable versions of this form can be found on the accompanying CD-ROM.)

It is probably important for us to explain our position with respect to negative consequences such as time-out or other forms of punishment. First, we do not believe that time-out or other forms of punishment are necessary. It is our experience that even the most persistent and severe behavior can be changed effectively without relying on negative consequences. If the procedures described in this book are followed with fidelity, then we are quite sure that positive change will occur. If challenging behavior occurs in the course of intervention, and it usually will, then we recommend that such occurrences be viewed as errors or mistakes. Errors are corrected through instruction, not punishment. The behavior intervention plan should be developed to account for these occurrences (see Chapter 6).

SUMMARIZING THE FUNCTIONAL BEHAVIORAL DATA

The first responsibility of team members in completing the FBA is for each person to independently complete the three checklists. Everybody who has interacted with or observed the child for at least 1 week should complete the checklists. This includes members of the PTR-YC team, and it can also include individuals who are not part of the team but who are involved with the child in a professional or nonprofessional capacity. All observations are potentially valuable. Completing the checklists does not require much time—probably not more than 10 or 15 minutes per person.

When the checklists are completed, they should be compiled and summarized in a team meeting. The meeting involves reviewing each checklist and entering summary information on the PTR-YC Functional Behavioral Assessment Summary Table in Figure 5.6. (*Note:* Blank fillable and printable versions of this form can be found on the accompanying CD-ROM.). The table includes columns for each of the three components, so the information for Prevent, Teach, and Reinforce, respectively, is entered in the pertinent column. One member of the team is responsible for entering the information in brief summary statements on the form as all team members review and discuss the data (the information on the checklists). The idea is to synthesize the information and seek to identify patterns in the data. Although all observations are valid, and although it is understandable that there will be differences in individuals' observations and perceptions, it is useful to note con-

Implementer's Tip

Identify the major patterns or themes of the information collected from team members to include in the PTR-YC Functional Behavioral Assessment Summary Table.

FORM
7

PTR-YC Functional Behavioral Assessment Checklist: Reinforce

Challenging behavior: _____   Person responding: _____   Child: _____

| 1.   What consequence(s) usually follow the child's challenging behavior? |

| ___ Sent to time-out
___ Sent out of the room
___ Sent to quiet spot
___ Calming/soothing
___ Talking about what just
    happened | ___ Gave personal space
___ Gave assistance
___ Verbal redirect
___ Delay in activity
___ Activity changed
___ Activity terminated
___ Removed from activity | ___ Verbal reprimand
___ Reviewed classroom rules
___ Physical prompt
___ Peer reaction
___ Physical restraint
___ Removal of reinforcers (e.g.,
    toys, items, attention)
___ Natural consequences (specify)
    _____ |

Other: _____

| 2.   Does the child enjoy praise from adults and children? Does the child enjoy praise from some people more
      than others? |

___ Yes (specify people) _____

___ No

| 3.   What is the likelihood of the child's appropriate behavior (e.g., participating appropriately, cooperating,
      following directions) resulting in acknowledgment or praise from adults or children? |

| ___ Very likely | ___ Sometimes | ___ Seldom | ___ Never |

| 4.   What is the likelihood of the child's challenging behavior resulting in acknowledgment (e.g., reprimands,
      corrections, restating classroom rules) from adults and children? |

| ___ Very likely | ___ Sometimes | ___ Seldom | ___ Never |

| 5.   What items and activities are most enjoyable to the child? What items or activities could serve as special
      rewards? |

| ___ Social interaction with adults
___ Social interaction with peers
___ Playing a game
___ Teacher's helper
___ Extra time outside
___ Extra praise and attention from adults
___ Tangibles (e.g., stickers, stamps) | ___ High fives
___ Praise from peers
___ Praise from adults
___ Music
___ Puzzles
___ Special activity
___ Special helper | ___ Extra time in preferred activity
___ Computer time
___ Art activities (e.g., drawing pic-
    tures, painting)
___ Objects/toys (specify)
    _____
___ Food (specify)
    _____ |

Other(s):_____

Additional comments not addressed:

Figure 5.5.   PTR-YC Functional Behavioral Assessment Checklist: Reinforce. (*Note:* Blank fillable and printable versions can be found on the accompanying CD-ROM.)

sistencies in the antecedents and consequences that are recorded on the different checklists. Such consistencies are central to the FBA process.

DEVELOPING HYPOTHESIS STATEMENTS

The PTR-YC Functional Behavioral Assessment Summary Table and the patterns it reveals set the stage for the team to develop hypothesis statements. Hypothesis statements are a concise and useful way to summarize the team's understanding of the challenging behavior and the way that the challenging behavior is currently influenced by the environment. Hypothesis statements are the culmination of the individualized FBA, and they lead directly to the development of the behavior intervention plan.

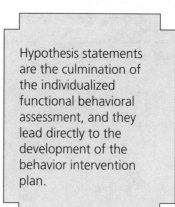

Hypothesis statements are the culmination of the individualized functional behavioral assessment, and they lead directly to the development of the behavior intervention plan.

Hypothesis statements take a simple A-B-C form—antecedent, behavior, and consequence. The information can be taken directly from the PTR-YC Functional Behavioral Assessment Summary Table. Antecedents come from the prevent column, behavior comes from the team's definition of the child's challenging behavior, and consequence comes from the teach and the reinforce columns. Another useful way to look at the form of hypothesis statements is to describe the equation as the following.

> When (something in the environment occurs), then (description of the behavior); as a result, (the typical consequence that reinforces the behavior).

The team specifies the *when* as the antecedent events that are observed to lead to the challenging behavior. The team describes *then* as the child's challenging behavior, and *as a result* is the statement of what the child often receives as a consequence. The following are examples of hypothesis statements.

- *When* Jill is asked to engage in a fine motor activity, *then* she will scream and/or engage in other disruptive behaviors; *as a result*, she will avoid having to perform the fine motor task.

- *When* Mahmud is on the playground and a peer gets within 3 feet and attempts to play with toys, *then* Mahmud will hit or kick the peer; *as a result*, the peer will withdraw and leave Mahmud alone.

- *When* Thomas has gone for a period (usually at least 10 minutes) without adult attention, *then* he may repeatedly slap his head; *as a result*, he will usually receive adult attention in the form of holding, soothing, and comforting.

It is important to appreciate that it may be necessary to prepare more than one hypothesis statement. For example, the FBA for Thomas (a boy with severe intellectual disabilities and some sensitivities to certain loud noises) revealed that there were a number of circumstances associated with his challenging behavior, and the function (maintaining consequence) was different in some of those circumstances. In the example cited above, Thomas's slapping was reinforced by adult attention. In the following hypothesis statement, the head slapping was reinforced by escape from an unpleasant sound.

- *When* Thomas encounters noises, including music or laughter, that are excessively loud or high pitched, *then* he may repeatedly slap his head; *as a result*, he will be removed by an adult from the offending noise.

Additional examples of hypothesis statements and the process of developing them are included in the case examples in the following appendix.

PTR-YC Functional Behavioral Assessment Summary Table

Child: _____   Date: _____

Behavior	Prevent data	Teach data	Reinforce data
Challenging behavior			
Desirable behavior			

Hypothesis: When _____ ,

then _____ ;

as a result, _____ .

Figure 5.6.   PTR-YC Functional Behavioral Assessment Summary Table. (*Note:* Blank fillable and printable versions can be found on the accompanying CD-ROM.)

FIGURE 5.7	**Self-Evaluation Checklist for Functional Behavioral Assessment**		

	Yes	No
1. Has the team carefully assessed the status of classroom practices, as indicated in the beginning of the chapter?	☐	☐
2. Have steps been taken to improve the implementation of classroomwide practices, as described in this chapter and at the beginning of Chapter 6?	☐	☐
3. Did the team decide who will complete the three checklists for the individualized functional behavioral assessment (FBA)? (*Remember:* the checklists should be completed by all relevant team members as well as outside individuals who have regular contact with the child.)	☐	☐
4. Were the completed checklists reviewed by the team and summarized on the PTR-YC Functional Behavioral Assessment Summary Table?	☐	☐
5. Were hypotheses developed to summarize the team's understanding of the function of the child's challenging behavior and the ways that the behavior is influenced by the environment?	☐	☐
6. Have the observation period and the primary data collectors been specified?	☐	☐

If the answer to each of these questions is "yes," then the team should proceed to the next step.

Figure 5.7. Self-Evaluation Checklist for Functional Behavioral Assessment.

When the steps described in this chapter are completed, the team should take a moment to review and fill out the Self-Evaluation Checklist for Functional Behavioral Assessment (see Figure 5.7). It is important that all steps are scored as "yes" before moving to the next chapter.

APPENDIX

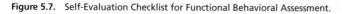

Case Examples

MEETING 3: HASANI

PTR-YC Assessment

The next meeting for Hasani's team involved gathering the data from the PTR-YC functional behavioral assessment (FBA), developing a hypothesis, and using that data to drive intervention planning. Each team member brought their PTR-YC Behavior Rating Scale data and their completed PTR-YC Functional Behavioral Assessment Checklists to the third meeting. The facilitator reviewed the current data from the PTR-YC Behavior Rating Scale with a short discussion about how this system was working for people, what was going well, and whether there were any current challenges. The team was recording consistent data, meaning they were rating things in a similar fashion, and no issues were found with the collection of this information.

The facilitator took out an extra blank copy of the PTR-YC Functional Behavioral Assessment Checklists for recording the combined information. The team decided to share their responses from the PTR-YC assessment in a round robin fashion. The first person read the question and shared his or her response; each subsequent member shared any additions and comments for that item. The facilitator kept the discussion moving forward while the recorder took all the notes on the blank copy. The team decided to complete the PTR-YC Functional Behavioral Assessment Summary Table while discussing the assessment. Figures 5.1A–5.3A show the final PTR-YC assessment that was compiled at this meeting.

As the team went through each item on the PTR-YC assessment, they recorded the relevant information on the PTR-YC Functional Behavioral Assessment Summary Table (see Figure 5.4A). This organizational table assisted the team in recognizing triggers and patterns in behavior, possible functions for challenging behavior, and reinforcers that appear to sustain challenging behavior, as well as ideas for how to reinforce the desired behavior.

By organizing the information (data) gathered from the PTR-YC assessment, the team could see two things very clearly: 1) they had identified many skills to teach and would need to prioritize, and 2) the function of the challenging behavior—does not respond—seemed to be escape, avoid, delay, or terminate a nonpreferred activity or transition. This information was used to create a hypothesis statement for Hasani's challenging behavior.

At the close of the meeting, the team reviewed the Self-Evaluation Checklist for Functional Behavioral Assessment (see Figure 5.7) to make sure all steps were completed. The team members recognized how this process was strengthening the team and providing a focus, a common understanding, and a common language with common goals. The team felt cohesive. The final step for this meeting was to review what each team member needed to complete for the final meeting before beginning implementation of the behavior plan. Each team member agreed to review the intervention strategies and choose one prevent, one teach, and one reinforce strategy to decrease the challenging behavior and one reinforce strategy to support the desired behavior.

MEETING 3: JOEL

PTR-YC Assessment

Joel's team independently completed the PTR-YC FBA over the next week. The team made several attempts to get input from Gary, Joel's father, but he did not have time to provide the information for the meeting. Sally, the educational specialist, had previously begun to build a relationship with Gary when his work schedule was less hectic and offered to be the main contact from the team. Sally made sure Gary knew what was happening at meetings and how he could contribute when he was able. Sally also communicated to Gary that his input would be helpful to develop strategies for home when he was ready.

The team members came prepared for the third meeting with the PTR-YC Behavior Rating Scale for review and their completed PTR-YC Functional Behavioral Assessment Checklists. When looking at the data, the team began to realize that Joel rarely hit more than 10 times; in fact, there were no recordings of a 5 in the baseline data and only one 4 recorded. The team mostly recorded 3 (hit 5–7 times). This surprised the team as they truly thought that Joel hit others more than 10 times per day.

The team was anxious to look at more data from the PTR-YC assessment. The team decided to have Sally facilitate because she had some additional observation data to share. Sally had a blank copy of the PTR-YC Functional Behavioral Assessment Checklists for recording the group answers, and she also had the PTR-YC Functional Behavioral Assessment Summary Table out so they could fill in the information as they recorded the team's responses on the

FORM 5

PTR-YC Functional Behavioral Assessment Checklist: Prevent

Challenging behavior: _Does not respond_   Person responding: _Team_   Child: _Hasani_

1. Are there times of the day when challenging behavior is most likely to occur? If yes, what are they?				
X Morning __ Afternoon	__ Before meals X Evening	__ During meals __ Naptime	__ After meals	__ Preparing meals

Other: _____

2. Are there times of the day when challenging behavior is least likely to occur? If yes, what are they?				
__ Morning X Afternoon	X Before meals __ Evening	X During meals __ Naptime	__ After meals	__ Preparing meals

Other: _____

3. Are there specific activities when challenging behavior is very likely to occur? If yes, what are they?			
X Arrival __ Dismissal X Large-group times X Small-group times	__ Naptime __ Toileting/diapering __ Special event (specify) _____	X Peer interactions __ Centers/free play __ Meals	__ Snack X Transitions (specify) _____

Other: _Family members also identified the morning and bedtime routines to be activities with a high likelihood of challenging behavior._

4. Are there specific activities when challenging behavior is least likely to occur? What are they?			
__ Arrival X Dismissal __ Large-group times __ Small-group times	__ Naptime __ Toileting/diapering __ Special event (specify) _____	__ Peer interactions X Centers/free play X Meals	X Snack __ Transitions (specify) _____

Other: _____

5. Are there other children or adults whose proximity is associated with a high likelihood of challenging behavior? If so, who are they?		
__ Siblings __ Family member(s) __ Care provider(s) __ Other adults	Specify:_____ Specify:_____ Specify:_____ Specify:_____	__ Teacher __ Parent __ Other children (specify) _____

Other: _____

6. Are there other children or adults whose proximity is associated with a low likelihood of challenging behavior? If so, who are they?		
__ Siblings __ Family member(s) __ Care provider(s) __ Other adults	Specify:_____ Specify:_____ Specify:_____ Specify:_____	__ Teacher __ Parent __ Other children (specify) _____

Other: _____

(page 1 of 2)

(continued)

Figure 5.1A. Hasani's PTR-YC Functional Behavioral Assessment Checklist: Prevent. (*Note:* Blank fillable and printable versions of this form can be found on the accompanying CD-ROM.)

Figure 5.1A. *(continued)*

FORM 5   PTR-YC Functional Behavioral Assessment Checklist: Prevent *(continued)*

7. Are there specific circumstances that are associated with a high likelihood of challenging behavior?

___ Asked to do something _X_ Given a direction ___ Reprimand or correction ___ Being told "no" ___ Sitting near specific peer _X_ Change in schedule ___ Getting peer/adult attention	___ Seated for meal _X_ Playing with others ___ Sharing ___ Taking turns ___ Playing by self ___ Novel/new task ___ One-to-one time with adult	_X_ Transition _X_ End of preferred activity ___ Removal of preferred item _X_ Beginning of non-preferred activity ___ Activity becomes too long	___ Structured time ___ Unstructured time ___ Down time (no task specified) ___ Teacher is attending to someone else _X_ During a non-preferred activity

Other: _____

---

8. Are there conditions in the physical environment that are associated with a high likelihood of challenging behavior (e.g., too warm, too cold, too crowded, too much noise, too chaotic, weather conditions)?

___ Yes (specify) _____

_X_ No

---

9. Are there circumstances that occur on some days and not other days that may make challenging behavior more likely?

_X_ Illness ___ Allergies ___ Physical condition ___ Change in diet	___ No medication ___ Change in medication ___ Hunger ___ Parties or social event	___ Change in caregiver _X_ Fatigue _X_ Change in routine ___ Parent not home	___ Home conflict ___ Sleep deprivation ___ Stayed with noncustodial parent

Other: _____

Additional comments not addressed:

(page 2 of 2)

FORM 6

PTR-YC Functional Behavioral Assessment Checklist: Teach

Challenging behavior: _Does not respond_   Person responding: _Team_   Child: _Hasani_

1. Does the challenging behavior seem to be exhibited in order to gain attention from other children?
___ Yes (specify peers) _____ _X_ No

2. Does the challenging behavior seem to be exhibited in order to gain attention from adults? If so, are there particular adults whose attention is solicited?
___ Yes (specify adults) _____ _X_ No

3. Does the challenging behavior seem to be exhibited in order to obtain objects (e.g., toys, games, materials, food) from other children or adults?
___ Yes (specify objects) _____ _X_ No

4. Does the challenging behavior seem to be exhibited in order to delay a transition from a preferred activity to a nonpreferred activity?
_X_ Yes (specify transitions) _Arrival_ _____ ___ No

5. Does the challenging behavior seem to be exhibited in order to terminate or delay a nonpreferred (e.g., difficult, boring, repetitive) task or activity?
_X_ Yes (specify nonpreferred tasks or activities) _Tabletop activities, circle time, large groups_ ___ ___ No

6. Does the challenging behavior seem to be exhibited in order to get away from a nonpreferred child or adult?
___ Yes (specify peers or adults) _____ _X_ No

7. What social skills(s) could the child learn in order to reduce the likelihood of the challenging behavior occurring in the future?

___ Getting attention appropriately _X_ Sharing—giving a toy _X_ Sharing—asking for a toy _X_ Taking turns _X_ Beginning interactions with peers and adults _X_ Responding or answering peers and adults	_X_ Engaging in interactions (staying on topic with peers and adults in a back-and-forth exchange) ___ Giving a play idea ("You be the mommy") _X_ Playing appropriately with toys and materials with peers	___ Accepting positive comments and praise ___ Making positive comments ___ Giving praise to peers ___ Waiting for acknowledgment or reinforcement _X_ Skills to develop friendships

Other: _____

(page 1 of 2)

(continued)

Figure 5.2A. Hasani's PTR-YC Functional Behavioral Assessment Checklist: Teach. (*Note:* Blank fillable and printable versions of this form can be found on the accompanying CD-ROM.)

Figure 5.2A.   *(continued)*

FORM 6   **PTR-YC Functional Behavioral Assessment Checklist: Teach** *(continued)*

8. What problem-solving skill(s) could the child learn in order to reduce the likelihood of the challenging behavior occurring in the future?

___ Controlling anger ___ Controlling impulsive behavior _X_ Strategies for calming down _X_ Asking for help _X_ Using visuals to support independent play	___ Self-management ___ Playing independently _X_ Playing cooperatively _X_ Following directions _X_ Following schedules and routines ___ Accepting "no" ___ Managing emotions	_X_ Getting engaged in an activity _X_ Staying engaged in activities ___ Choosing appropriate solutions ___ Making choices from appropriate options ___ Following through with choices

Other: _____

9. What communication skill(s) could the child learn in order to reduce the likelihood of the challenging behavior occurring in the future?

_X_ Asking for a break _X_ Asking for help _X_ Responding to others _X_ Requesting wants and needs	_X_ Communicating effectively with words _X_ Communicating effectively with pictures ___ Communicating effectively with sign language	_X_ Expressing emotions (e.g., frustration, anger, hurt) appropriately _X_ Saying, "No" or "Stop"

Other: _____

Additional comments not addressed:

(page 2 of 2)

FORM 7

PTR-YC Functional Behavioral Assessment Checklist: Reinforce

Challenging behavior: *Does not respond*   Person responding: *Team*   Child: *Hasani*

---

1. What consequence(s) usually follow the child's challenging behavior?

___ Sent to time-out	X Gave personal space	___ Verbal reprimand
___ Sent out of the room	X Gave assistance	___ Reviewed classroom rules
___ Sent to quiet spot	X Verbal redirect	___ Physical prompt
___ Calming/soothing	X Delay in activity	___ Peer reaction
___ Talking about what just happened	X Activity changed	___ Physical restraint
	X Activity terminated	___ Removal of reinforcers (e.g., toys, items, attention)
	X Removed from activity	___ Natural consequences (specify) _____

Other: _____

---

2. Does the child enjoy praise from adults and children? Does the child enjoy praise from some people more than others?

X Yes (specify people) *Amara, Jerry, occupational therapist, lead teacher* _____

___ No

---

3. What is the likelihood of the child's appropriate behavior (e.g., participating appropriately, cooperating, following directions) resulting in acknowledgment or praise from adults or children?

___ Very likely	X Sometimes	___ Seldom	___ Never

---

4. What is the likelihood of the child's challenging behavior resulting in acknowledgment (e.g., reprimands, corrections, restating classroom rules) from adults and children?

X Very likely	___ Sometimes	___ Seldom	___ Never

---

5. What items and activities are most enjoyable to the child? What items or activities could serve as special rewards?

___ Social interaction with adults	___ High fives	X Extra time in preferred activity
___ Social interaction with peers	___ Praise from peers	___ Computer time
___ Playing a game	___ Praise from adults	X Art activities (e.g., drawing pictures, painting)
___ Teacher's helper	___ Music	___ Objects/toys (specify)
X Extra time outside	___ Puzzles	_____
___ Extra praise and attention from adults	X Special activity	X Food (specify)
X Tangibles (e.g., stickers, stamps)	___ Special helper	*Sweets, cake*

Other(s):_____

Additional comments not addressed:

Figure 5.3A. Hasani's PTR-YC Functional Behavioral Assessment Checklist: Reinforce. (*Note:* Blank fillable and printable versions of this form can be found on the accompanying CD-ROM.)

FORM 8

PTR-YC Functional Behavioral Assessment Summary Table

Child: _____Hasani_____   Date: __September_____

Behavior	Prevent data	Teach data	Reinforce data
Challenging behavior Does not respond	Times: Morning and evening routines, arrival, small group, large group, peer interactions, transitions Specific circumstances: Given a direction, playing with other peers, start of and during nonpreferred activity, end of preferred activity, change in routine or schedule, illness	Function: To delay or terminate making a transition, to delay or terminate nonpreferred activity	Gave personal space and assistance, verbal redirect, delay in activity, activity changed, activity terminated, removed from activity
Desirable behavior Engagement	Times: During meals, dismissal, centers, snack Specific circumstances: One-to-one with adults, during preferred activities	Social skills: Responding or answering peers and adults, sharing (giving a toy and requesting), taking turns, beginning interactions, engaging in interactions, playing appropriately with toys, skills to develop friendships Problem solving: Strategies to calm down, asking for help, using visuals, playing cooperatively, following directions, following schedule, getting engaged, staying engaged	Extra time outside, tangibles (e.g., stickers, stamps), special activities, extra time in preferred activities, art activities (e.g., painting), food, sweets

Hypothesis: When __Hasani is asked to do a nonpreferred activity or make a transition__ ,

then __she does not respond to adults or peers__ ;

as a result, __the activity or transition is delayed, changed, or terminated__ .

Figure 5.4A.   Hasani's PTR-YC Functional Behavioral Assessment Summary Table. (*Note:* Blank fillable and printable versions of this form can be found on the accompanying CD-ROM.)

checklists. Another team member was chosen to take any additional notes and make copies for everyone. Last, a time keeper was designated as the team had a lot to cover in this 1-hour meeting.

As the team compiled the data from the assessments, they noted that Joel received a lot of adult attention when he hit other adults and/or peers. Adults reacted by stating rules, redirecting, reprimanding, and talking about what happened and what Joel should do instead. Much of this attention was negative attention, and the team members had not previously viewed such attention as reinforcing. In their discussion, however, they realized it was very reinforcing, even though it was negative. This also led to a discussion about how Joel did not handle positive comments and positive praise well. Although the team initially thought the function of the hitting behavior was to escape the activity, the data revealed far more adult attention than expected. The team also thought it might be necessary to teach Joel how to accept positive praise and positive comments. This conversation was noted in the extra notes provided with this meeting.

Sally also shared her own observation data. She observed this hitting behavior occurring consistently at arrival time. Joel had hit someone within the first 5 minutes every day at arrival. Again, the team made note of arrival time and the consistency of hitting. This conversation helped the team develop the hypothesis. Once the data were compiled and the team agreed on the hypothesis, the team was ready to develop individual interventions based on this hypothesis statement for Joel. Figures 5.5A–5.7A show the PTR-YC assessment that was compiled at this meeting.

For the next meeting, the team would read the interventions chapter and choose a prevent, teach, and reinforce strategy for the targeted behaviors. Team members were instructed to record their answers on the intervention menu. Sally was responsible for making sure Gary received all the information from the meeting along with instructions on how to participate in the intervention planning meeting. Gary was also encouraged to complete the PTR-YC Functional Behavioral Assessment Checklists. The next meeting was set for 1 week, and the team continued to collect data on the PTR-YC Behavior Rating Scale. Joel's PTR-YC Functional Behavioral Assessment Summary Table is shown in Figure 5.8A.

MEETING 3: JESSI

PTR-YC Assessment

Lucy, Jessi's foster mother, brought the PTR-YC Functional Behavioral Assessment Checklists that she filled out with Kay, Jessi's foster father; Lauren, the classroom assistant, brought her checklists; and Elle, the classroom teacher, brought her checklists as well as the director's checklists for Jessi's third meeting. The PTR-YC Behavior Rating Scale for the past week was discussed, and Elle and Lauren realized as they looked at the data that Jessi's behavior did not occur as often as they thought. Looking at Jessi's challenging behavior in terms of the operational definition and seeing the behaviors as a cluster of behaviors instead of each behavior as a separate event made it easier to record a pretty accurate estimate of how many times the challenging behavior occurred each day. Because the challenging behavior was not occurring as often as they originally thought, the team discussed whether they should adjust the anchors on the PTR-YC Behavior Rating Scale; the conclusion was that they would just leave the anchors as they are for now. It was clear that Jessi needed a lot of prompting and adult support to be able to follow the daily schedule, which was her desirable behavior.

The team decided to go through each element of the PTR-YC Functional Behavioral Assessment Checklists and record the information on the PTR-YC Functional Behavioral Assessment Summary Table (see Figures 5.9A–5.12A). They went through each item and summarized the information combined from all the checklists, including the checklists from those who could not be present. The elements that contributed to the challenging behavior became clearer as the information was combined and recorded onto the summary table, and it be-

FORM 5

PTR-YC Functional Behavioral Assessment Checklist: Prevent

Challenging behavior: _Hitting others_　　Person responding: _Team_　　Child: _Joel_

---

1. Are there times of the day when challenging behavior is most likely to occur? If yes, what are they?

X Morning X Afternoon	___ Before meals ___ Evening	___ During meals ___ Naptime	___ After meals	___ Preparing meals

Other: _____

---

2. Are there times of the day when challenging behavior is least likely to occur? If yes, what are they?

___ Morning ___ Afternoon	___ Before meals ___ Evening	X During meals ___ Naptime	___ After meals	___ Preparing meals

Other: _____

---

3. Are there specific activities when challenging behavior is very likely to occur? If yes, what are they?

X Arrival ___ Dismissal X Large-group times X Small-group times	___ Naptime ___ Toileting/diapering ___ Special event (specify) _____	___ Peer interactions ___ Centers/free play ___ Meals	___ Snack X Transitions (specify) _____

Other: _Any activity that he does not prefer to do. His preferences seem to change as well._

---

4. Are there specific activities when challenging behavior is least likely to occur? What are they?

___ Arrival ___ Dismissal ___ Large-group times ___ Small-group times	___ Naptime ___ Toileting/diapering ___ Special event (specify) _____	___ Peer interactions ___ Centers/free play X Meals	X Snack ___ Transitions (specify) _____

Other: _Playing with blocks or cars, although sometimes he will hit to get toys from his peers_

---

5. Are there other children or adults whose proximity is associated with a high likelihood of challenging behavior? If so, who are they?

___ Siblings ___ Family member(s) ___ Care provider(s) ___ Other adults	Specify:_____ Specify: _____ Specify: _____ Specify: _____	___ Teacher ___ Parent ___ Other children (specify) _____

Other: _____

---

6. Are there other children or adults whose proximity is associated with a low likelihood of challenging behavior? If so, who are they?

___ Siblings ___ Family member(s) ___ Care provider(s) X Other adults	Specify:_____ Specify: _____ Specify: _____ Specify: _Mary, classroom assistant_	X Teacher ___ Parent ___ Other children (specify) _____

Other: _____

(page 1 of 2)

Figure 5.5A. Joel's PTR-YC Functional Behavioral Assessment Checklist: Prevent. (*Note:* Blank fillable and printable versions of this form can be found on the accompanying CD-ROM.)

FORM 5 PTR-YC Functional Behavioral Assessment Checklist: Prevent *(continued)*

7. Are there specific circumstances that are associated with a high likelihood of challenging behavior?

X Asked to do something	___ Seated for meal	X Transition	___ Structured time
X Given a direction	___ Playing with others	X End of preferred activity	___ Unstructured time
___ Reprimand or correction	X Sharing	X Removal of preferred item	___ Down time (no task specified)
X Being told "no"	X Taking turns	X Beginning of non-preferred activity	X Teacher is attending to someone else
___ Sitting near specific peer	___ Playing by self	___ Activity becomes too long	X During a non-preferred activity
___ Change in schedule	___ Novel/new task		
X Getting peer/adult attention	___ One-to-one time with adult		

Other: _____

8. Are there conditions in the physical environment that are associated with a high likelihood of challenging behavior (e.g., too warm, too cold, too crowded, too much noise, too chaotic, weather conditions)?

___ Yes (specify) _____

X No

9. Are there circumstances that occur on some days and not other days that may make challenging behavior more likely?

___ Illness	___ No medication	___ Change in caregiver	___ Home conflict
___ Allergies	___ Change in medication	X Fatigue	X Sleep deprivation
___ Physical condition	___ Hunger	X Change in routine	___ Stayed with noncustodial parent
___ Change in diet	___ Parties or social event	___ Parent not home	

Other: *The team notices that sometimes Joel seems very tired.*

Additional comments not addressed:

(page 2 of 2)

FORM 6

PTR-YC Functional Behavioral Assessment Checklist: Teach

Challenging behavior: _Hitting others_   Person responding: _Team_   Child: _Joel_

1. Does the challenging behavior seem to be exhibited in order to gain attention from other children?	

___ Yes (specify peers) _____
_X_ No

2. Does the challenging behavior seem to be exhibited in order to gain attention from adults? If so, are there particular adults whose attention is solicited?

_X_ Yes (specify adults) _Gary, Shelly_____
___ No

3. Does the challenging behavior seem to be exhibited in order to obtain objects (e.g., toys, games, materials, food) from other children or adults?

_X_ Yes (specify objects) _Toys, especially novel_____
___ No

4. Does the challenging behavior seem to be exhibited in order to delay a transition from a preferred activity to a nonpreferred activity?

_X_ Yes (specify transitions) _Anything he does not seem to want to do, but this changes from day to day_
___ No

5. Does the challenging behavior seem to be exhibited in order to terminate or delay a nonpreferred (e.g., difficult, boring, repetitive) task or activity?

_X_ Yes (specify nonpreferred tasks or activities) _Any nonpreferred activity such as small-group activities_
___ No

6. Does the challenging behavior seem to be exhibited in order to get away from a nonpreferred child or adult?

___ Yes (specify peers or adults) _____
_X_ No

7. What social skills(s) could the child learn in order to reduce the likelihood of the challenging behavior occurring in the future?

_X_ Getting attention appropriately _X_ Sharing—giving a toy _X_ Sharing—asking for a toy _X_ Taking turns ___ Beginning interactions with peers and adults ___ Responding or answering peers and adults	___ Engaging in interactions (staying on topic with peers and adults in a back-and-forth exchange) ___ Giving a play idea ("You be the mommy") _X_ Playing appropriately with toys and materials with peers	_X_ Accepting positive comments and praise _X_ Making positive comments _X_ Giving praise to peers _X_ Waiting for acknowledgment or reinforcement ___ Skills to develop friendships

Other: _____

(page 1 of 2)

Figure 5.6A. Joel's PTR-YC Functional Behavioral Assessment Checklist: Teach. (*Note:* Blank fillable and printable versions of this form can be found on the accompanying CD-ROM.)

FORM 6 **PTR-YC Functional Behavioral Assessment Checklist: Teach** *(continued)*

8. What problem-solving skill(s) could the child learn in order to reduce the likelihood of the challenging behavior occurring in the future?

X Controlling anger	X Self-management	X Getting engaged in an activity
X Controlling impulsive behavior	___ Playing independently	___ Staying engaged in activities
X Strategies for calming down	X Playing cooperatively	___ Choosing appropriate solutions
___ Asking for help	X Following directions	___ Making choices from appropriate options
___ Using visuals to support independent play	X Following schedules and routines	___ Following through with choices
	X Accepting "no"	
	___ Managing emotions	

Other: _____

9. What communication skill(s) could the child learn in order to reduce the likelihood of the challenging behavior occurring in the future?

___ Asking for a break	X Communicating effectively with words	X Expressing emotions (e.g., frustration, anger, hurt) appropriately
___ Asking for help	___ Communicating effectively with pictures	___ Saying, "No" or "Stop"
___ Responding to others	___ Communicating effectively with sign language	
X Requesting wants and needs		

Other: _____

Additional comments not addressed:

FORM 7

PTR-YC Functional Behavioral Assessment Checklist: Reinforce

Challenging behavior: _Hitting others_   Person responding: _Team_   Child: _Joel_

---

1. What consequence(s) usually follow the child's challenging behavior?

X Sent to time-out	___ Gave personal space	X Verbal reprimand
X Sent out of the room	X Gave assistance	X Reviewed classroom rules
X Sent to quiet spot	X Verbal redirect	___ Physical prompt
___ Calming/soothing	X Delay in activity	___ Peer reaction
X Talking about what just happened	X Activity changed	___ Physical restraint
	X Activity terminated	___ Removal of reinforcers (e.g., toys, items, attention)
	X Removed from activity	___ Natural consequences (specify) _____

Other: _____

---

2. Does the child enjoy praise from adults and children? Does the child enjoy praise from some people more than others?

X Yes (specify people) _Gary, Sally_ _____

___ No

---

3. What is the likelihood of the child's appropriate behavior (e.g., participating appropriately, cooperating, following directions) resulting in acknowledgment or praise from adults or children?

___ Very likely	X Sometimes	___ Seldom	___ Never

---

4. What is the likelihood of the child's challenging behavior resulting in acknowledgment (e.g., reprimands, corrections, restating classroom rules) from adults and children?

X Very likely	___ Sometimes	___ Seldom	___ Never

---

5. What items and activities are most enjoyable to the child? What items or activities could serve as special rewards?

X Social interaction with adults	___ High fives	X Extra time in preferred activity
___ Social interaction with peers	___ Praise from peers	___ Computer time
___ Playing a game	___ Praise from adults	___ Art activities (e.g., drawing pictures, painting)
X Teacher's helper	___ Music	X Objects/toys (specify)
___ Extra time outside	___ Puzzles	_Trucks and cars_
___ Extra praise and attention from adults	X Special activity	___ Food (specify)
X Tangibles (e.g., stickers, stamps)	X Special helper	_____

Other(s): _____

Additional comments not addressed:

Figure 5.7A.   Joel's PTR-YC Functional Behavioral Assessment Checklist: Reinforce. (*Note:* Blank fillable and printable versions of this form can be found on the accompanying CD-ROM.)

FORM 8

PTR-YC Functional Behavioral Assessment Summary Table

Child: _Joel_   Date: _October_

Behavior	Prevent data	Teach data	Reinforce data
Challenging behavior *Hitting others*	*Times: Morning and afternoon, especially arrival* *Activities: Large- and small-group, transitions* *Specific circumstances: Asked to do something, given a direction, being told "no," sharing, taking turns, beginning of and during nonpreferred activities, end of preferred activities, getting attention, teacher attending to others*	*Function: To delay making a transition and get adult attention*	*Consequences: Verbal redirect, gave assistance, talked about what just happened, reviewed classroom rules, delay or change in activity, time-out or sent to quiet spot, verbal reprimand, removed from activity or activity terminated*
Desirable behavior *Participates in nonpreferred classroom activities*	*Times: During meals* *Activities: Snack* *People: Teacher and classroom assistant* *Specific circumstances: One-to-one with adults, during preferred activities*	*Social skills: Getting attention appropriately, sharing (giving a toy and requesting), taking turns, playing appropriately with toys, accepting and giving positive praise, waiting for reinforcement* *Problem solving: Controlling anger, controlling impulses, strategies to calm down, self-managment, accepting "no," playing cooperatively, following directions, getting engaged in activities*	*Reinforcement: Social interaction with adults, tangibles (e.g., stickers, stamps), special activities, special helper, extra time in preferred activities, objects and toys (e.g., cars, trucks)*

Hypothesis: When _Joel is asked to participate in the arrival activities_ ,
then _he will begin hitting peers and/or adults_ ;
as a result, _he gets attention through reprimands, redirects, talking about what happened, or restating rules_ .

Figure 5.8A. Joel's PTR-YC Functional Behavioral Assessment Summary Table. (*Note:* Blank fillable and printable versions of this form can be found on the accompanying CD-ROM.)

<table>
<tr><td>FORM
5</td><td colspan="2">PTR-YC Functional Behavioral Assessment Checklist: Prevent</td></tr>
</table>

Challenging behavior: _Physical aggression toward self or others_ Person responding: _Team_ Child: _Jessi_

---

1. Are there times of the day when challenging behavior is most likely to occur? If yes, what are they?

X Morning X Afternoon	___ Before meals ___ Evening	___ During meals ___ Naptime	___ After meals	___ Preparing meals

Other: _____

---

2. Are there times of the day when challenging behavior is least likely to occur? If yes, what are they?

___ Morning ___ Afternoon	___ Before meals ___ Evening	X During meals X Naptime	___ After meals	___ Preparing meals

Other: _During music time and/or when she has something that makes noise_

---

3. Are there specific activities when challenging behavior is very likely to occur? If yes, what are they?

___ Arrival ___ Dismissal X Large-group times X Small-group times	___ Naptime ___ Toileting/diapering ___ Special event (specify) _____	X Peer interactions X Centers/free play ___ Meals	___ Snack X Transitions (specify) _Ending story or songs_

Other: _____

---

4. Are there specific activities when challenging behavior is least likely to occur? What are they?

___ Arrival ___ Dismissal ___ Large-group times ___ Small-group times	___ Naptime ___ Toileting/diapering ___ Special event (specify) _____	___ Peer interactions ___ Centers/free play X Meals	X Snack ___ Transitions (specify) _____

Other: _Music time with instruments, reading with adults_

---

5. Are there other children or adults whose proximity is associated with a high likelihood of challenging behavior? If so, who are they?

___ Siblings ___ Family member(s) ___ Care provider(s) ___ Other adults	Specify:_____ Specify:_____ Specify:_____ Specify:_____	___ Teacher ___ Parent ___ Other children (specify) _____

Other: _____

---

6. Are there other children or adults whose proximity is associated with a low likelihood of challenging behavior? If so, who are they?

___ Siblings ___ Family member(s) ___ Care provider(s) ___ Other adults	Specify:_____ Specify:_____ Specify:_____ Specify:_____	X Teacher X Parent ___ Other children (specify) _____

Other: _____

(page 1 of 2)

Figure 5.9A.   Jessi's PTR-YC Functional Behavioral Assessment Checklist: Prevent. (*Note:* Blank fillable and printable versions of this form can be found on the accompanying CD-ROM.)

FORM 5   **PTR-YC Functional Behavioral Assessment Checklist: Prevent** *(continued)*

7. Are there specific circumstances that are associated with a high likelihood of challenging behavior?

☒ Asked to do something ☒ Given a direction ☐ Reprimand or correction ☐ Being told "no" ☐ Sitting near specific peer ☐ Change in schedule ☐ Getting peer/adult attention	☐ Seated for meal ☒ Playing with others ☒ Sharing ☒ Taking turns ☐ Playing by self ☐ Novel/new task ☐ One-to-one time with adult	☒ Transition ☒ End of preferred activity ☒ Removal of preferred item ☐ Beginning of non-preferred activity ☐ Activity becomes too long	☐ Structured time ☒ Unstructured time ☒ Down time (no task specified) ☒ Teacher is attending to someone else ☐ During a non-preferred activity

Other: _____

8. Are there conditions in the physical environment that are associated with a high likelihood of challenging behavior (e.g., too warm, too cold, too crowded, too much noise, too chaotic, weather conditions)?

___ Yes (specify) _____

☒ No

9. Are there circumstances that occur on some days and not other days that may make challenging behavior more likely?

☒ Illness ☐ Allergies ☒ Physical condition ☐ Change in diet	☐ No medication ☐ Change in medication ☒ Hunger ☐ Parties or social event	☐ Change in caregiver ☒ Fatigue ☒ Change in routine ☐ Parent not home	☐ Home conflict ☒ Sleep deprivation ☒ Stayed with noncustodial parent

Other: *On days with a seizure, after visitation with Mom and Dad during the week*

Additional comments not addressed:

(page 2 of 2)

FORM 6

PTR-YC Functional Behavioral Assessment Checklist: Teach

Challenging behavior: _Aggressive behavior toward self or others_   Person responding: _Team_   Child: _Jessi_

1. Does the challenging behavior seem to be exhibited in order to gain attention from other children?
_X_ Yes (specify peers) _Sometimes Mandy (she likes to help Jessi all the time)_   ___ No
2. Does the challenging behavior seem to be exhibited in order to gain attention from adults? If so, are there particular adults whose attention is solicited?
_X_ Yes (specify adults) _All adults that will spend time with her_   ___ No
3. Does the challenging behavior seem to be exhibited in order to obtain objects (e.g., toys, games, materials, food) from other children or adults?
_X_ Yes (specify objects) _Objects that make noise, certain books_   ___ No
4. Does the challenging behavior seem to be exhibited in order to delay a transition from a preferred activity to a nonpreferred activity?
_X_ Yes (specify transitions) _Ending story/reading, ending singing time, putting noisy toys away_   ___ No
5. Does the challenging behavior seem to be exhibited in order to terminate or delay a nonpreferred (e.g., difficult, boring, repetitive) task or activity?
___ Yes (specify nonpreferred tasks or activities) _____   _X_ No
6. Does the challenging behavior seem to be exhibited in order to get away from a nonpreferred child or adult?
___ Yes (specify peers or adults) _____   _X_ No

7. What social skills(s) could the child learn in order to reduce the likelihood of the challenging behavior occurring in the future?

_X_ Getting attention appropriately ___ Sharing—giving a toy _X_ Sharing—asking for a toy _X_ Taking turns _X_ Beginning interactions with peers and adults _X_ Responding or answering peers and adults	___ Engaging in interactions (staying on topic with peers and adults in a back-and-forth exchange) ___ Giving a play idea ("You be the mommy") ___ Playing appropriately with toys and materials with peers	___ Accepting positive comments and praise ___ Making positive comments ___ Giving praise to peers ___ Waiting for acknowledgment or reinforcement ___ Skills to develop friendships

Other: _____

(page 1 of 2)

Figure 5.10A. Jessi's PTR-YC Functional Behavioral Assessment Checklist: Teach. (*Note:* Blank fillable and printable versions of this form can be found on the accompanying CD-ROM.)

FORM 6   PTR-YC Functional Behavioral Assessment Checklist: Teach *(continued)*

8. What problem-solving skill(s) could the child learn in order to reduce the likelihood of the challenging behavior occurring in the future?

___ Controlling anger	___ Self-management	_X_ Getting engaged in an activity
___ Controlling impulsive behavior	_X_ Playing independently	_X_ Staying engaged in activities
___ Strategies for calming down	___ Playing cooperatively	___ Choosing appropriate solutions
_X_ Asking for help	_X_ Following directions	_X_ Making choices from appropriate options
___ Using visuals to support independent play	_X_ Following schedules and routines	_X_ Following through with choices
	_X_ Accepting "no"	
	___ Managing emotions	

Other: _____

9. What communication skill(s) could the child learn in order to reduce the likelihood of the challenging behavior occurring in the future?

___ Asking for a break	___ Communicating effectively with words	_X_ Expressing emotions (e.g., frustration, anger, hurt) appropriately
_X_ Asking for help	_X_ Communicating effectively with pictures	_X_ Saying, "No" or "Stop"
___ Responding to others	___ Communicating effectively with sign language	
_X_ Requesting wants and needs		

Other: _____

Additional comments not addressed:

△ FORM 7

PTR-YC Functional Behavioral Assessment Checklist: Reinforce

Challenging behavior: _Does not respond_   Person responding: _Team_   Child: _Jessi_

1. What consequence(s) usually follow the child's challenging behavior?

___ Sent to time-out	_X_ Gave personal space	___ Verbal reprimand
___ Sent out of the room	_X_ Gave assistance	___ Reviewed classroom rules
___ Sent to quiet spot	_X_ Verbal redirect	_X_ Physical prompt
_X_ Calming/soothing	_X_ Delay in activity	_X_ Peer reaction
___ Talking about what just happened	___ Activity changed	___ Physical restraint
	___ Activity terminated	___ Removal of reinforcers (e.g., toys, items, attention)
	_X_ Removed from activity	___ Natural consequences (specify) _____

Other: _____

2. Does the child enjoy praise from adults and children? Does the child enjoy praise from some people more than others?

_X_ Yes (specify people) _Almost anyone_ _____

___ No

3. What is the likelihood of the child's appropriate behavior (e.g., participating appropriately, cooperating, following directions) resulting in acknowledgment or praise from adults or children?

___ Very likely	_X_ Sometimes	___ Seldom	___ Never

4. What is the likelihood of the child's challenging behavior resulting in acknowledgment (e.g., reprimands, corrections, restating classroom rules) from adults and children?

_X_ Very likely	___ Sometimes	___ Seldom	___ Never

5. What items and activities are most enjoyable to the child? What items or activities could serve as special rewards?

_X_ Social interaction with adults	___ High fives	___ Extra time in preferred activity
___ Social interaction with peers	___ Praise from peers	___ Computer time
___ Playing a game	_X_ Praise from adults	___ Art activities (e.g., drawing pictures, painting)
___ Teacher's helper	_X_ Music	_X_ Objects/toys (specify)
___ Extra time outside	___ Puzzles	_Noise-making toys_
_X_ Extra praise and attention from adults	___ Special activity	___ Food (specify) _____
___ Tangibles (e.g., stickers, stamps)	___ Special helper	

Other(s): _Being read to while sitting in an adult's lap_ _____

Additional comments not addressed:

Figure 5.11A. Jessi's PTR-YC Functional Behavioral Assessment Checklist: Reinforce. (*Note:* Blank fillable and printable versions of this form can be found on the accompanying CD-ROM.)

	FORM 8	PTR-YC Functional Behavioral Assessment Summary Table

Child: _Jessi_   Date: _January 19_

Behavior	Prevent data	Teach data	Reinforce data
Challenging behavior *Physical aggression toward self or others*	*Times: Morning and afternoon* *Activities: Large group, small group, peer interactions, centers/free play, transitions (ending story or songs)* *Specific circumstances: Asked to do something, given a direction, playing with others, sharing, taking turns, transition, end of preferred activity, removal of preferred item, unstructured time, down time, teacher is attending to someone else* *Occasional circumstances: Illness, physical condition, hunger, fatigue, change in routine, sleep deprivation, stayed with noncustodial parent, day with seizure, visitation during the week*	*Function: When Jessi cannot have something she wants; when Jessi cannot have undivided attention from an adult*	*Consequences: Calming/soothing, gave personal space, gave assistance, verbal redirect, delay in activity, removed from activity, physical prompt, peer reaction*

(page 1 of 2)

(continued)

Figure 5.12A. Jessi's PTR-YC Functional Behavioral Assessment Summary Table. (*Note:* Blank fillable and printable versions of this form can be found on the accompanying CD-ROM.)

Figure 5.12A. *(continued)*

FORM 8   **PTR-YC Functional Behavioral Assessment Summary Table** *(continued)*

Behavior	Prevent data	Teach data	Reinforce data
Desirable behavior *Requests with pictures/gestures*	*Times: During meals, naptime* *Activities: Meals, snack, music time with instruments, reading with adults* *People: Teacher and parent* *Specific circumstances: One-to-one with adults, during preferred activities*	*Social skills: Getting attention appropriately, sharing (asking for a toy), taking turns, beginning interactions with adults, responding/ answering adults* *Problem solving: Asking for help, playing independently, following directions, following schedules and routines, accepting "no," getting engaged in an activity, staying engaged in activities, making choices from appropriate options, following through with choices* *Communication skills: Asking for help, requesting wants and needs, communicating effectively with pictures, expressing emotions, saying "no" or "stop"*	*Reinforcement: Social interaction with adults, extra praise and attention from adults, praise from adults, music, noise-making toys, being read to while sitting in an adult's lap*

Hypothesis: When *Jessi can't have a desired item from a peer* ,
then *she will engage in physical aggression toward herself or others* ;
as a result, *she gets the desired item*

Hypothesis: When *Jessi wants attention from adults and does not get it or when it ends* ,
then *she will engage in physical aggression toward herself or others* ;
as a result, *she gets attention from adults or extends the amount of attention* .

(page 2 of 2)

came evident that there were two different situations that resulted in challenging behavior—when Jessi could not have something she wanted and when she could not have undivided attention from an adult. The team created two hypothesis statements, and they began to realize that they wanted to change the desirable behavior that they wanted to target. Instead of Jessi being able to follow the daily schedule, they realized that it would be more beneficial for her to be able to say that she wanted something or to have undivided attention from an adult. The team decided on a new desirable behavior (asking for something) and created a new operational definition (will use pictures and/or gestures to request an item or for attention from an adult). They changed their rating scale, created new anchors, agreed to continue collecting data on the challenging behavior, and began taking data on the new desirable behavior. Jessi's revised PTR-YC Behavior Rating Scale is shown in Figure 5.13A. The team then decided they would read through all the intervention strategies, choose at least one strategy from each of the categories (prevent, teach, reinforce) that they would like to see as a part of the behavior intervention plan, and agreed to meet on Friday to create the behavior intervention plan.

MEETING 3: ETHAN

PTR-YC Assessment

Because Joan, the center director and classroom teacher, and Carol, the teaching assistant, set aside 15 minutes in the morning before the children began to arrive to work on the PTR-YC steps for Ethan, they decided that they would begin filling out the PTR-YC Functional Behavioral Assessment Checklists together. On Tuesday, they met and were able to get through the prevent checklist. Veronica, Ethan's grandmother, returned her checklist to the center on Monday, and Joan and Carol used her information to begin the process. As they went through each item on the prevent checklist, Joan and Carol agreed on the items based on their conversation and what Veronica reported on her checklist. They were in agreement on many items, but Joan and Carol could identify more areas of concern because they saw the behavior all the time. As they discussed the items, Joan recorded their combined answers on a blank PTR-YC Functional Behavioral Assessment Checklist while Carol recorded the prevent data responses on the PTR-YC Functional Behavioral Assessment Summary Table. They decided that they would send a copy of the PTR-YC Functional Behavioral Assessment Checklist: Prevent and PTR-YC Functional Behavioral Assessment Summary Table home to Veronica to share the additional information and ask if she had any feedback. On Wednesday, they met and completed the teach checklist and filled in the teach data on the summary table. They began the reinforce checklist but did not get very far before children arrived at the center. On Thursday morning, Joan and Carol finished with the checklists and summary table and developed a hypothesis. It was easy for them to create a hypothesis statement because they had spent the past few days going through the checklists. Carol made a copy of the PTR-YC Functional Behavioral Assessment Checklist: Reinforce and PTR-YC Functional Behavioral Assessment Summary Table to send home to Veronica to get her feedback about the hypothesis statement. Joan and Carol also briefly looked at their frequency graph to see how often Ethan had disruptive behavior over the past 3 days and figured they would need a few more days of data. Figures 5.14A–5.17A show Ethan's checklists and summary table.

Joan and Carol were also discussing what classroom practices they wanted to implement, and they wanted to implement them all, but they knew they could not do them all right away. They decided to begin with increasing their positive attention to the 5:1 ratio because that was something they could do right away and it would not require putting any materials together.

FORM 4

PTR-YC Behavior Rating Scale

Child: _Jessi_   Rater: _Elle and Lauren_   Observation period: _All day_   Month: _January_

Date/time

Desirable behavior														
Requests with pictures/ gestures	5	5	5	5	5	5	5	5	5	5	5	5	5	5
	4	4	4	4	4	4	4	4	4	4	4	4	4	4
	3	3	3	3	3	3	3	3	3	3	3	3	3	3
	2	2	2	2	2	2	2	2	2	2	2	2	2	2
	1	1	1	1	1	1	1	1	1	1	1	1	1	1
Challenging behavior														
Physical aggression to self or others	5	5	5	5	5	5	5	5	5	5	5	5	5	5
	4	4	4	4	4	4	4	4	4	4	4	4	4	4
	3	3	3	3	3	3	3	3	3	3	3	3	3	3
	2	2	2	2	2	2	2	2	2	2	2	2	2	2
	1	1	1	1	1	1	1	1	1	1	1	1	1	1

Desirable behavior: _Requests with pictures/gestures_
5 = _Verbal reminder to use pictures_
4 = _Gestural prompt to use pictures_
3 = _Initial physical guidance to use pictures_
2 = _Partial physical guidance to use pictures_
1 = _Hand-over-hand guidance to use pictures_

Challenging behavior: _Physical aggression to self or others_
5 = _8 or more times per day_
4 = _6 or 7 times per day_
3 = _4 or 5 times per day_
2 = _2 or 3 times per day_
1 = _0 or 1 time per day_

Figure 5.13A. Jessi's revised PTR-YC Behavior Rating Scale with blank areas to be completed by the classroom teacher and assistant. (*Note:* Blank fillable and printable versions of this form can be found on the accompanying CD-ROM.)

FORM 5

PTR-YC Functional Behavioral Assessment Checklist: Prevent

Challenging behavior: _Disruptive behavior_ Person responding: _Team_ Child: _Ethan_

1. Are there times of the day when challenging behavior is most likely to occur? If yes, what are they?

X Morning	___ Before meals	___ During meals	___ After meals	___ Preparing meals
X Afternoon	___ Evening	___ Naptime		

Other: _____

2. Are there times of the day when challenging behavior is least likely to occur? If yes, what are they?

___ Morning	X Before meals	X During meals	X After meals	___ Preparing meals
___ Afternoon	___ Evening	___ Naptime		

Other: _____

3. Are there specific activities when challenging behavior is very likely to occur? If yes, what are they?

___ Arrival	___ Naptime	X Peer interactions	___ Snack
___ Dismissal	___ Toileting/diapering	X Centers/free play	___ Transitions (specify)
___ Large-group times	___ Special event (specify)	___ Meals	
___ Small-group times	_____		_____

Other: _____

4. Are there specific activities when challenging behavior is least likely to occur? What are they?

___ Arrival	___ Naptime	___ Peer interactions	X Snack
___ Dismissal	X Toileting/diapering	___ Centers/free play	___ Transitions (specify)
X Large-group times	___ Special event (specify)	X Meals	
X Small-group times	_____		_____

Other: _____

5. Are there other children or adults whose proximity is associated with a high likelihood of challenging behavior? If so, who are they?

___ Siblings	Specify:_____	___ Teacher
___ Family member(s)	Specify:_____	___ Parent
___ Care provider(s)	Specify:_____	___ Other children (specify)
___ Other adults	Specify:_____	_____

Other: _____

6. Are there other children or adults whose proximity is associated with a low likelihood of challenging behavior? If so, who are they?

___ Siblings	Specify:_____	X Teacher
___ Family member(s)	Specify:_____	X Parent
___ Care provider(s)	Specify:_____	___ Other children (specify)
___ Other adults	Specify:_____	_____

Other: _____

(page 1 of 2)

(continued)

Figure 5.14A. Ethan's PTR-YC Functional Behavioral Assessment Checklist: Prevent. (*Note:* Blank fillable and printable versions of this form can be found on the accompanying CD-ROM.)

Figure 5.14A. *(continued)*

FORM 5   **PTR-YC Functional Behavioral Assessment Checklist: Prevent** *(continued)*

7. Are there specific circumstances that are associated with a high likelihood of challenging behavior?

___ Asked to do something	___ Seated for meal	___ Transition	___ Structured time
___ Given a direction	_X_ Playing with others	___ End of preferred activity	_X_ Unstructured time
___ Reprimand or correction	_X_ Sharing	_X_ Removal of preferred item	_X_ Down time (no task specified)
_X_ Being told "no"	_X_ Taking turns	___ Beginning of non-preferred activity	_X_ Teacher is attending to someone else
___ Sitting near specific peer	___ Playing by self	___ Activity becomes too long	___ During a non-preferred activity
___ Change in schedule	___ Novel/new task		
___ Getting peer/adult attention	___ One-to-one time with adult		

Other: _____

8. Are there conditions in the physical environment that are associated with a high likelihood of challenging behavior (e.g., too warm, too cold, too crowded, too much noise, too chaotic, weather conditions)?

___ Yes (specify) _____

_X_ No

9. Are there circumstances that occur on some days and not other days that may make challenging behavior more likely?

_X_ Illness	___ No medication	___ Change in caregiver	___ Home conflict
___ Allergies	___ Change in medication	_X_ Fatigue	_X_ Sleep deprivation
___ Physical condition	___ Hunger	___ Change in routine	___ Stayed with noncustodial parent
___ Change in diet	___ Parties or social event	___ Parent not home	

Other: _____

Additional comments not addressed:

(page 2 of 2)

PTR-YC Functional Behavioral Assessment Checklist: Teach

FORM 6

Challenging behavior: *Disruptive behavior*   Person responding: *Team*   Child: *Ethan*

1. Does the challenging behavior seem to be exhibited in order to gain attention from other children?

    X Yes (specify peers) *Whoever has what he wants*

    ___ No

2. Does the challenging behavior seem to be exhibited in order to gain attention from adults? If so, are there particular adults whose attention is solicited?

    ___ Yes (specify adults) _____

    X No

3. Does the challenging behavior seem to be exhibited in order to obtain objects (e.g., toys, games, materials, food) from other children or adults?

    X Yes (specify objects) *Blocks, the red cars, water table toys, certain art materials, certain books*

    ___ No

4. Does the challenging behavior seem to be exhibited in order to delay a transition from a preferred activity to a nonpreferred activity?

    ___ Yes (specify transitions) _____

    X No

5. Does the challenging behavior seem to be exhibited in order to terminate or delay a nonpreferred (e.g., difficult, boring, repetitive) task or activity?

    ___ Yes (specify nonpreferred tasks or activities) _____

    X No

6. Does the challenging behavior seem to be exhibited in order to get away from a nonpreferred child or adult?

    ___ Yes (specify peers or adults) _____

    X No

7. What social skills(s) could the child learn in order to reduce the likelihood of the challenging behavior occurring in the future?

X Getting attention appropriately	___ Engaging in interactions (staying on topic with peers and adults in a back-and-forth exchange)	___ Accepting positive comments and praise
X Sharing—giving a toy		___ Making positive comments
X Sharing—asking for a toy		___ Giving praise to peers
X Taking turns	X Giving a play idea ("You be the mommy")	___ Waiting for acknowledgment or reinforcement
X Beginning interactions with peers and adults	___ Playing appropriately with toys and materials with peers	X Skills to develop friendships
___ Responding or answering peers and adults		

Other: _____

(page 1 of 2)

(continued)

Figure 5.15A. Ethan's PTR-YC Functional Behavioral Assessment Checklist: Teach. (*Note:* Blank fillable and printable versions of this form can be found on the accompanying CD-ROM.)

Figure 5.15A. *(continued)*

FORM 6   **PTR-YC Functional Behavioral Assessment Checklist: Teach** *(continued)*

8. What problem-solving skill(s) could the child learn in order to reduce the likelihood of the challenging behavior occurring in the future?

_X_ Controlling anger	_X_ Self-management	___ Getting engaged in an activity
_X_ Controlling impulsive behavior	___ Playing independently	___ Staying engaged in activities
_X_ Strategies for calming down	_X_ Playing cooperatively	_X_ Choosing appropriate solutions
_X_ Asking for help	___ Following directions	___ Making choices from appropri-
___ Using visuals to support indepen-	_X_ Following schedules and	ate options
dent play	routines	___ Following through with choices
	_X_ Accepting "no"	
	_X_ Managing emotions	

Other: _____

9. What communication skill(s) could the child learn in order to reduce the likelihood of the challenging behavior occurring in the future?

___ Asking for a break	_X_ Communicating effec-	_X_ Expressing emotions (e.g.,
_X_ Asking for help	tively with words	frustration, anger, hurt)
___ Responding to others	___ Communicating effec-	appropriately
_X_ Requesting wants and needs	tively with pictures	___ Saying, "No" or "Stop"
	___ Communicating effec-	
	tively with sign language	

Other: _____

Additional comments not addressed:

(page 2 of 2)

FORM 7

PTR-YC Functional Behavioral Assessment Checklist: Reinforce

Challenging behavior: _Does not respond_   Person responding: _Team_   Child: _Ethan_

---

1. What consequence(s) usually follow the child's challenging behavior?

___ Sent to time-out	_X_ Gave personal space	_X_ Verbal reprimand
___ Sent out of the room	_X_ Gave assistance	___ Reviewed classroom rules
_X_ Sent to quiet spot	_X_ Verbal redirect	_X_ Physical prompt
_X_ Calming/soothing	___ Delay in activity	_X_ Peer reaction
_X_ Talking about what just happened	___ Activity changed	___ Physical restraint
	___ Activity terminated	_X_ Removal of reinforcers (e.g., toys, items, attention)
	_X_ Removed from activity	___ Natural consequences (specify) _____

Other: _____

---

2. Does the child enjoy praise from adults and children? Does the child enjoy praise from some people more than others?

_X_ Yes (specify people) _Almost anyone_

___ No

---

3. What is the likelihood of the child's appropriate behavior (e.g., participating appropriately, cooperating, following directions) resulting in acknowledgment or praise from adults or children?

___ Very likely	___ Sometimes	_X_ Seldom	___ Never

---

4. What is the likelihood of the child's challenging behavior resulting in acknowledgment (e.g., reprimands, corrections, restating classroom rules) from adults and children?

_X_ Very likely	___ Sometimes	___ Seldom	___ Never

---

5. What items and activities are most enjoyable to the child? What items or activities could serve as special rewards?

___ Social interaction with adults	___ High fives	___ Extra time in preferred activity
___ Social interaction with peers	___ Praise from peers	___ Computer time
___ Playing a game	_X_ Praise from adults	___ Art activities (e.g., drawing pictures, painting)
_X_ Teacher's helper	___ Music	_X_ Objects/toys (specify)
___ Extra time outside	___ Puzzles	_____
_X_ Extra praise and attention from adults	___ Special activity	___ Food (specify)
___ Tangibles (e.g., stickers, stamps)	___ Special helper	_____

Other(s):_____

Additional comments not addressed:

Figure 5.16A. Ethan's PTR-YC Functional Behavioral Assessment Checklist: Reinforce. (*Note:* Blank fillable and printable versions of this form can be found on the accompanying CD-ROM.)

FORM 8

PTR-YC Functional Behavioral Assessment Summary Table

Child: _Ethan_   Date: _March 13_

Behavior	Prevent data	Teach data	Reinforce data
Challenging behavior _Disruptive behavior_	_Times: Morning and afternoon_ _Specific activities: Peer interactions, centers/free play_ _Specific circumstances: Being told "no," playing with others, sharing, taking turns, removal of preferred item, unstructured time, down time, teacher is attending to someone else, illness, fatigue, sleep deprivation_	_Function: To obtain objects_	_Sent to quiet spot, calming/soothing, talking about what just happened, gave personal space, gave assistance, verbal redirect, removed from activity, verbal reprimand, physical prompt, peer reaction, removal of reinforcers_
Desirable behavior _Engagement_	_Times: Before, during, or after meals_ _Specific activities: Large group, small group, toileting, meals, snacks_ _Specific circumstances: Teacher, parent proximity_	_Social skills: Getting attention appropriately, sharing (giving a toy and asking for a toy), taking turns, beginning interactions with peers, giving a play idea, skills to develop friends_ _Problem solving: Controlling anger, controlling impulsive behavior, strategies to calm down, asking for help, self-management, playing cooperatively, following schedules and routines_	_Praise, teacher helper, extra praise and attention from adults, praise from adults, objects/toys_

Hypothesis: When _Ethan cannot have something he wants from a peer_ ,
then _he will engage in disruptive behavior (see operational definition)_ ;
as a result, _he receives adult attention and help in obtaining objects_ .

Figure 5.17A. Ethan's PTR-YC Functional Behavioral Assessment Summary Table. (_Note:_ Blank fillable and printable versions of this form can be found on the accompanying CD-ROM.)

PTR-YC Intervention

6

This chapter describes the process of selecting intervention strategies, developing the behavior intervention plan, and getting prepared to implement the plan. This step follows the assessment processes described in Chapter 5, and the elements of the plan should be logically linked to the information obtained from the assessment strategies.

Like Chapter 5, this chapter has two main sections. The first section concerns classroom practices. These practices can and should be implemented before completion of the functional behavioral assessment (FBA) and development of the individualized behavior intervention plan. Implementation of high-quality classroom practices has the potential to reduce challenging behaviors or to affect the circumstances in which challenging behaviors occur. Therefore, we encourage teams to implement these practices as quickly and as diligently as possible.

The second section involves the components of the individualized behavior intervention plan—prevent, teach, and reinforce. After introducing the process and rationale behind selecting optimal strategies, the process by which strategies are selected is described. We then describe considerations for developing the plan and for preparing to implement the plan in the classroom. Descriptions of evidence-based strategies in the categories of prevent, teach, and reinforce are provided in the appendix at the end of the book. We encourage all team members to be familiar with these descriptions before selecting specific strategies to include in the child's plan.

CLASSROOMWIDE PRACTICES

There are five classroomwide practices that can lead to improved behavior by all of the children in the classroom, including children who have been identified as having challenging behaviors. We strongly recommend that these five classroomwide strategies be implemented before and along with the individualized strategies we describe later in this chapter. In the following pages, we describe these five practices in some detail and provide examples to illustrate their implementation.

Five-to-One Ratio of Positive Attention

The 5:1 ratio of positive attention is based on research that has shown that children are better behaved in preschool settings when adults spend the majority of their time attending to positive behavior and not challenging behavior (Kontos, 1999; Zanolli, Saudargas, & Twardosz, 1997). At one level, it may seem as if maintaining a 5:1 ratio is simple and straightforward. If it was, then everyone would do it. Another thing that we know about challenging behavior is that it has many negative consequences for the "behaver." Among these is the tendency for adults to minimize their time with the child in positive, growth-enhancing interactions. Many teachers have explained this phenomenon this way: "I just decided to leave him alone for fear that something would set him off." Of course, over time this can result in the child receiving a 1:5 ratio of positives to negatives!

In Ms. Adkins' class, Rebecca was a spitter (5 to 10 times per day). This behavior was disruptive and disturbing to staff, children, and parents. Ms. Adkins and her team were also aware that they spent the majority of their time with Rebecca dealing with the aftermath of her spitting. As one of the classroom assistants said, "I guess I can't really recall the last time I said something to Rebecca about what she was doing well." Realizing that the team needed to do a 180-degree turn regarding the positive-to-negative ratio with Rebecca, they decided to give themselves a goal and a constant reminder. Their goal was for the team to catch Rebecca appropriately behaving 30 times during the 3-hour preschool day. The three team members each wore a carpenter's apron with 10 poker chips placed in one side pocket of the apron, and they moved a chip to the other pocket each time they made a positive comment to Rebecca about her appropriate behavior.

When implementing the 5:1 ratio, remember the following:

- All members of the team must contribute to maintaining the 5:1 ratio.

- As with Ms. Adkins' example, it is always helpful to have a specific goal for the team and a reminder.

- The only interactions that count in the positive (or 5) category are encouraging comments to the child about his or her behavior. Requests nicely stated (e.g., "Come here please") count in the negative (or 1) column. Other examples of negative comments include giving directions, making requests, or asking questions, even if stated in a positive tone or nicely asked.

- Even if shifting to the 5:1 ratio by itself does not result in a satisfactory change in challenging behavior for specific children, remember that this is still a necessary step to ultimate PTR-YC success down the road.

- Many practitioners report that getting to 5:1 changed themselves in significant ways. It would not be unusual to feel more positive about yourself and the child in question at the end of the day and to realize that the child in question does not actually behave poorly all the time. Also, it would not be unusual to realize that children in the class start to emulate your positive comments with each other, including the child with challenging behaviors.

Using Predictable Schedules

One of the most simple but effective classroomwide strategies for reducing challenging behavior is to maximize children's ability to predict what comes next (Christie, 1988; Wien, 1996). Developing a daily schedule and directly teaching children what comes next is a great place to start. Having a daily schedule that truly operates to reduce challenging behaviors is not just about having a poster on the wall and doing the same thing every day. It is about maintaining a routine and keeping all of the children informed about the routine.

Ms. Lydia's daily schedule is as follows.
- *Arrival and tabletop activities*
- *Opening circle*
- *Choice time/centers*
- *Story circle*
- *Snack*
- *Outdoor play/indoor gross motor*
- *Small-group time*

- *Closing circle*
- *Dismissal*

With notable exceptions (e.g., holiday parties, field trips) these routines occur in the order listed each school day. Ms. Lydia decided not to attach strict time limits on her routines because this content would not be understood by all children, and she and her team wanted the flexibility to lengthen or shorten a routine given children's levels of interest on any particular day.

From the first day of school and throughout the year, Ms. Lydia begins opening circle time with a review of the daily schedule, usually turning this into a fun game in which children guess what comes next, or Ms. Lydia gives a wrong answer and the children can correct her with what routine really does come next. This schedule review is a nice preliteracy activity as well. Throughout the day and right before a transition is about to occur, she and her team will ask individual children what routine is next on the schedule.

When a schedule change will occur on the following day, Ms. Lydia and her team review the upcoming change with the children at closing circle time and again at opening circle time the following day.

When implementing schedules, remember to do the following:

- Prominently display the daily schedule at children's eye level.

- Use words and pictures to represent entries on the schedule.

- Design your schedule so that you can either remove an item to indicate its completion, cover up the item to indicate its completion, or provide other ways to indicate that activities are finished.

- Review the schedule daily with the whole group and with individual children prior to making a transition.

- Preview upcoming changes with children.

- Keep things new and exciting. A predictable schedule does not mean doing the exact thing every day.

Establishing Routines within Routines

The predictability of a general schedule does not provide enough structure to prevent some children's challenging behaviors. As mentioned in Chapter 5, it is often helpful to specify other levels of predictability with one's overall classroom schedule (Strain, Bovey, Wilson, & Roybal, 2009), and this is where the idea of routines within routines within routines comes into play.

Sign-in is one daily routine in Mr. Donald's preschool class in which children come individually to a large poster board and sign in using their name, name approximation, letters, or general marks, depending on their developmental level. The first thing that happens in this routine is that Mr. Donald will approach one child at an arrival tabletop activity, hand him a marker, and say, for example, "Tim, time to sign in. Pick a friend and go sign in together." This sequence represents a routine within the sign-in routine. Mr. Donald has also taught the children that there is a routine to follow next. Children have been taught to approach the friend of their choice, tap him or her on the shoulder, look at him or her, say the child's name, and ask him or her to "come sign in." Mr. Donald used a picture sequence to teach this multistep process, with children in his class performing each step of the process. He went over the sequence at opening circle time for the first 2 weeks of class prior to actually instituting the sign-in routine. His main goal was to give children opportunities for peer interaction and to get to know each other's name. When he first instituted the routine, Mr. Donald was available to help remind children of the sequences if they needed assistance.

Routines within routines can and should be utilized for each major component of the day. Remember the following as your team works to create these routines within routines within routines:

- Think carefully about the developmental goals you have for a general routine (e.g., peer interaction, language, fine motor skills), and make sure the routines within the routine actually provide opportunities for children to practice skills related to the goal.

- Always mediate with picture sequences. Picture sequences are a permanent reminder for children regarding your behavioral expectations, and they help children understand each step of each routine.

- Directly teach the sequences using fun activities such as puppets, role-playing with adults purposefully making mistakes, and children taking turns modeling for each other.

Directly Teach Behavioral Expectations

Another classroomwide tactic for addressing challenging behavior is to make certain that all children know precisely what behavioral expectations you have for each routine (Lane, Wehby, & Cooley, 2006; Walker, Ramsey, & Gresham, 2004). For many preschool teams, it is vital to agree about these expectations. We recommend that teams specify no more than three expectations for any one routine.

Ms. Alice and the other team members generated the following behavioral expectations for each daily routine in the preschool classroom in their 2½-hour day.

For arrival
- *Active engagement with materials*
- *Peer social interactions*

For opening circle
- *Maintaining attending behavior (sitting in the group)*
- *Active participation (watching, motor movement, verbal participation)*

For choice time
- *Peer social interactions*
- *Independent engagement with materials*

For snack
- *Peer social interactions*

For outdoor/gross motor
- *Motor participation with the group*

For closing circle and story
- *Maintaining attending behavior (sitting in the group)*
- *Active participation (watching, motor movement, verbal participation)*

Ms. Alice and her team took pictures of the children in their class demonstrating all the expectations, and the pictures were strategically posted around the classroom. At the beginning of the year, the staff reviewed the expectations for each upcoming routine prior to making a transition. The photographs were used to remind children of the expectations. When staff noticed an episode of rule follow-

ing, they made a point to publicly acknowledge this (e.g., "Amy, you sang every word of the song!"). Staff used the pictures to redirect children to the desired behavior when they were not following expectations.

Remember the following as your team works to directly teach behavioral expectations.

- Adjust the level of expectations across the year. For example, engagement at opening circle time for a 3-year-old group may be 5 minutes or less at the beginning of the year but double that or longer by the end of the year.

- Practice expectations beforehand. Practicing after rule infractions may be perceived as punitive by the children.

- Make sure that all children have an opportunity to practice behavioral expectations each day.

- Remember the 5:1 ratio and to catch children appropriately behaving.

Directly Teach Peer-Related Social Skills

Children with and without disabilities often lack key social skills necessary for success in preschool and later in life. Research has indicated a strong relationship between low peer status in childhood and later problems in adolescence and adulthood (Odom & Strain, 1986; Strain & Kohler, 1998). Children with social deficits often show similar patterns of behavior; they may be withdrawn and hesitant to interact with peers, socially aloof and unaware of their peers, or want to interact with their peers but do not have the skills to do so success-fully. Promoting children's social development to help prevent problems later in life is one of the primary goals of preschool. Simply placing a child with social delays (e.g., a child who is withdrawn, a child who has trouble initiating interactions with friends, a child who rarely responds when peers approach him or her) in an early childhood setting, however, does not automatically result in increasing positive social behaviors or peer acceptance. Actively teaching social skills involves careful planning around routines and activities, arranging the environment to support peer interaction, and implementing strategies such as peer-mediated interventions, adult cueing and prompting, and reinforcement.

Research indicates that by providing planned and systematic opportunities (i.e., oppor-tunities that consistently occur) for peer interactions, children engage in more social inter-actions throughout the day and have more opportunities to practice emerging social skills. (Strain & Bovey, 2011). Through interactions during routine activities such as snack, arrival time, and clean up time, children practice targeted social skills more often and learn the skills more rapidly. Research also documents improved generalization of social skills from targeted activities to other times of the day (Strain & Kohler, 1998). For example, an ex-tremely shy child who begins talking with a peer as they set up snack together might begin talking with this same peer during center time. Because social interactions are embedded into ongoing activities, children are able to gain access to natural reinforcers (e.g., friends), thus keeping motivation high to engage in these interactions. Many opportunities exist throughout the day to unobtrusively include peer interactions in ongoing routines within preschool and child care settings. One strategy is to examine the day and look at what the adults are doing with or for the children. Caregivers can create more opportunities for peer interactions by having a child do those tasks instead. For example, instead of an adult set-ting up snack, children might work in pairs to put out napkins, cups, and plates, or children might work together to make an art collage or pass out book bags at the end of the day.

Circle time always begins the same way in Ms. Judy's preschool classroom. As the children sit down for circle time, Ms. Judy pulls Thomas's name out of the job can. Thomas gets up and takes the basket filled with sun pictures and proceeds to pass a sun out to each child. After Thomas sits down, the class sings "Oh Mr. Sun," using the pictures as props for motor movement and imitation. Ms. Judy takes Haley's name out of the can as the song ends and has her take the basket and collect all of the suns. Haley, however, has trouble independently completing this task, so an adult provides her with some physical assistance to go to every child. An adult also verbally prompts Haley to tell the children to "put the sun in." This job of passing out and collecting the suns used to be done by an adult, but the caregivers decided that it was a simple task that a child could easily do. They realized that having a child pass out and collect the materials created 2 peer social interactions for each child, and it created 12–15 peer interactions in less than 1 minute for the child who hands out or picks up the props. The teachers also know that these interactions will occur every day.

The caregivers have created a similar situation at snack—the children pass out the cups, plates, snack (when appropriate), and juice. Instead of having an adult sit at the snack tables with the children, the adults designate a snack captain and drink captain for each table. Monique has been selected as the snack captain for her table. Once all the children are seated and they have sung their snack song, Ms. Judy gives Monique a stack of napkins. Adults then cue the children who need prompting to ask Monique for a napkin. Once the napkins are passed out, Monique is given a plate with the snacks on it. Again, the adults cue the children to ask Monique for a snack, and she passes the plate to each child so he or she can take a snack. Meanwhile, Marcus, the drink captain, is given the cups and a small pitcher of juice. While some children are asking Monique for snack, others are asking Marcus for juice. Teachers facilitate these interactions and make sure everyone asks for snack and juice—whether it is by verbalizing a request; gesturing; or using pictures, signs, or other ways to communicate.

Teachers and other caregivers need to ask themselves the following questions when trying to create opportunities for peer interaction.

- What social skills goals do I have for the individual children in my class? What are my expectations for the children in my care?

- What do I typically do with or for the children?

- Could a child do this job?

- Is this activity something that frequently happens? This question is important because we want to create opportunities that occur often, thus providing a wealth of opportunities over the course of a day, week, month, and school year.

- Can I ensure that support will be available so that all children can be successful in carrying out this task?

By asking these questions and looking at their daily schedule, caregivers can identify opportunities during natural activities and routines to support or encourage peer interactions. Ms. Judy and her classroom team have successfully used these strategies through the passing out of the suns before singing their opening song and through their snack time routine. It is important that caregivers are available to facilitate peer interactions and provide cues (e.g., general or specific verbal cues, gestures, visual cues) or assistance (e.g., helping a child hand napkins to peers or pass a plate of snacks to a friend), if necessary. For example, an adult assisted Haley in collecting the suns by verbally cueing her to ask the other children for their suns. Also, an adult provided physical assistance as Haley walked around the group collecting the props. Opportunities for peer interaction should be identified within different activities throughout the day to provide practice and mastery of peer-related social skills.

Caregivers can see how many opportunities for peer interaction can be created throughout the day by looking at some activities that typically take place in preschool or child care settings.

- A child could be designated as the class greeter during arrival time, saying hello to classmates as they come in and asking them a simple question such as, "Who do you want to play with today?" or "Which book do you vote to read today during circle time, *Brown Bear* or *Snowy Day?*"

- A child can pass out and collect props from each child at circle or storytime.

- A child can invite a peer to take his or her place at the activity he or she just completed instead of the adult inviting another child (e.g., Angelo might ask Blair if she wants to use the headset to listen to music now that he is done).

- A child can pass out snack items to each child at the table.

- One child might be the "teacher" and ask his or her peers, "Where do you want to play?" as children disperse for center time.

- A child can ask a playmate to go to a center with him or her (e.g., Kate might invite Alyssa to go to housekeeping with her).

One convenient aspect of creating opportunities for social interaction within routines is that little effort is necessary to create these opportunities. They simply become part of the daily routine. In addition, these jobs are typically done by adults, so it is fairly easy for an adult to provide assistance to a child as needed. Also, as caregivers raise their expectations that children will interact with one another, children typically rise to the occasion and begin engaging with and helping one another, taking on more responsibility during activities. Finally, it is important that adults provide feedback so children realize what behaviors are expected from them. It is also important that adults praise children for their efforts to interact with peers.

Summary

We wish to emphasize the importance of the five universal classroom practices, and we encourage you and your team to implement them as conscientiously as possible. We have seen on numerous occasions that the implementation of these practices can lead to surprising and dramatic reductions in challenging behavior to the extent that individualized and relatively effortful interventions are no longer needed.

> Implementing the five universal classroom practices can lead to surprising and dramatic reductions in challenging behavior to the extent that individualized and relatively effortful interventions are no longer needed.

Some challenging behaviors do persist even when high-quality classroom practices are used. Children with these challenging behaviors are in need of individualized, assessment-based intervention strategies. Therefore, at this point we turn to a discussion of the PTR-YC model and the steps that must be followed to implement it with fidelity.

INDIVIDUALIZED INTERVENTIONS AND THE BEHAVIOR INTERVENTION PLAN

It is time to develop a behavior intervention plan for children with persistent challenging behavior for whom an FBA has been completed. The behavior intervention plan in the PTR-YC model always includes at least one strategy from each of the three core components—prevent, teach, and reinforce. A description of recommended, evidence-based strategies for each of the core components is provided in the appendix at the end of the book. The specific strategies that your team will choose to include in the behavior intervention plan should be based on a few considerations.

The first and most important consideration is the extent to which the strategy is logically linked to the hypothesis statements that resulted from the FBA. The greater the linkage between the assessment data and the intervention strategy, the more likely it will be that the intervention is effective and efficient. For example, if your hypothesis for a challenging behavior is that the behavior's function is for the child to avoid making a transition to a nonpreferred activity, then the intervention strategy that you implement needs to address this function. A second consideration is the preference of the team members, especially those team members who will be responsible for implementing the selected strategies. Team members' preferences are usually determined by the ease with which the strategy can be implemented and by the degree with which the strategy can fit within the ongoing context of the classroom routines. This consideration has a lot to do with fidelity and the extent to which the strategy will be used with the frequency and quality needed to be optimally effective. A third consideration is the extent to which the strategy's effectiveness is supported by the research literature. The research literature is the best guide to strategies that can be effective, but it does not cover everything and it cannot indicate exactly which strategy will be most effective with your particular child with challenging behavior. Also, nobody can expect that early childhood professionals will be familiar with the entire literature on strategies for challenging behavior. We can offer a start, however. All of the strategies that are described in the appendix at the end of the book have support in the published research literature. There are published demonstrations in which the strategy described was shown to be effective in reducing challenging behavior with preschool-age children. The strategies have been demonstrated in stand-alone evaluations or as components of multifaceted, evidence-based intervention packages.

Prevent

In selecting strategies for the prevent component, the primary notion to keep in mind is that 1) the team should choose strategies that will remove or ameliorate antecedent events that are associated with (or trigger) challenging behavior, and 2) the team should add antecedent events that are associated with desirable, prosocial behavior. The PTR-YC Functional Behavioral Assessment Summary Table and the hypothesis statements should provide the information needed to guide these selections. There are many ways to accomplish these objectives, as the array of prevent menu items will make obvious. For example, the choice-making strategy may enable the child to avoid some triggers and engage with activities or materials that promote appropriate behavior. Providing individualized, visual schedules might alleviate a child's anxiety or concern regarding unpredictability, and it might reassure a child that preferred activities will occur soon. Prevent strategies can be powerful, and many teams decide to select two or three strategies if they are logically connected to the hypotheses and can be smoothly accommodated in the classroom routine.

Teach

In many ways, the teach component is the heart of the PTR-YC intervention because it is most responsible for helping the child develop new skills that will eventually enable him or her to successfully deal with the social environment without recourse to challenging behaviors. Guidance for determining the specifics of the teach strategies also comes from the PTR-YC Functional Behavioral Assessment Summary Table and from the hypotheses. Although there are many kinds of skills that may be appropriate selections for the teach component, the most common and most powerful is teaching replacement skills. A replacement skill is a communicative behavior that serves the same purpose (or function) as the challenging behavior. For example, if the function of a young boy's screaming behavior is to obtain a teacher's attention, then a replacement skill might be having the boy verbally call for the teacher. Once the boy learns to make the verbal request, his new skill will replace the screaming. This practice of teaching a communicative replacement for challenging behavior is known as functional communication training, and it can be an effective strategy if correctly used.

In addition to replacement skills, other behaviors can be taught as part of the behavior intervention plan. Some behaviors are important to teach because they are physically incompatible with the child's challenging behavior. For instance, if a child is sharing and playing quietly with a peer, then it is unlikely that the child will be engaging in challenging behavior. So, the behavior to be taught could include social interaction skills, cooperative play, or parallel play, depending on the context in which challenging behavior usually occurs. Other targets for the teach component might include self-regulation (specifically, self-monitoring), tolerating delay for a preferred activity, emotional literacy, and problem solving.

Reinforce

Reinforce is the third component of the behavior intervention plan. The primary objective is to implement strategies that will remove reinforcers for challenging behavior and to make sure that reinforcers follow desirable behavior. The PTR-YC Functional Behavioral Assessment Summary Table and hypothesis statements should be helpful in identifying the existing consequences and suggesting the kinds of changes that should be made. As discussed previously, achieving a 5:1 ratio of positive attention to negative attention is an important objective. Other reinforce strategies might involve changing the kinds of reinforcers that are used, however, and modifying the ways that adults respond to the occurrences of challenging behavior.

Summary of PTR-YC Intervention Strategies

The intervention menu in Table 6.1 provides a simple listing of the procedural options described in the appendix at the end of the book for each of the three core components. (*Note:* A printable version of this table [Form 9] can be found on the accompanying CD-ROM.) This list will help team members consider the strategies to include in the child's behavior intervention plan. Each entry on the menu is described in some detail in the appendix at the end of the book, and team members should be familiar with the options before making decisions about the composition of the behavior intervention plan. Also, sometimes team members may recommend an intervention strategy that is not on the list. This is quite acceptable

Table 6.1. PTR-YC menu of intervention strategies

Prevent strategies	Teach strategies	Reinforce strategies
Provide choices	Teach communication skills	Reinforce desirable behavior
Intersperse difficult or nonpreferred tasks with easy or preferred tasks	Embed multiple instructional opportunities	Reinforce physically incompatible behavior
Use visual supports and schedules	Peer-related social skills	Remove reinforcement for challenging behavior
Embed preferences into activities	Self-monitoring	Emergency intervention plan
Enhance predictability with schedules	Tolerate delay of reinforcement	
Alter physical arrangement of the classroom	Teach independence with visual schedules	
Remove triggers for challenging behaviors		

because we recognize that the list is not exhaustive of all possibilities. Although we have attempted to include the strategies that are most common and have been demonstrated in research to be effective in some circumstances, we appreciate that there may be other evidence-based strategies that can be identified and that there may be special strategies that have been shown to be effective with your particular child. We encourage teams to be flexible and creative, but our encouragement comes with two caveats: 1) the strategy should fit in one of the three components—prevent, teach, or reinforce—and teams should agree about the category in which it would go; and 2) the strategy should be accompanied by careful, objective evaluation (data) to be sure that it is being effective.

Three important things to keep in mind:

1. At least one strategy needs to be selected from each core component.
2. Each strategy should be linked to the FBA and hypothesis statements.
3. There needs to be agreement that team members are capable of implementing the strategy as intended.

There are three important things to remember as teams consider the intervention menu and begin to decide which strategies will be included on the individual child's behavior intervention plan. First, at least one strategy needs to be selected from each of the core components. Second, the strategy should be logically associated with the FBA and the hypothesis statements. Third, the team members should agree that the strategy can be implemented without undue compromises to ongoing responsibilities. In particular, the individuals who will be most responsible for implementation should agree that they will be able to implement the strategy with integrity and often enough to be effective. This latter point is essential because the strategy cannot be effective if it is not implemented as intended.

DEVELOPING THE BEHAVIOR INTERVENTION PLAN

When the team has identified the strategies that will comprise the behavior intervention plan, it is time to plan for all aspects of implementation, including the written document that will describe the behavior intervention plan. The written document includes two parts. The first is the cover page, which is a summary of the behavior intervention plan and is designed to be posted in strategic places in the classroom and shared with all team members and outside personnel who may be involved in the plan's implementation. The second part is comprised of subsequent pages that lay out the specifics of the implementation strategies. The specifics include descriptions of the steps involved in each strategy (or scripts), materials that may be needed (e.g., picture schedules), directions on when and how often the strategy should be used, who will be the primary person to implement the strategy, and what kind of consequences will be used when the child is successful. We realize that this may seem like a lot of planning and even a lot of writing; however, we emphasize that the more the team thinks about and anticipates the issues involved in implementation, the more likely it will be that the plan is implemented as intended and the intervention is effective. The more chronic, severe, and persistent the challenging behavior, the more important it is to be well prepared.

Before we describe the preparation of the behavior intervention plan document, we will review some of the considerations that the team should ponder in this important planning phase. These considerations are points that should be addressed on the behavior intervention plan after agreement is reached in team discussions.

A number of prevent strategies require materials to be obtained or developed. For example, new materials might include picture schedules or pictorial menus for children to make choices. Other prevent strategies might require timers, charts, checklists, or new curricular items. It is important to determine how such materials will be obtained or created and who will be responsible to see that they are in place.

Teach strategies must be planned so that team members have a clear idea of the teaching techniques that will be used. If prompts are to be used, then it is important to determine what kind of prompt will initially be used to get the child to respond and how that prompt will be gradually removed so that the child is demonstrating the behavior by him- or herself. If the child is going to be taught to use a new communicative behavior, then it is crucial that all team members understand the behavioral objective and the child's current ability to produce the behavior. Effective teaching requires many opportunities in the natural context during the day, and these opportunities must be anticipated and planned.

Reinforce strategies sometimes require that an assessment is conducted to determine exactly what kind of consequence(s) are powerful enough to motivate the child to consistently engage in the desirable behavior. The team needs to be sure that the reinforcers scheduled for the child are used on a regular basis in the initial stages of implementation so that the likelihood of behavior change is optimized. It may be necessary in a few cases to obtain special items to use as reinforcers, and the team will need to determine who will be responsible for obtaining these special items.

The team must determine how the strategy will be implemented, by whom, where, and how often. It is important to appreciate that behavior change occurs as a result of many opportunities to practice desired behavior with high-quality supports in place. Challenging behavior is not always easy to overcome, but children can be successful if their environments are designed to support positive behavior and if individualized interventions are well planned and carefully implemented.

PTR-YC Behavior Intervention Plan Summary Form

The first page of the behavior intervention plan, the PTR-YC Behavior Intervention Plan Summary, summarizes the core features of the individualized intervention plan (see Figure 6.1). (*Note:* Blank fillable and printable versions of this form can be found on the accompanying CD-ROM.) This form has lines for the child's name and classroom. Below these lines is a list of the classroom practices described at the beginning of this chapter. The list is intended as a reminder to use these practices. Although the practices are for all of the children in the classroom, they may be particularly important for the child who has difficulties with challenging behavior. Furthermore, if one or more of the practices is particularly important for the focus child, the team might decide to circle or highlight those practices on this form as a special emphasis and reminder.

The remainder of the form is for the individual strategies—prevent, teach, and reinforce. There is space for more than one strategy per category, although some children may have only one strategy under one or more categories. A brief description of the strategy should be inserted in the first block of space under each category. Implementation notes, which might include details such as when to use a teaching strategy or when to make sure that a visual schedule is available, should be inserted under the brief description block. Examples are shown in the case studies in the appendix at the end of the chapter.

The summary form is the first page of the behavior intervention plan. Subsequent pages provide the details needed for consistent and accurate implementation and can include specifications of 1) materials to be used, 2) activities and routines in which the strategy is to be implemented, 3) personnel responsible for implementation, and 4) a list of steps to be followed to correctly implement the strategy. The list of steps is referred to as a task analysis and includes descriptions of the steps that are followed to implement the strategy. Examples of task analyses for strategies in each of the three core categories are shown in Table 6.2. In addition, illustrations are included in the case studies in the appendix at the end of the chapter.

△ FORM 10

PTR-YC Behavior Intervention Plan Summary

Child: _____   Class: _____

Classroom practices for all children:

☐ Show positive attention: 5:1 ratio.

☐ Teach behavioral expectations for each routine.

☐ Teach positive peer-related social skill.

☐ Use predictable schedules.

☐ Use predictable routines within routines.

Intervention strategies

	Prevent	Teach	Reinforce
Brief description			
Implementation notes			

Figure 6.1.   PTR-YC Behavior Intervention Plan Summary. (*Note:* Blank fillable and printable versions of this form can be found on the accompanying CD-ROM.)

Table 6.2.   Examples of task analyses

Prevent: Providing choice during coloring for Sarah, who often exhibits challenging behavior when presented with fine motor activities.

- Prepare visual chart displaying three different pictures for coloring.
- Present chart to child and ask, "Which picture do you want to color?"
- When child indicates a preference, immediately provide that picture with the crayons.
- Praise child for making the choice and for engaging in the coloring activity.
- If activity is a long one (for this particular child), then allow Sarah to choose two steps from three to complete.

Teach: Teaching communication skills (functional communication training) for Steve, who is nonverbal and engages in tantrums if he is expected to sit in one place for extended periods of time.

- An adult (teacher or aide) is in close proximity to Steve during morning circle and all other group sitting activities.
- When Steve begins to fidget (a precursor to tantrums), an adult moves close and prompts Steve to use the sign for break (fists moving apart) while saying, "Steve wants a break."
- As soon as the break sign is displayed, an adult smiles and encourages Steve to get up and move to another location in the classroom.

Reinforce: Reinforce desirable behavior for Mahmoud, who is in need of more positive responses to peer initiations.

- An adult sets a silent timer (buzzer) to go off every 5 minutes.
- When the timer gives the signal, an adult looks for the next occasion when Mahmoud appropriately (positively) responds to a peer's initiation.
- An adult provides a positive acknowledgement to Mahmoud and the peer for doing so well (using rewards that are known to be effective for both children).

PREPARING FOR IMPLEMENTATION:
TRAINING, COACHING, AND ONGOING SUPPORT

Implementing a behavior intervention plan is not always easy. It requires change in the way that adults provide guidance and the way they interact with the child who has challenging behaviors. Change can be hard. Change can be hard for the child, and it can be hard for the adults. But change is important, and change is possible. The purpose of PTR-YC is to make it as simple as possible.

Two things are important to remember as the behavior intervention plan is implemented.

1. All children can learn to engage in positive, prosocial behaviors and desist from patterns of challenging behavior. This change can be difficult for some children, but it is important to emphasize that all children can make the change if the environment is well designed and if there are necessary interventions and supports in place.

2. All teachers (and other classroom personnel) can implement the intervention strategies indicated on a high-quality behavior intervention plan. This can be difficult for some teachers, but it is important to emphasize that all teachers can implement a behavior intervention plan if the environment is well designed and if the teacher receives necessary preparation and support.

What are the supports that need to be in place to enable the teachers and other classroom personnel to implement the behavior intervention plan with integrity, consistency, and quality? The answer differs from teacher to teacher, classroom to classroom, behavior intervention plan to behavior intervention plan, and child to child. The goal, however, is always the same—for the teachers and other implementers to be competent, confident, and comfortable in their ability to implement all of the behavior intervention plan strategies with accuracy, integrity, and fluency.

Some teachers will be perfectly comfortable with some strategies from the very beginning. Some strategies are so simple that they do not require much effort or special competence to implement. But other strategies may be more involved, and some teachers may lack the relevant experience needed to effectively implement the strategy. We expect this will be the case in many circumstances. And when this is the case, then some assistance will be needed to help the teachers gain the competence and confidence needed for fluent implementation. The team will need to plan for necessary training, coaching, and ongoing support in such cases.

> **Implementer's Tip**
>
> Plan for success. If a teacher seems to initially need more support to become comfortable and confident with implementing strategies, then it is best to plan to provide extra support. This front-loading of support will set everyone up for success.

There are many ways that training can be provided, and the preferences of the teachers should be a primary consideration. The most effective training will be individualized, however, so it is focused on the needs of the child, the teachers, and the specific intervention strategies. Also, the training should be provided in context, or at least have the majority occur in the classroom with actual practice and feedback. In this respect, ideal training includes a hefty proportion of on-site coaching in which the trainer (or coach) is present in the classroom when the intervention strategy is actually occurring. In practice, it is important to have a trusting and goal-oriented relationship between the trainer/coach and the teachers who are receiving the assistance.

Trainers/coaches can be experienced personnel from within the same program or they can be external consultants or employees of a district or regional agency. Many configurations can be effective; however, it is always important to plan for ongoing monitoring and support. Simply because a teacher reaches a high level of competence during initial training does not mean that that same level will be maintained. Therefore, we always encourage programs to arrange for ongoing support to be built into training plans.

MONITORING FIDELITY

A behavior intervention plan must be consistently and accurately implemented if it is going to be effective. Even when team members have the best of intentions, we have found that implementation fidelity is not something that automatically happens. It has to be monitored. If fidelity is lacking, then it needs to be corrected, especially during the first days of intervention; however, it can also be important after intervention has been in place for several weeks.

The procedure we recommend for monitoring fidelity uses the PTR-YC Fidelity of Strategy Implementation, as shown in Figure 6.2. (*Note:* Blank fillable and printable versions of this form can be found on the accompanying CD-ROM.) This form is primarily used to remind teachers and other personnel who are involved in implementing the behavior intervention plan about the need to faithfully and frequently implement the strategies, but it is also used for troubleshooting. We recommend that the form be used at least 2 times per week during the first 3 weeks of implementation and then once per week thereafter, assuming that good progress is being made. One form should be completed for each adult in the classroom who is responsible for implementing all or parts of the behavior intervention plan. The form may be completed by the person who is doing the implementation (as a self-evaluation) or by another person in the classroom who is available to observe the implementation. The form is to be used as follows.

1. Create a template of the form to be used for all observations for the PTR-YC implementation for a particular child. This is done by writing out a brief description of the strategies and the essential steps for implementation in the designated places on the form. When more than one strategy per component is on the behavior intervention plan, the

PTR-YC Fidelity of Strategy Implementation

Child: _____ Interventionist: _____ Observer: _____

Date: _____ Observation period: _____

	Were all steps implemented as intended?		Did the child respond as intended?		Was the strategy implemented as frequently as intended?	
Prevent strategy Steps: 1. 2. 3. 4. 5.	Yes	No	Yes	No	Yes	No
Teach strategy Steps: 1. 2. 3. 4. 5.	Yes	No	Yes	No	Yes	No
Reinforce strategy Steps: 1. 2. 3. 4. 5.	Yes	No	Yes	No	Yes	No

Figure 6.2. PTR-YC Fidelity of Strategy Implementation. (*Note:* Blank fillable and printable versions of this form can be found on the accompanying CD-ROM.)

form can be extended to accommodate more than one strategy, or an additional page of the form can be created. When the strategies and steps are listed, multiple copies can be made for use with different interventionists and different dates.

2. Indicate the date, the interventionist, the observer, and the observation period. The observation period should conform to the period in which the behavior intervention plan is being implemented. This might be the entire time that the child is in the class (i.e., all day) or it might just be a specific routine during which intervention is being focused.

3. The observer should mark "yes" or "no" for the three questions for each strategy when the observation period is completed.

> **Implementer's Tip**
>
> Describing the strategies should be relatively simple and should come from the steps outlined in the behavior intervention plan. If teams are struggling with this, then it means a further breakdown of steps needed to implement the strategy is necessary. It is important to make sure the steps needed to implement strategies are well defined.

- *Were all steps implemented as intended?* If the interventionist consistently failed to implement important steps listed on the behavior intervention plan for a particular strategy, then the observer should mark "no." If the interventionist implemented the steps of the strategy as intended, then the observer should mark "yes."

- *Did the child respond as intended?* There is a general expectation about how a child should respond to an intervention. For example, if a teacher provides a prompt for the child to use a communicative request, then the expectation is for the child to respond by using the request. The observer should mark "yes" or "no," depending on the child's response (or lack of response).

- *Was the strategy implemented as frequently as intended?* The team should have a good idea about how often a strategy should be implemented during a day or a routine. Strategies of instruction and reinforcement should be implemented as often as there are appropriate opportunities. Prevent strategies are usually restricted to specific circumstances, but they should typically be used during each of these circumstances to be optimally effective. The observer should mark "yes" or "no," depending on how frequently the strategy was implemented.

The completed forms should be kept in a designated file and reviewed at team meetings and whenever concerns regarding progress are raised. These issues are discussed further in Chapter 7.

When the steps described in this chapter are completed, the team should take a moment to review and fill out the Self-Evaluation Checklist for Implementation in Figure 6.3. It is important that all steps are scored as "yes" before moving to the next chapter.

Self-Evaluation Checklist for Intervention

	Yes	No
1. Has the team carefully assessed the status of classroom practices, and have steps been taken to improve the implementation of classroomwide practices?	☐	☐
2. Did the team members review the descriptions of the possible intervention strategies for prevent, teach, and reinforce (listed in the PTR-YC Menu of Intervention Services)?	☐	☐
3. Did the team decide on intervention strategies to include in the child's behavior intervention plan?	☐	☐
4. Did the team complete the PTR-YC Behavior Intervention Plan Summary?	☐	☐
5. Did the team complete the additional pages (including the task analysis) of the child's behavior intervention plan?	☐	☐
6. Did the team determine what training and ongoing support would be provided for the classroom personnel responsible for implementing the behavior intervention plan?	☐	☐

If the answer to each of these questions is "yes," then the team should proceed to the next step.

Figure 6.3. Self-Evaluation Checklist for Intervention.

APPENDIX
Case Examples

MEETING 4: HASANI

PTR-YC Intervention

The next meeting for Hasani's team involved creating the behavior intervention plan. The team members came to this meeting with multiple strategy ideas. They decided to write down all the strategy ideas and put them up on a sticky wall sorted into three categories—prevent, teach, and reinforce. Once the team agreed on which interventions to implement, they decided to target arrival time because there were opportunities for preferred and nonpreferred activities. The team also was not sure if they would be able to provide this level of support for Hasani throughout the entire day, so they wanted to try the strategy at the beginning of the day first to see if she was responding to the interventions. The team needed time to get the visuals ready and to role-play how to implement the strategies. They decided to take 3 days to get prepared and would begin implementing on Monday. Figures 6.1A and 6.2A show Hasani's PTR-YC Behavior Intervention Plan Summary and behavior intervention plan.

<table>
<tr><td>

FORM 10

PTR-YC Behavior Intervention Plan Summary
</td></tr>
</table>

Child: _Hasani_   Class: _Busy Bees_

Classroom practices for all children:

☐ Show positive attention: 5:1 ratio.

☐ Teach behavioral expectations for each routine.

☐ Teach positive peer-related social skill.

☐ Use predictable schedules.

☐ Use predictable routines within routines.

Intervention strategies

	Prevent	Teach	Reinforce
Brief description	Use visual supports and schedules.	Teach independence with visual schedules.	Reinforce desirable behavior.
Implementation notes	Target arrival time: Set up greetings with visuals for a scripted response. Use the visual supports to prompt at least two more responses during arrival time.	Prompt for responses with visuals at greeting, beginning tabletop activities, and sign-in.	Increase positive attention to 5:1 ratio and make extra deposits when responding will be required. Give behavior-specific praise when desired behavior is present.

Figure 6.1A. Hasani's PTR-YC Behavior Intervention Plan Summary. (*Note:* Blank fillable and printable versions of this form can be found on the accompanying CD-ROM.)

FIGURE 6.2A

Behavior Intervention Plan

Child: Hasani

Age: 2½ years old

Parents: Amara and Jerry

Classroom: Busy Bees

Date of plan: September 20

Challenging behavior: When presented with a request that is familiar, Hasani does not respond within 5 seconds.

Function of challenging behavior: Delay or terminate transition or nonpreferred activity.

Hypothesis statement: When Hasani is asked to do a nonpreferred activity or make a transition to another activity, then she does not respond to adults and peers; as a result, the activity or transition is delayed, changed, or terminated.

	Prevent	Teach	Reinforce
Strategy	Use of visual supports and schedules	Teach independence with visual schedules	Reinforce desirable behavior
When to implement	Target arrival time	Target greeting, beginning tabletop activities, and sign-in	Any time Hasani is engaged in an activity or responds to a request or interaction
Steps involved	When Hasani finishes putting her things in her cubby upon arrival, show Hasani the minischedule (in cubby) with pictures of scripted greeting response. Guide her to a teacher or peer and prompt her through the greeting script; provide as much support as necessary for Hasani to participate. Provide verbal praise for each step that Hasani does (even if she does not do it on her own), and flip each picture over to indicate that the step is complete. Repeat previous steps for at least one peer. Repeat previous steps for at least three teachers or peers during arrival time. When Hasani has greeted three individuals, have Hasani put her minischedule back in her cubby.	Visuals should be present, accessible, and available at each relevant area. Guide Hasani to the appropriate area and go directly to the visuals. Prompt Hasani (as necessary) to use visuals to engage in the activity—initially make each step brief and require no more than three steps. As each step is completed, turn the picture over to indicate the step is complete. Provide verbal praise for each completed step and extra praise when the activity is complete. Repeat steps for next two activities, providing as much support as Hasani requires to be successful.	Provide behavior-specific praise as immediately as possible; provide extra praise when a response is required. This can be combined with physical affection (e.g., hugs, tickles), singing ABCs, or access to art activities when appropriate and available.

Figure 6.2A. Hasani's behavior intervention plan.

MEETING 4: JOEL

PTR-YC Intervention

The intervention meeting for Joel's team took almost 2 hours; it ran a bit longer than expected. Although attempts were made to include Gary, Joel's father, in this meeting, he had not responded. This meeting was facilitated by Sally, the educational specialist, with a recorder and time keeper appointed.

Sally began with a brief discussion of what the arrival time looked like because this was consistently a problem for Joel. As the discussion continued, Sally realized that the arrival sequence was not clearly defined and suggested the team review the classroom practices section of the PTR-YC manual. The team saw many areas that needed to improve. They decided to create two implementation phases—general classroom practices and individual supports.

The team would target three classroom practices during the first phase—using positive comments on a 5:1 ratio, using predictable schedules, and using routines within routines. The first phase would take 2 weeks, with the first week focused on developing the materials needed to implement the classroom strategies and the individual strategies. The second week would involve implementing the classroom strategies, and the third week would focus on the individual strategies. The team decided to begin with the 5:1 positive attention strategy.

The team spent time talking about the consequences—those that have maintained the hitting behavior and the new consequences that would be needed to support teaching a new skill. Sally facilitated this discussion and helped the team see how their own reactions to hitting were actually supporting Joel's behavior because it gave him a lot of adult attention. Although one team member in particular was uncomfortable with this discussion, the PTR-YC Functional Behavioral Assessment Checklists (see Figures 5.5A–5.7A) and Summary Table (see Figure 5.8A) supported this maintaining consequence. The team felt it was important to minimize the attention given to Joel related to hitting. Because hitting is a behavior the team felt could not be ignored, they developed a response that everyone would follow if hitting was about to occur or did occur. The team would not mention the behavior of hitting. Team members would instead redirect Joel to participate in the activity if they could catch him right before he hit. The team generated a list of the warning signs that were subtle behaviors that gave clues that Joel might hit another person; this was easily generated by the team and readily agreed on. If Joel did hit, then the team would interrupt the hitting and redirect Joel to an appropriate activity (without talking about it) while giving their attention to the child who was hit. The team role-played and practiced with each other on how and when to give their attention to Joel.

Visual supports and a direct teaching method were developed as part of the individual intervention to support Joel. The team realized that the way that they gave attention to Joel would affect the impact of this intervention, and they would need to make sure that they all provided attention in a similar, scripted way. Figures 6.3A and 6.4A show Joel's PTR-YC Behavior Intervention Plan Summary and his behavior intervention plan.

MEETING 4: JESSI

PTR-YC Intervention

Jessi's team met to design the behavior intervention plan, and each member came to the meeting with ideas. They first discussed the new PTR-YC Behavior Rating Scale (see Figure 5.13A) and how it was going. The teacher and assistant felt much more comfortable with the new desirable behavior (even though it had only been 2 days) and were anxious to identify strategies to begin implementing to get her to more effectively communicate. Her challenging behavior was staying around the same rate, but the teacher and assistant felt that it was not as intense as it had been in the past.

FORM
10

PTR-YC Behavior Intervention Plan Summary

Child: _Joel_   Class: _Bears_

Classroom practices for all children:

☒ Show positive attention: 5:1 ratio.

☐ Teach behavioral expectations for each routine.

☐ Teach positive peer-related social skill.

☒ Use predictable schedules.

☒ Use predictable routines within routines.

Intervention strategies

	Prevent	Teach	Reinforce
Brief description	Provide choices. Use visual supports and schedules.	Teach independence with visual schedules.	Physically reinforce incompatible behavior
Implementation notes	Target arrival time: Set up an individual schedule for Joel with all arrival activities (visual support). Joel can choose two of the three activities in which to participate. Visual supports should include two to three behavioral expectations for each activity and should be posted in the relevant area.	Directly teach Joel to follow the schedule and have him remove the activities as he completes them. Also, refer to the behavioral expectations and give specific praise when Joel is following the behavioral expectations.	Make deposits in 5:1 ratio. Challenging behavior: Do not comment on hitting or attempts to hit. Immediately redirect him to use his words instead. Desired behavior: Immediately comment on all attempts to participate in activities.

Figure 6.3A. Joel's PTR-YC Behavior Intervention Plan Summary. (*Note:* Blank fillable and printable versions of this form can be found on the accompanying CD-ROM.)

Behavior Intervention Plan

Child: Joel

Parent: Gary

Team members: Gary; teacher; classroom assistant; and Sally, the educational specialist

Method of home–school communication: Joel's back-and-forth book

Hypothesis: When Joel is asked to participate in the arrival activities, then he will begin hitting peers and/or adults; as a result, he gets adult attention through reprimanding, redirecting, talking about what happened, or restating rules.

Implementation Phases

Right away: Begin implementing 5:1 ratio of positive to negative attention.

Week 1: Develop and prepare materials for classroom and individual interventions.

Week 2: Begin implementation of classroom strategies.

Week 3: Begin implementation of individualized strategies.

Joel's warning signs: Voice becomes louder; takes things from others without asking; says, "No"; sometimes will look at the individual or item the individual is holding with "the look."

Prevent strategy: Provide choices and use visual supports and schedules.

Materials needed: Choice board with small photographs of three expectations for entering the classroom on one side and three choices for arrival activities on the other side. The photographs are laminated and attached to the board with Velcro so that pictures can be moved and repositioned.
    An adult will be designated to meet Joel at the door and follow these steps.

1. As soon as Joel enters the classroom off the bus, present Joel with his visual schedule of what he is supposed to do as he enters the room. These include the following: say, "Hi" to the teacher, put my backpack in my cubby, and sign in.

2. Ask Joel what he wants to do first.

3. He can choose by saying what he wants, pointing to the picture, or taking the picture off and handing it to the teacher.

4. As he completes each step, he is allowed to put the picture in the "finished" envelope.

5. Once these tasks are complete, his last step is to choose an arrival activity.

6. On the other side of the choice board, show him three of the arrival activities that he can choose from and ask him to choose one.

Teach strategy: Teach independence with visual schedules.
    An adult will be designated to work with Joel during arrival activities until he can do so independently and with no incidents of hitting.

1. Using the choice board, show Joel the three pictures of the available activities and briefly describe what the activities are.

2. Ask Joel, "Where do you want to play first?"

3. If Joel points to, says, or hands you the picture of an activity, then prompt him to go to that area.

4. If Joel does not pick or indicate an activity, then give him one of the pictures and guide him (if necessary) to the appropriate area.

5. When Joel gets to the activity, remind him of the expectations for the activity, referring to the pictures of the expectations posted in that area.

6. If he does not follow the steps, then provide as much assistance as needed to go through the expectations.

7. As he is going through the expectations, provide verbal praise for attempts and active participation in the activity.

8. Have him put that activity's picture in the "finished" envelope once the activity is over and he has finished the steps or has participated for 2 minutes, and prompt him to choose the next activity.

9. Repeat Steps 3–7.

10. Have him put the activity's picture in the "finished" envelope once that activity is over, and he then has free choice time until large-group time.

Figure 6.4A.   Joel's behavior intervention plan.

FIGURE 6.4A **Behavior Intervention Plan** *(continued)*

Reinforce strategy: Physically reinforce incompatible behavior.

Any time that Joel is participating in a classroom activity that he does not seem interested in, he will receive verbal praise and occasionally will also receive a small fish cracker. Any attempts and even partial participation should result in verbal praise for Joel. The adult will stay in close proximity to Joel and will be available to provide praise, crackers, or any physical assistance that he may need. This will last for the first 2 minutes of the activity.

1. Joel will choose an activity from his visual schedule and go to the appropriate area.

2. When Joel arrives at the activity, set the timer for 2 minutes.

3. Once Joel starts engaging in the activity, provide specific verbal praise for what he is doing ("I like how you're coloring" or "Wow, you are trying so hard to use those scissors!").

4. Occasionally give him a fish cracker along with the verbal praise as long as it does not interfere with the particular activity (if he is drawing, coloring, cutting, or participating in any other activity that requires two hands, then it would be better to use the fish crackers at a later time).

5. Provide the verbal praise and/or fish crackers as much as possible during the 2-minute time period. The team will decide how to fade the verbal praise and fish crackers once he is able to do this more independently (based on data recorded on the PTR-YC Behavior Rating Scale).

6. Joel should be given the option to leave the activity or to continue once the 2 minutes is over. If Joel stays at the activity, then it is not necessary for the adult to remain and provide the same level of reinforcement at that time. If Joel leaves the activity, then he will be prompted to choose the next activity from his visual schedule if he does not do so on his own.

Using Data

The team will meet every 2 weeks to review data and progress once the classroom practices have been implemented. All information will be sent home and shared with Joel's family. After the initial PTR-YC Fidelity of Strategy Implementation is completed, subsequent fidelity checks will occur as needed. If Joel's behavior does not improve, if his behavior becomes variable, or if his behavior becomes worse, then the team will complete the PTR-YC Fidelity of Strategy Implementation to determine if the strategies are implemented as intended. There are no plans for regular fidelity checks at this time.

The team looked at the PTR-YC Menu of Intervention Strategies (see Table 6.1) and was in immediate agreement that using visual supports would definitely be the prevent strategy to implement. It was also clear that teaching communication was what they wanted to target with Jessi for the teach strategy and that they would want to embed multiple instructional opportunities. The team decided to implement two strategies for the reinforce component—remove reinforcement for challenging behavior and reinforce desirable behavior. The team then discussed the best time to implement the strategies to increase Jessi's desirable communication skills, and the team decided they wanted to try implementing the strategies throughout the day instead of targeting just one activity, routine, or time of day. The team agreed that if it became too overwhelming, then they would discuss targeting a specific activity, routine, or time of day to implement the strategies.

The team then discussed implementing classroom practices, and the decision was easy when they looked at them in terms of what they could do to help Jessi be more successful in their classroom. Because Jessi responded so well to positive attention, as well as thinking about how it could positively affect several of the other students, it was an easy decision to begin implementing the 5:1 ratio of positive to negative attention. The team also decided that using predictable schedules and routines within routines would be helpful for all the children, and it did not require much for them to be able to implement these strategies. Although the team recognized that there was a lot to implement, they agreed that they would do their best to implement them all and reevaluate the situation if it became too much. Decisions would ultimately be made based on how the teacher and assistant felt about implementation and the affect that it had on Jessi and the other children. Figures 6.5A and 6.6A show Jessi's PTR-YC Behavior Intervention Plan Summary and her behavior intervention plan.

FORM
10

PTR-YC Behavior Intervention Plan Summary

Child: _Jessi_ _____   Class: _Ms. Elle and Ms. Lauren_ _____

Classroom practices for all children:

☒ Show positive attention: 5:1 ratio.

☐ Teach behavioral expectations for each routine.

☐ Teach positive peer-related social skill.

☒ Use predictable schedules.

☒ Use predictable routines within routines.

Intervention strategies

	Prevent	Teach	Reinforce
Brief description	Use visual supports and schedules.	Teach communication skills. Embed multiple instructional opportunities.	Challenging behavior: Remove reinforcement for challenging behavior. Desired behavior: Reinforce desirable behavior.
Implementation notes	Jessi and each adult will have a key ring with pictures of Jessi's favorite things in the classroom as well as the adults in order to provide as many opportunities as possible to use the pictures to prevent challenging behaviors.	Jessi and each adult will have a key ring with pictures of Jessi's favorite things in the classroom as well the adults in order to provide as many opportunities as possible to use the pictures to teach her how to appropriately ask for what she wants.	Feedback will be given verbally (e.g., concise and specific feedback), physically (e.g., hugs, high fives, pats on the back), and with gestures (e.g., smiles, thumbs up) to help Jessi understand the feedback as much as possible.

Figure 6.5A.   Jessi's PTR-YC Behavior Intervention Plan Summary. (*Note:* Blank fillable and printable versions of this form can be found on the accompanying CD-ROM.)

Behavior Intervention Plan

Team members: Lucy and Kay (foster parents), social worker, biological parents, Elle (teacher), Lauren (assistant), and the center director

Long-term vision: We want Jessi to be happy and to meet her potential.

Hypotheses

- When Jessi cannot have a desired item from a peer, then she will engage in physical aggression toward herself or others, as a result, she gets the desired item.

- When Jessi wants attention from adults (sitting in their lap, hugs, kisses) and does not get it, or when the attention from an adult ends, then she will engage in physical aggression toward herself or others, as a result, she gets attention from adults or extends the amount of attention from adults.

Materials needed: Photographs of the most common interactions that Jessi likes, laminated, hole-punched on one corner, and put on a key ring. Multiple copies of photograph key rings need to made so that Jessi and each teacher can have one, as well as a set for home and at least one extra set to keep in the classroom. Photographs should be updated as necessary.

Prevent strategy: Use visual supports and schedules.

1. Present visual support or visual schedule to Jessi.

2. Have her respond to the visual support or follow the visual schedule as independently as possible.

3. Once the task is complete, have her put the picture representing the task or activity into the "all done" box to indicate that the step is over.

4. Provide verbal praise for following directions.

Teach strategy: Teach communication skills.

1. Determine what Jessi is requesting.

2. Find the appropriate picture on the photograph key ring (hers or yours).

3. Show the picture, and guide one of her hands to touch the picture.

4. As soon as she touches the picture with your assistance, provide the interaction that is depicted in that picture.

5. Provide specific verbal praise while she is gaining access to what she requested.

Teach strategy: Embed multiple instructional opportunities.
See the behavior matrix for identified times to embed instructional opportunities.

1. When the identified opportunity arises, prompt Jessi to use her pictures.

2. Help her find the correct picture.

3. Prompt, as needed, for her to point to the picture.

4. As soon as she points, provide access to her request.

5. Provide verbal praise for using her pictures to "ask" for things.

Reinforce strategy: Remove reinforcement for challenging behavior.

1. When Jessi exhibits any challenging behavior, do not look at her or say anything.

2. If the challenging behavior is toward a peer, then provide your attention to the peer.

3. While you are not responding to the challenging behavior, you can pull out your photograph key ring or physically prompt Jessi to use her photograph key ring without making eye contact or talking with her about it.

4. Once you can prompt her to use her picture to make a request, immediately respond to her request (use steps to reinforce desirable behavior).

Reinforce strategy: Reinforce desirable behavior.

1. When Jessi points to or holds up a picture from her photograph key ring, provide access to what is depicted in that photograph as immediately as possible.

2. As you are providing the attention that she requested, also provide verbal praise for using her pictures and asking for what she wanted.

(continued)

Figure 6.6A. Jessi's behavior intervention plan.

Figure 6.6A. *(continued)*

FIGURE 6.6A   **Behavior Intervention Plan** *(continued)*

Behavior matrix to embed multiple instructional opportunities: These are the planned times to target teaching communication skills, but additional opportunities can be created by the teacher or may naturally occur. These opportunities are the minimal opportunities that Jessi should have during the morning.

Activity	Create opportunity to
Arrival	Request hug
Large group	Request to sit on teacher's lap
Centers	Request items from peers
Snack	Request to sit by teacher
Storytime	Request specific book
Outdoor play	Request items from peers
Small group	Request items from others
Closing circle	Request high fives from peers

MEETING 4: ETHAN

PTR-YC Intervention

Deciding on Ethan's interventions took a few days and was done similarly to how the team went through the PTR-YC Functional Behavioral Assessment Checklists. Joan, the center director and classroom teacher, sent a copy of the PTR-YC Menu of Intervention Strategies and the descriptions of the interventions home to Veronica, Ethan's grandmother, to get her input on what strategies to implement before they were scheduled to meet to discuss interventions. Veronica e-mailed Joan with a few comments but said that she would be okay with whatever strategies they decided on because they were going to be doing it. Because Joan had read through the interventions prior to beginning the process, she had Carol, the teaching assistant, read the descriptions of the interventions and pick one or two that she thought would be best to implement. As Joan and Carol looked at the options for the prevent strategies, they agreed that it would make sense to use visual supports and schedules. They decided that they could help Ethan see what he was supposed to do in certain situations (by posting pictures of how friends treat each other) and use the pictures to help him understand what he should be doing instead. Joan and Carol also thought this might be helpful for a couple of other children in their classroom and were eager to see if the other children would benefit from these pictures. They reviewed the teach strategies during their next meeting and identified that teaching peer-related social skills was an easy and logical choice based on the prevent strategy that they identified the day before. They chose to implement reinforce desirable behavior for the reinforce strategy. Over the following two mornings before the children arrived, Joan and Carol wrote out the steps for how they were going to implement each strategy for Ethan's behavior intervention plan. They made a copy of the PTR-YC Behavior Intervention Plan Summary (see Figure 6.7A) to send home to Veronica and agreed to try out the new strategies that day. They decided that they would both try the strategies during choice time to see if they needed to make any adjustments or if their plan was not clear enough. Joan and Carol both felt confident in being able to implement the plan.

FORM 10	**PTR-YC Behavior Intervention Plan Summary**

Child: _Ethan_   Class: _Ms. Joan and Ms. Carol_

Classroom practices for all children:

☐ Show positive attention: 5:1 ratio.

☐ Teach behavioral expectations for each routine.

☐ Teach positive peer-related social skill.

☐ Use predictable schedules.

☐ Use predictable routines within routines.

Intervention strategies

	Prevent	Teach	Reinforce
Brief description	Use visual supports and schedules.	Peer-related social skills.	Reinforce desirable behavior.
Implementation notes	Refer to posted pictures of appropriate ways to interact with peers before choice time begins. Increase the positive attention toward all the children by pointing out when children are appropriately interacting with each other and publicly reinforcing them as a way to prompt Ethan to use the same skills and prevent his disruptive behavior.	Introduce skills and provide opportunities for role playing during large-group time. Use Ethan as part of the role play as much as possible.	Stay in close proximity to Ethan during free choice time in order to be able to provide immediate feedback for using the new skills.

Figure 6.7A. Ethan's PTR-YC Behavior Intervention Plan Summary. (*Note:* Blank fillable and printable versions of this form can be found on the accompanying CD-ROM.)

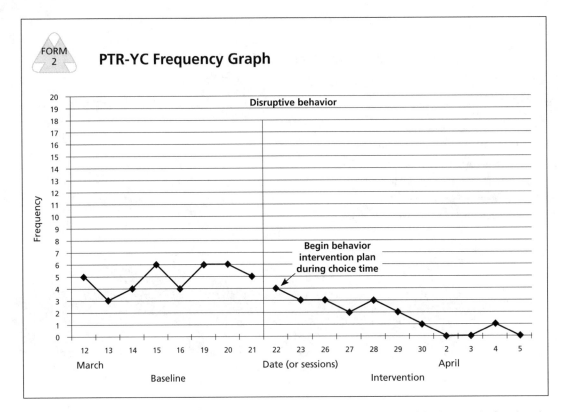

Figure 6.8A.   Ethan's PTR-YC Frequency Graph. (*Note:* Blank fillable and printable versions of this form can be found on the accompanying CD-ROM.)

In the short time that they started the PTR-YC process for Ethan and began implementing the positive attention as a classroom practice, Joan and Carol had seen a positive change in the behavior of all the children. Although Ethan's behavior had improved as well, he still continued to have some instances of disruptive behavior, and Joan and Carol were anxious to begin their interventions. They continued to keep frequency data since beginning this process and were hopeful that Ethan would make great progress (see Figure 6.8A). They also decided to begin tracking the intensity of how Ethan responds to his peers and created a PTR-YC Behavior Rating Scale to be able to track the frequency of Ethan's disruptive behavior and the intensity of his responses to his peers (see Figure 6.9A). Figure 6.10A shows Ethan's behavior intervention plan.

PTR-YC Behavior Rating Scale

Child: _Ethan_   Rater: _Joan and Carol_   Observation period: _Choice time_   Month: _March_

	Date/time																
Desirable behavior *Positive responses to peers*	5	5	5	5	5	5	5	5	5	5	5	5	5	5	5	5	5
	4	4	4	4	4	4	4	4	4	4	4	4	4	4	4	4	4
	3	3	3	3	3	3	3	3	3	3	3	3	3	3	3	3	3
	2	2	2	2	2	2	2	2	2	2	2	2	2	2	2	2	2
	1	1	1	1	1	1	1	1	1	1	1	1	1	1	1	1	1
Challenging behavior	5	5	5	5	5	5	5	5	5	5	5	5	5	5	5	5	5
	4	4	4	4	4	4	4	4	4	4	4	4	4	4	4	4	4
	3	3	3	3	3	3	3	3	3	3	3	3	3	3	3	3	3
	2	2	2	2	2	2	2	2	2	2	2	2	2	2	2	2	2
	1	1	1	1	1	1	1	1	1	1	1	1	1	1	1	1	1

Desirable behavior: _Positive responses to peers_

5 = _Independently asks peer nicely, with hand out_

4 = _Asks nicely, with hand out, with teacher facilitation_

3 = _Gets teacher assistance_

2 = _Yells and/or screams at peers_

1 = _Yells, screams, takes items, destroys things_

Challenging behavior:

5 = _____

4 = _____

3 = _____

2 = _____

1 = _____

Figure 6.9A. Ethan's PTR-YC Behavior Rating Scale with blank areas to be completed by the teacher and assistant. (*Note:* Blank fillable and printable versions of this form can be found on the accompanying CD-ROM.)

FIGURE 6.10A

Behavior Intervention Plan

Long-term vision: Ethan will be an active and positive member of the classroom and will be ready for any milestone.

Hypothesis statement: When Ethan cannot have something that he wants from a peer, then he will engage in disruptive behavior (taking toys from peers without asking, yelling "no" to peers, tattling to teachers, crying, pulling a peer's hair, destroying a peer's play, and yelling profanities); as a result, he receives adult attention and help in obtaining objects.

Prevent strategy: Use visual supports and schedules.

Materials needed: Pictures of appropriate ways to interact with peers to post (pictures have already been taken but need to be printed and posted)

Personnel responsible: Joan and Carol will choose and post pictures together. The person designated to stay in close proximity will alternate between Joan and Carol each day.

1. Before the children make the transition to choice time, review how the children should interact with each other when they want something that another child has. Refer to the posted pictures as you review the steps.

2. The designated person for the day should be in close proximity to Ethan during choice time and should point out when Ethan or any of the other children demonstrate appropriate skills.

Teach strategy: Peer-related social skills.

Materials needed: Posted pictures of appropriate ways to interact with each other. Props (toys, classroom materials) needed for role plays, can with Popsicle sticks.

Personnel responsible: Person who is teaching this lesson each day.

1. During each large-group time (daily, in the morning), there will be time to discuss a social skill and role-play it.

2. Using the pictures as reference, review the social skill identified for that day.

3. Use the can with Popsicle sticks with each child's name on it. For this activity, mark the ends of Ethan's Popsicle stick so it can be chosen more often and he can have more practice. Choose two children to role-play the appropriate way to interact in the situation.

4. Tell each child what role they are playing and provide any appropriate props.

5. Facilitate the role play as necessary.

6. Repeat Steps 3–5, but this time have the children role-play the wrong way to interact in the situation.

7. Once the role plays have been done, review the steps again as a whole group.

Reinforce strategy: Reinforce desirable behavior.

Materials needed: None

Personnel responsible: Person designated to be in close proximity to Ethan for that day. This will alternate between Joan and Carol. Stay in close proximity to Ethan and make sure you can see and hear him playing. Provide specific and targeted verbal praise for any attempts or successful uses of the appropriate skills. The following is an example of how this is done.

1. Ethan is playing near a peer and wants one of the blocks.

2. Ethan puts his hand out to the peer (to indicate he wants a block).

3. Teacher facilitates the peer handing the block to Ethan.

4. Ethan receives the block.

5. Teacher provides verbal praise to Ethan for putting out his hand (e.g., "Ethan, you asked for the block and JJ gave it to you!")

6. Teacher provides verbal praise to the peer for using the appropriate skill ("JJ, you were a great friend for sharing your block with Ethan!").

    Data will be reviewed each Friday to monitor progress.

Figure 6.10A. Ethan's behavior intervention plan.

Using Data and Next Steps

This chapter deals with monitoring the behavior intervention plan implementation and using data to make informed decisions about what steps to take, depending on how the child's behavior responds to intervention. Sometimes the behavior intervention plan works perfectly and the data show immediate improvements that continue until challenging behavior is no longer an issue and the child has shown dramatic growth in positive social interactions. However, sometimes this is not the case. Sometimes change is not evident, and sometimes change is too gradual to make the difference that is needed. This chapter addresses these possible scenarios and offers suggestions for the steps that the team can take to make revisions and further progress.

IMPLEMENTATION AND PROGRESS MONITORING

The following should occur before implementation is initiated: 1) a team is assembled, 2) goals are defined; 3) data is obtained on the baseline levels of a targeted challenging behavior and a targeted social-communicative behavior, 4) classroom practices are assessed and improvements are made, 5) a functional behavioral assessment is completed, 6) a behavior intervention plan is developed, and 7) necessary training and coaching is arranged. These are the steps described in Chapters 3–6. The important step that we would like to emphasize at this point is the collection of progress monitoring data.

Prior to implementing the carefully designed behavior intervention plan, there should be at least 3 days of data that have been collected and summarized on a simple graph. It is best if there is more than a week of data, but 3 days is the minimum. The data should be in the form of the PTR-YC Behavior Rating Scale (as described in Chapter 4) or, in some cases, frequency counts. The data that have been collected will reveal important information. The data on challenging behavior will reveal one of several possible patterns:

1. *High, stable levels of challenging behavior.* The data in this pattern confirm that the level of challenging behavior is unacceptably high and will continue at a high rate unless something is done (see Figure 7.1). The behavior intervention plan should be implemented right away in this pattern. The behavior intervention plan should also be implemented right away if the pattern shows that the challenging behavior is getting worse (see Figure 7.2).

2. *Low levels of challenging behavior.* This pattern indicates that the level of challenging behavior is quite low and suggests questions about the purpose of the behavior intervention plan (see Figure 7.3). There are a number of possible explanations. The first explanation is that the behavior, in fact, has decreased to the point that it is no longer a concern that requires an individualized intervention, at least at the present time. This may be because improved classroom practices have had a beneficial effect or perhaps a different change has occurred that somehow resulted in improved behavior. The team should decide if more days of data should be collected and if the behavior intervention plan should be placed on hold.

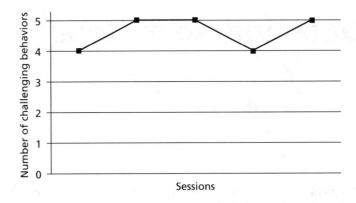

Figure 7.1.   Frequency graph showing high, stable levels of challenging behavior.

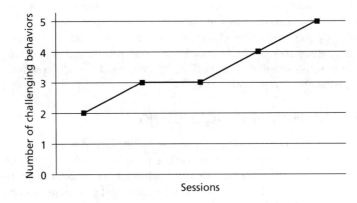

Figure 7.2.   Frequency graph showing increasing levels of challenging behavior.

Another explanation is that the behavior is actually still continuing at an alarming level but, for some reason, the data are not reflecting what is happening. This could be because the definition of the behavior needs to be improved or the data are not being collected at the appropriate time. Either way, if the data are not capturing the behavior of concern, then the data collection strategy needs to be revised. Such a revision should be immediately accomplished, and data should be obtained until the levels of the data are consistent with the levels anecdotally reported by the teacher and other team members.

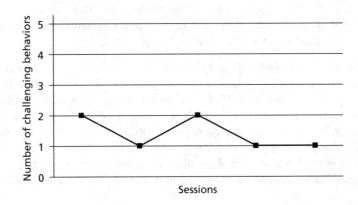

Figure 7.3.   Frequency graph showing low levels of challenging behavior.

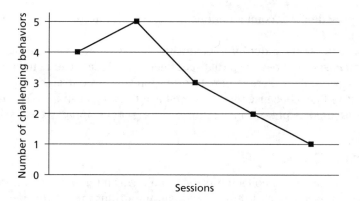

Figure 7.4. Frequency graph showing decreasing levels of challenging behavior.

3. *Decreasing trend of challenging behavior.* Sometimes challenging behavior occurs at high levels when data collection begins, but then it decreases over time (see Figure 7.4). This could be because of a positive change that has occurred in the classroom or in the way that teachers are interacting with the child. Data should continue to be collected, but implementation of the behavior intervention plan should be postponed until the data indicate that the behavior is again a significant concern.

4. *An inconsistent pattern of challenging behavior.* Another pattern is one in which the challenging behavior appears to be high on some days but nonexistent on other days. If this pattern persists, then two things should occur (see Figure 7.5). First, the team should try to find out what is different on the good and bad days that might be responsible for the differences. This pattern often signifies that some kind of stressor (or setting event) has occurred prior to the child coming to school that has affected the child during the day so that otherwise innocuous events came to serve as triggers setting off challenging behavior. It is possible that such stressors might have been missed during the functional behavioral assessment. If so, the team might wish to expand on the behavioral assessment to identify the possible stressor. For example, the stressor might be exhaustion due to inadequate sleep or a difficult exchange during the early morning hours. If the event can be identified, then it might be possible to elimi-

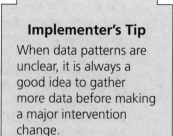

Implementer's Tip

When data patterns are unclear, it is always a good idea to gather more data before making a major intervention change.

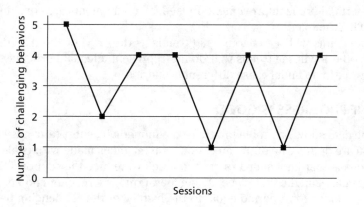

Figure 7.5. Frequency graph showing inconsistent levels of challenging behavior.

nate it or provide for accommodations in the classroom (e.g., providing an early rest time on arrival).

Second, the team should implement the behavior intervention plan as planned, with special emphasis on those days that had been a problem. The behavior intervention plan should proceed unless there is new information that is contraindicative of specific strategies. This is unlikely because the evidence-based strategies in PTR-YC are not the type that would be affected by preexisting setting events (see the appendix at the end of the book).

DATA-BASED DECISION MAKING

The data that have been collected prior to behavior intervention plan implementation are referred to as baseline, and they provide an important means for determining the extent to which intervention is effective. A useful way to separate baseline from intervention is to draw a vertical line on the graph at the end of baseline and then continue collecting data during intervention in exactly the same way that you were collecting the data before intervention.

Data-based decision making depends on comparing the data trends that occur in intervention with the data that were collected in baseline. Intervention should obviously result in lower levels of challenging behavior and higher levels of desirable behavior. The speed with which this change can be expected to occur varies from child to child and from behavior intervention plan to behavior intervention plan. Sometimes it takes a while for a child to learn new desirable behaviors, and this depends on the child's characteristics as well as the quality of the instructional interactions and the frequency with which instruction occurs during the day. The higher the quality and the more frequent the instruction, the more rapid the behavior change.

> Data-based decision making depends on comparing the data trends that occur in intervention with the data that were collected in baseline.

Some improvement in challenging behavior should be evident in the first few sessions or days because the behavior intervention plan in PTR-YC includes multiple components. The change in reinforce strategies often produces improvements more rapidly than the teach strategies, and the prevent strategies can result in changes that are almost immediate. Therefore, teams can expect to see favorable changes quite rapidly in most cases of PTR-YC implementation. We hasten to add here that just because the prevent or reinforce strategies might help change occur quickly, this does not mean that the teach component is less important. On the contrary, the teach component is probably the most important component for long-term, durable improvement. Indeed, all components are considered to be essential in the PTR-YC model.

Some teams will see encouraging trends as they review the data during intervention, whereas others will see trends that do not represent adequate progress. The following describes what to do under these different scenarios.

WHAT TO DO IF PROGRESS IS GOOD

When the data show favorable progress, the immediate, short-term answer is to keep doing what you are doing. One of the most common mistakes made with challenging behavior interventions is that implementers are too quick to reduce the supports that have produced behavior change in the first place. As a general rule, we recommend keeping PTR-YC interventions in place for a period equal to the history of the challenging behavior. So, if challenging behavior has been present for 6 months, then we recommend keeping PTR-YC in place for 6 months as well. Teams may want to consider at that point in time whether the future interests of the child are best served by systematically reducing elements of the PTR-YC plan. For example, let's say that the child is about to move to a kindergarten setting in which the ratio of adults to children is such that some components of the PTR-YC plan may be impractical. It would make sense to systematically reduce supports rather than to have them simply disappear immediately.

Moreover, teams may want to consider whether elements of the plan could be altered in such a way that the child him- or herself is now implementing components in a self-management fashion. For example, say that the initial reinforce component called for adults to positively comment on the child's behavior when he or she was actively engaged in class activities. The team may want to eventually consider if teaching the child to self-evaluate and self-reinforce is a viable next step. PTR-YC encourages teams to eventually think about strategies to enhance children's independent performance.

When considering reductions in the type and/or intensity of PTR-YC supports, teams need to keep close tabs on children's challenging and desirable behaviors. When any decrement in behavior occurs, no matter how small, we recommend slowing the process if not reinstating the full plan for a period of time.

In the past, many teams have expanded on the PTR-YC process after challenging behavior has been resolved. Teams have used this careful planning process to guide plans for teaching new skills not directly related to challenging behavior. Understand that the teach strategies in this manual are not just for desirable (and replacement) behaviors per se but can be used far more broadly.

> Teams need to keep close tabs on children's challenging and desirable behaviors when considering reductions in the type and/or intensity of PTR-YC supports. If the full plan is not going to be reinstated for a period of time, then slow the process down when any decrement in behavior occurs.

WHAT TO DO IF PROGRESS IS UNSATISFACTORY

Data on PTR-YC suggests that close adherence to the recommended steps in the process will yield satisfactory behavior change in the vast majority of cases. One cannot guarantee uniform success with PTR-YC, however, given the certainty of some level of uncertainty in the behavioral sciences. What is possible, however, is to provide a number of tried and true solutions when behavior change is not satisfactory.

In this section, we examine a sequence of steps that teams should follow to improve children's behavior change when initial tactics have not been successful. We *strongly* suggest that the recommended steps be implemented in the order given. To do otherwise risks the unnecessary expenditure of time and resources.

Step 1: Determine if the behavior intervention plan tactics have been implemented with fidelity. Chapter 6 describes recommendations for the collection of fidelity data—data on whether the intervention plans are being delivered as intended. These data systems for fidelity assessment are sufficiently detailed and intensive in application in most cases to determine if the behavior intervention plan practices are in place. We see that subtle shifts in procedures have occurred over time in some cases, however, or that some members of the team are implementing with fidelity, whereas others are not.

Procedurally, we recommend that teams come to a definitive determination regarding fidelity by

- Reviewing the specific practices that comprise the PTR model for the specific case with all team members who are implementers. Each implementer should be encouraged during a team meeting to describe his or her understanding of each intervention component, explain when and where it is to be implemented, and demonstrate how he or she implements each intervention component in a role-playing format with fellow team members. The team may conclude at this point, or more members may need further coaching to have a skill set that would permit high-fidelity implementation of all components.

- Once the team is certain that all implementers are sufficiently competent to deliver PTR-YC, another meeting should be scheduled to examine the current fidelity data collection procedures and make resource allocations necessary to implement data collection for three to five intervention sessions per day. The goal for this data collection is to assess each implementer's behavior for the entire period of time that the interventions are scheduled to occur. In addition to using the established fidelity data systems, we also encourage a designated team member to make narrative records of implementer's behaviors that may be related to the target child's behaviors but are not part of the PTR-YC plan. Many teams may find that this entire process can be substantially aided by video recordings. Teams may conclude that PTR-YC is indeed being implemented as intended. If so, then we recommend proceeding to Step 2. If any fidelity concerns appear, no matter how small, we recommend resolving these prior to moving to the next step.

Step 2: Determine if the supposed reinforcers are operating. Young children change their minds a lot. They particularly change their minds about what will motivate them to change their behavior when the clear contingency is in place to first do this behavior, then gain access to the person, material, toy, or event. In many cases, the determination of reinforcers is quite straightforward. However, when initial plans have gone awry, we recommend the use of a paired-comparison strategy to maximize the probability that selected reinforcers will operate as such. Procedurally, the team should make a careful reinforcer reappraisal by

- Interviewing all care providers to determine their judgment as to what things the child in question most enjoys.

- Following up this interview with informal observations (2 days) to see if the child seeks out the suggested items or others as well.

- Meeting as a team to create a list of 8–10 (maximum) potential reinforcers (the original selected reinforcers may or may not make this list, depending on findings).

- Presenting the child with all possible pairs from the potential reinforcer list over the course of 2 days. When the child makes a selection, mark down the item selected. The team will have created a hierarchy of preferred items once all possible pairs have been presented—from the item most often selected to the item least often selected. We recommend choosing only the top one or two items to use in the context of PTR-YC. Assuming that the top one or two items were not originally used in the PTR-YC plan, we suggest that the team give the new "R" version a 5–10 session per day trial before determining that it is necessary to move to Step 3.

- The other side of the "R" coin is also worth a second look. Not only is it essential to have a powerful reinforcer available for new behaviors, but it is also equally important to ensure that the child is not being inadvertently reinforced for continued challenging behavior. The most common examples we see are instances in which the intensity or salience of reinforcement has been reduced as planned, but children are still receiving some level of continued feedback for challenging behavior. For example, the teacher may no longer engage a child in conversation when challenging behavior occurs (removing attention when the function of challenging behavior is thought to be attention), but he or she still looks at the child when challenging behavior occurs. Teams may well want to devote a day or two of observation to ensure that subtle but still important consequences do not follow challenging behavior.

Step 3: Recheck the function(s) of challenging behavior. Teams will find on rare occasions that the original determination of function was in error. It is time to reexamine the original hypothesis regarding the function of challenging behavior when teams have determined that powerful reinforcers are in place and that the behavior intervention plan is generally implemented with fidelity. Teams are encouraged to utilize the PTR-YC Functional Behavioral Assessment Checklists and Summary Table in Chapter 5, keeping in mind that the original hypothesis may be incorrect, but this time in a meeting context. New functions may emerge or not. If new functions are determined, then teams should proceed with redeveloping a new behavior intervention plan as previously outlined.

As we acknowledged in Chapter 1, there may be circumstances in which the influences underlying a child's challenging behaviors are too difficult for a preschool-based team to adequately assess or too intransigent for a classroom-based intervention. Although we believe that these circumstances are quite rare, it is nevertheless apparent that they exist. When they do, it is appropriate and necessary to enlist outside expertise. Sometimes simply having an experienced consultant assist with the functional behavioral assessment and behavior intervention plan design can be sufficient, or a comprehensive multidisciplinary approach may be needed at other times. Regardless, we urge your team to pursue whatever measures are necessary to find and implement procedures to achieve a successful resolution.

Remember that functions can change over time and that the same behavior can serve different functions in different classroom contexts.

OVERALL SUMMARY AND TEAM IMPLEMENTATION GUIDE

PTR-YC is a model of positive assessment and intervention designed to help young children with serious challenging behaviors learn adaptive social skills and reduce their challenging behaviors. The objective is to help guide these young children toward an improved, healthy trajectory of social-emotional development so that they will be able to succeed in their overall development, their enjoyment of friendships, and in all phases of their upcoming journey to kindergarten, elementary school, and beyond.

We are confident that PTR-YC can be an effective approach for you and your team; however, its effectiveness will depend on your team's ability to faithfully follow the process in a step-by-step manner. To help with this process, we offer the PTR-YC Team Implementation Guide (see Figure 7.6). (*Note:* Blank fillable and printable versions of this form can be found on the accompanying CD-ROM.) This guide is intended to help teams organize their information in one document and provide a summary of the steps and requirements described in this manual. The guide follows the Self-Evaluation Checklists at the end of Chapters 3–6, so it is not necessary for teams to use both. It is provided as an option for teams who wish to use it.

We are confident that PTR-YC can be an effective approach for you and your team; however, its effectiveness will depend on your team's ability to faithfully follow the process in a step-by-step manner.

△ FORM 12

PTR-YC Team Implementation Guide

Step 1: Teaming and Goal Setting

Child's name: _____ Age: _____ Date of plan: _____

Location/setting (e.g., Head Start, early childhood special education classroom, community preschool): _____

_____

Team members (list all team members, including at least one family member): _____

_____

Operational definition of initial challenging behavior: _____

_____

Operational definition of initial desirable behavior: _____

_____

Step 2: Data Collection

How are the behaviors going to be measured (circle one)?   Behavior rating scale   Frequency counts

(If using the behavior rating scale, have the anchors been carefully defined and written
on the sheet?)   Yes   No

(If using frequency counts, has the procedure has been specified and written down?)   Yes   No

When will data be collected (observation period)? _____

Who is going to collect data (identify a primary data collector)? _____

Location of permanent data logs and graphs: _____

Person responsible for maintaining the logs and graphs: _____

Step 3: PTR-YC Assessment

Has current use of classroom practices been assessed?   Yes   No

What steps have been taken to improve the implementation of classroomwide practices?

_____

_____

Who completed the three PTR-YC Functional Behavioral Assessment Checklists?

_____

Were completed checklists reviewed by the team and summarized on the PTR-YC Functional
Behavioral Assessment Summary Table?   Yes   No

Hypothesis statement(s): _____

_____

_____

_____

Figure 7.6. PTR-YC Team Implementation Guide. (*Note:* Blank fillable and printable versions of this form can be found on the accompanying CD-ROM.)

FORM 12   **PTR-YC Team Implementation Guide** *(continued)*

Step 4: PTR-YC Intervention

Have classroom practices been assessed, and have steps been taken to improve implementation of classroomwide practices?	Yes	No
Did team members review the descriptions of intervention strategies (found in the appendix at the end of the book)?	Yes	No
Did team members decide on intervention strategies to implement, and did they complete the PTR-YC Behavior Intervention Plan Summary?	Yes	No
Did the team complete the additional pages (including the task analyses) of the child's behavior intervention plan?	Yes	No
Did the team determine what training and ongoing support would be provided for the classroom personnel responsible for implementing the behavior intervention plan?	Yes	No

Step 5: Using Data and Next Steps

How often are the data reviewed once intervention strategies have been implemented?_____

_____

Who reviews the data? _____

What decisions are made based on the data?_____

_____

_____

APPENDIX

Case Examples

MEETING 5: HASANI

Using Data and Next Steps

Hasani's parents have been active members on this team and have modified the strategy for home. They are also tracking Hasani's targeted behaviors for home using the PTR-YC Behavior Rating Scale. The family has shared all of the information and behavior intervention plan with outside service providers. Initial implementation began, and the team scheduled to meet 2 weeks after beginning implementation for progress monitoring.

Team members brought their data sheets and any other notes they had to review to the progress monitoring meeting. The team was functioning very consistently, and progress was noted at school and home. Outside service providers have noticed a marked improvement and have become more interested in learning about the PTR-YC process and strategies. The family is teaching the outside providers about this process, and consistency is beginning with outside services. The team decides to continue to meet every 2 weeks, with an open invitation for outside providers to attend as well. The team also begins a process of developing new goals and new skills to target as they began with so many skills to teach. They follow the same process with each minigoal and find that the time needed to develop plans was greatly reduced. Figures 7.1A and 7.2A show Hasani's progress from September to October.

MEETING 5: JOEL

Using Data and Next Steps

Joel's team decided to meet every 2 weeks to review progress and troubleshoot if necessary. Sally, the educational specialist, sent all the information home to Gary, Joel's father, with a note encouraging his involvement. Gary called Sally 3 days after this information went home. He said he was pleased with the plan and the explanations for every piece of the plan. He said he would like to learn a little more about the plan and what he might be able to do at home. Sally and the classroom teacher were able to meet with Gary the next week. They discussed the plan with Gary and shared the classroom arrival strategy. They went over what the bedtime routine was, and Sally agreed to create a visual schedule to send home for Gary to try. After some discussion about how Joel responds to attention from adults, Gary said that he would try to spend more time pointing out when Joel was doing the right thing instead of yelling at him when he was doing something wrong. Gary readily admitted that this would be difficult for him, especially at the end of the day, but that he would give it a try. Sally recommended trying to target the positive comments in the morning, which was a little less hectic than bedtime and when Gary was not as tired compared with the end of the day. The team created a list of things that Gary could use at home, including specific examples of opportunities to provide positive feedback and what Gary could say, which he posted on the refrigerator.

The team met after 2 weeks of implementing classroom strategies to discuss how they were working. Gary was able to join part of this meeting by telephone. Each team member talked about how they had changed how they spoke to children and they were all focused on the positive attention 5:1 ratio. Each member was excited about the impact of this strategy. Consistently using schedules and the established routine within the routines for arrival time had improved appropriate behavior in all the children in the class. The staff admitted they had changed how they responded to Joel's hitting immediately after the intervention meeting and had been responding more positively to him in general.

FORM 4

PTR-YC Behavior Rating Scale

Child: _Hasani_ Rater: _Team_ Observation period: _All day_ Month: _September_

Date/time

	12	13	14	15	16	19	20	21	22	23	26	27	28	29	30					
Desirable behavior _Engagement_	5	5	5	5	5	5	5	5	5	5	5	5	5	5	5	5	5	5	5	5
	4	4	4	4	4	4	4	4	4	4	4	4	4	4	4	4	4	4	4	4
	3	3	3	3	3	3	3	3	3	3	3	3	3	(3)	3	3	3	3	3	3
	2	2	2	2	2	2	2	2	2	2	(2)	(2)	(2)	2	(2)	2	2	2	2	2
	(1)	(1)	(1)	(1)	(1)	(1)	(1)	(1)	(1)	(1)	1	1	1	1	1	1	1	1	1	1
Challenging behavior _Does not respond_	(5)	(5)	(5)	(5)	(5)	(5)	(5)	(5)	(5)	(5)	(5)	(5)	5	5	5	5	5	5	5	5
	4	4	4	4	4	4	4	4	4	4	4	4	(4)	(4)	(4)	4	4	4	4	4
	3	3	3	3	3	3	3	3	3	3	3	3	3	3	3	3	3	3	3	3
	2	2	2	2	2	2	2	2	2	2	2	2	2	2	2	2	2	2	2	2
	1	1	1	1	1	1	1	1	1	1	1	1	1	1	1	1	1	1	1	1

←——— Baseline ———→ ←——— Intervention ———→

Desirable behavior: _Engagement_
5 = _Looks independently_
4 = _Looks with a prompt or reminder_
3 = _Looks with physical assistance_
2 = _Does not look or answer_
1 = _Walks away_

Challenging behavior: _Does not respond_
5 = _Does not respond at all_
4 = _Does not respond 75% of the time_
3 = _Does not respond 50% of the time_
2 = _Does not respond 25% of the time_
1 = _Responds to adults and peers_

Figure 7.1A. Hasani's PTR-YC Behavior Rating Scale for September. (Note: Blank fillable and printable versions of this form can be found on the accompanying CD-ROM.)

143

PTR-YC Behavior Rating Scale

Child: _Hasani_   Rater: _Team_   Observation period: _All day_   Month: _October_

Date/time

	3	4	5	6	7	10	11	12	13	14	17	18	19	20	21	24	25	26	27	28
Desirable behavior _Engagement_	5	5	5	5	5	5	5	5	5	5	5	5	5	5	5	5	5	5	5	5
	4	④	4	4	4	4	4	4	4	4	4	4	4	4	4	4	4	4	④	4
	3	3	3	③	③	3	3	③	③	③	3	③	3	③	③	③	③	③	3	③
	②	2	②	2	2	②	②	2	2	2	②	2	②	2	2	2	2	2	2	2
	1	1	1	1	1	1	1	1	1	1	1	1	1	1	1	1	1	1	1	1
Challenging behavior _Does not respond_	5	5	5	5	5	5	5	5	5	5	5	5	5	5	5	5	5	5	5	5
	④	4	4	4	4	4	4	4	4	4	4	4	4	4	4	4	4	4	4	4
	3	3	③	③	③	③	③	③	3	③	③	③	3	③	③	3	3	③	3	③
	2	2	2	2	2	2	2	2	②	2	2	2	②	2	2	②	②	2	②	2
	1	1	1	1	1	1	1	1	1	1	1	1	1	1	1	1	1	1	1	1

Desirable behavior: _Engagement_

5 = _Looks independently_

4 = _Looks with a prompt or reminder_

3 = _Looks with physical assistance_

2 = _Does not look or answer_

1 = _Walks away_

Challenging behavior: _Does not respond_

5 = _Does not respond at all_

4 = _Does not respond 75% of the time_

3 = _Does not respond 50% of the time_

2 = _Does not respond 25% of the time_

1 = _Responds to adults and peers_

Figure 7.2A. Hasani's PTR-YC Behavior Rating Scale for October. (*Note:* Blank fillable and printable versions of this form can be found on the accompanying CD-ROM.)

After sharing their experiences in a round robin fashion, Sally brought out the PTR-YC Behavior Rating Scale and PTR-YC Fidelity of Strategy Implementation (see Figures 7.3A–7.5A). The challenging behavior of hitting had already been reduced to a 2 (hits 1–4 times per day), and there were 2 days with no hitting at all. The team decided to go ahead and implement the intensive individualized intervention as they decided that the goal was to consistently reach a 1—no hitting. The team could also see that all classroom staff was implementing this strategy with fidelity, as it was designed to be implemented.

The team continued to meet every other week during the lunch hour so Gary could participate by telephone. Gary also began to see some positive results at home. Joel was participating more in classroom activities after a couple of weeks of the individualized interventions. The team continued to meet every 2 weeks to monitor Joel's progress and was able to add additional skills to teach Joel from the PTR-YC assessment. As the team was able to add more skills, Joel's engaged time during classroom activities increased, his language skills also improved, and the team was eventually able to eliminate the individualized strategies by the end of the traditional preschool year. The school team was able to improve and completely implement the classroomwide practices, and Joel was able to benefit from the general curriculum.

MEETING 5: JESSI

Using Data and Next Steps

Jessi's team decided to meet briefly every other Friday during nap/rest time once most of the children were sleeping. The director was available to help watch the children if needed and attended meetings when she could. The team discussed the overall improvements that had been made as a whole due to implementing the classroom practices, and they were starting to see some improvements in Jessi's ability to be a part of the daily classroom activities. It seemed as though the more specified routines and schedules were making a positive impact on Jessi's ability to participate in making transitions, but it was too soon to tell if she was directly benefiting from these changes. The teacher and assistant were pleased with the positive affect that the classroom practices had made with the rest of the children in the classroom.

When the team looked at the PTR-YC Behavior Rating Scale, it was not clear that the strategies had worked or that Jessi had made any individual progress (see Figures 7.6A and 7.7A). Although the data had not shown much progress, the teacher and assistant were certain that Jessi would make progress because they were seeing some improvement that the data sheet did not capture. Elle, the classroom teacher, would ask the director to do a short observation and complete the PTR-YC Fidelity of Strategy Implementation to make sure that they were correctly implementing the steps. It was agreed that they would continue with the current plan and would meet again in 2 weeks to look at the data again and discuss fidelity. The team discussed whether the strategies were too difficult to implement. Although it required a lot of work, the strategies were not too difficult, and the team agreed that the progress was worth the work. The team also knew that the amount of current work would decrease as their skills improved and as the children became more independent. The team agreed to continue to implement the classroom practices as well as the behavior intervention plan for Jessi and to meet again in 2 weeks.

The rating scale and fidelity data were reviewed at the next progress monitoring meeting. The director completed the PTR-YC Fidelity of Strategy Implementation and realized that not all the steps were being followed completely and reminded the team about the importance of following the specific steps of the plan (see Figure 7.8A). Elle and Lauren, the classroom assistant, agreed to post the steps for teaching communication around the classroom in certain places as a reminder. It seemed that adhering to the implementation steps helped Jessi to communicate with less prompting, and this helped everyone see the importance of maintaining fidelity of the plan. The team agreed that if there were decreases in Jessi's ability to

PTR-YC Behavior Rating Scale

Child: _Joel_   Rater: _Team_   Observation period: _Arrival_   Month: _October_

Date/time	9/30	10/3	10/4	10/5	10/6	10/7	10/10	10/11	10/12	10/13	10/14	10/17	10/18	10/19	10/20	10/21	10/24	10/25	10/26	10/27
Desirable behavior Participates in activities	1	1	1	1	1	1	1	2	1	1	2	1	2	2	2	2	2	3	3	2
Challenging behavior Hitting others	3	4	4	5	4	4	3	3	3	4	3	3	3	2	3	2	2	2	3	2
							Only track arrival						Begin 5:1				Begin classroom strategies			

Desirable behavior: _Participates in activities_

5 = _Independently participates in activity for 2 minutes_
4 = _Participates with visual prompts for 2 minutes_
3 = _Participates with partial assistance for 2 minutes_
2 = _Participates with full assistance for 2 minutes_
1 = _Hits adults or peers or leaves activity_

Challenging behavior: _Hitting others_

5 = _Hits 10 or more times_
4 = _Hits 7–9 times_
3 = _Hits 4–6 times_
2 = _Hits 1–3 times_
1 = _Hits 0 times_

Figure 7.3A. Joel's PTR-YC Behavior Rating Scale for October. (*Note:* Blank fillable and printable versions of this form can be found on the accompanying CD-ROM.)

FORM 4

PTR-YC Behavior Rating Scale

Child: _Joel_ Rater: _Team_ Observation period: _Arrival_ Month: _November_

Date/time	10/28	10/31	11/1	11/2	11/3	11/4	11/7	11/8	11/9	11/10	11/11	11/14	11/15	11/16	11/17	11/18	11/21	11/22	11/23	
Desirable behavior Participates in activities	5	5	5	5	5	5	5	5	5	5	5	5	5	5	5	5	5	5	5	5
	4	4	(4)	4	(4)	(4)	4	4	4	4	4	4	4	4	4	4	4	4	4	4
	(3)	(3)	3	(3)	3	3	3	3	3	3	3	3	3	3	3	3	3	3	3	3
	2	2	2	2	2	2	2	2	2	2	2	2	2	2	2	2	2	2	2	2
	1	1	1	1	1	1	1	1	1	1	1	1	1	1	1	1	1	1	1	1
Challenging behavior Hitting others	5	5	5	5	5	5	5	5	5	5	5	5	5	5	5	5	5	5	5	5
	4	3	3	4	3	4	4	4	4	4	4	4	4	4	4	4	4	4	4	4
	3	3	3	3	3	3	3	3	3	3	3	3	3	3	3	3	3	3	3	3
	(2)	2	(2)	(2)	(2)	2	2	2	2	2	2	2	2	2	2	2	2	2	2	2
	1	(1)	1	1	1	(1)	1	1	1	1	1	1	1	1	1	1	1	1	1	1

Notes:
- 10/31: Halloween; began individual strategies
- 11/11: Holiday

Desirable behavior: _Participates in activities_

5 = _Independently participates in activities_
4 = _Participates with visual prompts for 2 minutes_
3 = _Participates with partial assistance for 2 minutes_
2 = _Participates with full assistance for 2 minutes_
1 = _Hits adults or peers or leaves activity_

Challenging behavior: _Hitting others_

5 = _Hits 10 or more times_
4 = _Hits 7–9 times_
3 = _Hits 4–6 times_
2 = _Hits 1–3 times_
1 = _Hits 0 times_

Figure 7.4A. Joel's PTR-YC Behavior Rating Scale for November. (Note: Blank fillable and printable versions of this form can be found on the accompanying CD-ROM.)

△ FORM 11   **PTR-YC Fidelity of Strategy Implementation**

Child: _Joel_   Interventionist: _Teacher_   Observer: _K.W._

Date: _11/4_   Observation period: _Arrival_

	Were all steps implemented as intended?		Did the child respond as intended?		Was the strategy implemented as frequently as intended?	
Prevent strategy Steps: 1. Present Joel with the visual schedule. 2. Ask what he wants to do first. 3. Joel chooses one activity. 4. When the activity is complete, he puts the picture in the "finished" envelope. 5. When the tasks are complete, he is presented with a choice of arrival activities.	(Yes)	No	(Yes)	No	(Yes)	No
Teach strategy Steps: 1. Show Joel three choices available on the choice board and describe. 2. Ask Joel what he wants to do—help him choose if needed. 3. Review expectations for the activity. 4. Participate in the activity for at least 2 minutes. 5. When the activity is finished, Joel puts the picture in the "finished" envelope. 6. Repeat for second activity.	(Yes)	No	Yes	No	(Yes)	No
Reinforce strategy Steps: 1. Joel chooses an activity from the schedule and goes to the area. 2. Set timer for 2 minutes. 3. Provide specific verbal feedback for participation. 4. Provide occasional fish crackers for participation. 5. When 2 minutes are over, Joel can continue or leave the activity.	(Yes)	No	(Yes)	No	(Yes)	No

Figure 7.5A. Joel's PTR-YC Fidelity of Strategy Implementation. (*Note:* Blank fillable and printable versions of this form can be found on the accompanying CD-ROM.)

PTR-YC Behavior Rating Scale

Child: __Jessi__   Rater: __Elle and Lauren__   Observation period: __All day__   Month: __January__

Date/time	1/19	1/20	1/23	1/24	1/25	1/26	1/27	1/30	1/31	2/1	2/2	2/3	2/6	2/7	2/8	2/9	2/10	2/13	2/14	2/15
Desirable behavior *Request with pictures/gesture*	5 4 3 2 (1)	5 4 3 2 (1)	5 4 3 2 (1)	5 4 3 2 (1)	5 4 3 2 (1)	5 4 3 2 (1)	5 4 3 2 (1)	5 4 3 2 (1)	5 4 3 2 (1)	5 4 3 2 (1)	5 4 3 2 (1)	5 4 3 (2) 1	5 4 3 2 (1)	5 4 3 2 (1)	5 4 3 2 (1)	5 4 3 (2) 1	5 4 3 2 (1)	5 4 3 (2) 1	5 4 3 2 (1)	5 4 3 (2) 1
Challenging behavior *Physical aggression toward self/ others*	(5) 4 3 2 1	(5) 4 3 2 1	5 (4) 3 2 1	(5) 4 3 2 1	5 (4) 3 2 1	5 (4) 3 2 1	5 (4) 3 2 1	5 4 (3) 2 1	5 4 (3) 2 1	5 4 (3) 2 1	5 4 (3) 2 1	5 4 (3) 2 1	5 (4) 3 2 1	5 4 (3) 2 1	5 4 (3) 2 1	5 4 3 (2) 1	5 4 (3) 2 1	5 4 3 (2) 1	5 4 (3) 2 1	5 4 3 (2) 1

<— Baseline —>   <— Intervention —>

Desirable behavior: __Requests with pictures/gestures__
5 = __Verbal reminder to use pictures__
4 = __Gestural prompt to use pictures__
3 = __Initial physical guidance to use pictures__
2 = __Partial physical guidance to use pictures__
1 = __Hand-over-hand guidance to use pictures__

Challenging behavior: __Physical aggression to self or others__
5 = __8 or more times per day__
4 = __6 or 7 times per day__
3 = __4 or 5 times per day__
2 = __2 or 3 times per day__
1 = __0 or 1 time per day__

Figure 7.6A. Jessi's PTR-YC Behavior Rating Scale for January. (*Note:* Blank fillable and printable versions of this form can be found on the accompanying CD-ROM.)

FORM 4

PTR-YC Behavior Rating Scale

Child: _Jessi_   Rater: _Elle and Lauren_   Observation period: _All day_   Month: _February to March_

	Date/time	2/16	2/17	2/20	2/21	2/22	2/23	2/24	2/27	2/28	2/29	3/1	3/2	3/5	3/6	3/7	3/8	3/9	3/12	3/13	3/14
Desirable behavior Request with pictures/gesture		5	5	5	5	5	5	5	5	5	5	5	5	5	5	5	5	5	5	5	5
		4	4	4	4	4	4	4	4	4	4	4	4	4	4	4	4	4	4	4	4
		3	3	3	3	3	3	3	3	3	3	3	3	③	3	③	③	③	3	③	③
		②	②	2	2	2	②	②	2	②	②	②	②	2	②	2	2	2	②	2	2
		1	1	1	1	①	1	1	①	1	1	1	1	1	1	1	1	1	1	1	1
Challenging behavior Physical aggression toward self/others		5	5	5	5	5	5	5	5	5	5	5	5	5	5	5	5	5	5	5	5
		4	4	4	4	4	4	4	4	4	4	4	4	4	4	4	4	4	4	4	4
		3	3	3	3	3	3	3	3	3	3	3	3	3	3	3	3	3	3	3	3
		②	②	2	②	2	②	②	②	2	②	2	②	②	2	2	②	②	2	②	②
		1	1	1	1	①	1	1	1	①	1	①	1	1	①	①	1	1	①	1	1

Desirable behavior: _Requests with pictures/gestures_

5 = _Verbal reminder to use pictures_
4 = _Gestural prompt to use pictures_
3 = _Initial physical guidance to use pictures_
2 = _Partial physical guidance to use pictures_
1 = _Hand-over-hand guidance to use pictures_

Challenging behavior: _Physical aggression to self or others_

5 = _8 or more times per day_
4 = _6 or 7 times per day_
3 = _4 or 5 times per day_
2 = _2 or 3 times per day_
1 = _0 or 1 time per day_

Figure 7.7A. Jessi's PTR-YC Behavior Rating Scale for February and March. (*Note:* Blank fillable and printable versions of this form can be found on the accompanying CD-ROM.)

PTR-YC Fidelity of Strategy Implementation

FORM 11

Child: _Jessi_____ Interventionist: _Teacher_____ Observer: _K.W._____

Date: _2/6_____ Observation period: _Small group_____

	Were all steps implemented as intended?		Did the child respond as intended?		Was the strategy implemented as frequently as intended?	
Prevent strategy Steps: 1. Present visual support or visual schedule to Jessi. 2. Have her respond to visuals (assist as needed). 3. When task is complete, put visual in "all done" box. 4. Provide verbal praise for following directions. 5.	(Yes)	No	(Yes)	No	(Yes)	No
Teach strategy Steps: 1. Determine what Jessi is requesting. 2. Find the appropriate photo on the key ring. 3. Show the picture and physically prompt her to touch the picture. 4. As soon as she touches the picture, provide access. 5. Provide specific verbal feedback about her communication.	Yes	(No)	Yes	(No)	Yes	No
Reinforce strategy Steps: 1. Do not provide any attention for challenging behavior. 2. If it is toward a peer, provide attention to the peer. 3. Physically prompt her to find the correct picture without attending. 4. Provide access to what is on the picture. 5.	Yes	(No)	(Yes)	No	(Yes)	No

Figure 7.8A. Jessi's PTR-YC Fidelity of Strategy Implementation. (*Note:* Blank fillable and printable versions of this form can be found on the accompanying CD-ROM.)

communicate, then they would make sure they were following the procedures first before implementing any other strategies.

The team would always start their meetings by reviewing the data and celebrating their successes. Jessi continued to make slow but steady progress, and the classroom staff became more confident and competent working with Jessi and teaching her how to more effectively communicate. They were also able to include her more into their classroom activities, and the children began to interact with her more because Jessi was less physically aggressive toward the children. Shortly after implementing the behavior intervention plan and seeing some success, Jessi began receiving services through the school district, and the team shared their behavior intervention plan with the school and incorporated it into Jessi's individualized education program (IEP). Jessi attended the early childhood special education classroom in the morning and continued in Elle and Lauren's classroom in the afternoon. Jessi was beginning to make more measurable progress because she was receiving more individualized services between the two settings.

MEETING 5: ETHAN

Using Data and Next Steps

Ethan's team decided they would briefly meet each Friday to look at the data from the past week. It seemed that Ethan's behavior intervention plan was really working after only 2 weeks of implementation, and Joan, the center director and classroom teacher, and Carol, the teacher assistant, celebrated Ethan's progress. Although Ethan still had disruptive behavior, it did not seem as intense as before, and he seemed to be recovering from incidents almost immediately. The behavior intervention plan really seemed to be working, and because the teachers had also begun to implement using predictable schedules as a classroom practice, they found that Ethan was responding more positively to not being able to play with a particular toy if someone else had it. Joan and Carol had been heavily reinforcing Ethan's peers for engaging in a variety of appropriate behaviors when there were conflicts over toys or classroom materials as a way to increase their positive attention to all the children. It seemed that Ethan was noticing this and was slowly starting to imitate some of those same behaviors of his peers. Joan e-mailed a brief summary of Ethan's progress to Veronica, Ethan's grandmother.

Joan and Carol reviewed Ethan's data after 4 weeks of implementing his behavior intervention plan, and it was clear that the plan was working well. Joan and Carol were pleased with the progress that Ethan was making. Although Ethan still had some disruptive behavior, Joan and Carol felt that it was manageable. They also saw how the classroom practices were making a difference for Ethan as well as the other children and committed to implement the rest of the practices. Joan and Carol agreed that Ethan's behavior was manageable enough to stop with their data collection, but they knew that they would continue to implement the strategies because they were so effective. They agreed to spend their time putting together materials and plans to implement the rest of the classroom practices. Because Ethan's progress had gone so well, Veronica was in complete agreement to stop collecting individual data on Ethan's behavior unless it became worse again. As Joan was keeping Veronica informed of what they were doing and how well Ethan was doing, Veronica was also implementing some of the strategies at home, especially providing Ethan with immediate and specific feedback for his appropriate behavior and increasing her positive attention with him. Veronica provided less specific feedback than Ethan was getting at the center, but it seemed to be just as effective. Veronica's feedback included more facial expressions and body language, but Ethan seemed to respond just as effectively as he was in the classroom. Figure 7.9A shows Ethan's PTR-YC Behavior Rating Scale.

FORM 4 — PTR-YC Behavior Rating Scale

Child: _Ethan_ Rater: _Joan and Carol_ Observation period: _Choice time_ Month: _March/April_

Date/time	3/22	3/23	3/26	3/27	3/28	3/29	3/30	4/2	4/3	4/4	4/5	4/6	4/9	4/10	4/11	4/12	4/13	4/16	4/17	4/18
Desirable behavior Positive responses to peers	5	5	5	5	5	5	5	5	5	5	5	5	5	(5)	(5)	5	(5)	(5)	(5)	5
	4	4	4	4	(4)	4	(4)	(4)	(4)	4	(4)	(4)	(4)	4	4	(4)	4	4	4	(4)
	3	3	3	(3)	3	(3)	3	3	3	(3)	3	3	3	3	3	3	3	3	3	3
	2	(2)	(2)	2	2	2	2	2	2	2	2	2	2	2	2	2	2	2	2	2
	(1)	1	1	1	1	1	1	1	1	1	1	1	1	1	1	1	1	1	1	1
Challenging behavior Disruptive behavior	5	5	5	5	5	5	5	5	5	5	5	5	5	5	5	5	5	5	5	5
	4	4	4	4	4	4	4	4	4	4	4	4	4	4	4	4	4	4	4	4
	3	3	3	3	3	3	3	3	3	3	3	3	3	3	3	3	3	3	3	3
	2	2	2	2	2	(2)	(2)	2	2	2	2	2	(2)	2	2	(2)	2	2	2	2
	1	1	1	1	1	1	1	1	1	1	1	(1)	1	(1)	(1)	1	(1)	(1)	(1)	(1)

3/29—individual interventions began
4/6—stopped using frequency graph

Desirable behavior: _Positive responses to peers_
5 = _Independently asks peer nicely, with hand out_
4 = _Asks nicely, with hand out, with teacher facilitation_
3 = _Gets teacher assistance_
2 = _Yells and/or screams at peers_
1 = _Yells, screams, takes items, destroys things_

Challenging behavior: _Disruptive behavior_
5 = _4 times_
4 = _3 times_
3 = _2 times_
2 = _1 time_
1 = _0 times_

Figure 7.9A. Ethan's PTR-YC Behavior Rating Scale for March and April. (Note: Blank fillable and printable versions of this form can be found on the accompanying CD-ROM.)

153

References

Arndorfer, R.E., Miltenberger, R.G., Woster, S.H., Rortvedt, A.K., & Gaffaney, T. (1994). Home-based descriptive and experimental analysis of problem behaviors in children. *Topics in Early Childhood Special Education, 14*, 64–87.

Asher, S.R. (1995). The academic lives of neglected, rejected, popular, and controversial children. *Child Development, 66*, 754–763.

Asmus, J.M., Wacker, D.P., Harding, J., Berg, W., Derby, M., & Kacis, E. (1999). Evaluation of antecedent stimulus parameters for the treatment of escape-maintained aberrant behavior. *Journal of Applied Behavior Analysis, 32*, 495–513.

Bambara, L., & Kern, L. (Eds.). (2005). *Individualized supports for students with problem behaviors: Designing positive behavior plans.* New York, NY: Guilford Press.

Blair, K.C., Umbreit, J., & Bos, C.S. (1999). Using functional assessment and children's preferences to improve the behavior of young children with behavioral disorders. *Behavioral Disorders, 24*, 151–166.

Blair, K.C., Umbreit, J., Dunlap, G., & Jung, G. (2007). Promoting inclusion and peer participation through assessment-based intervention. *Topics in Early Childhood Special Education, 27*, 134–147.

Branson, D., & Demchak, M. (2011). Toddler teachers' use of teaching pyramid practices. *Topics in Early Childhood Special Education, 30*, 196–208.

Bredekamp, S., & Copple, C. (Eds.). (1997). *Developmentally appropriate practice in early childhood programs* (Rev. ed.). Washington, DC: National Association for the Education of Young Children.

Brown, W.H., McEvoy, M.A., & Bishop, J.N. (1991). Incidental teaching of social behavior: A naturalistic approach for promoting young children's peer interactions. *Teaching Exceptional Children, 24*, 35–38.

Brown, W.H., & Odom, S.L. (1995). Naturalistic peer interventions for promoting preschool children's social interactions. *Preventing School Failure, 39*, 38–43.

Carr, E.G., Dunlap, G., Horner, R.H., Koegel, R.L., Turnbull, A.P., Sailor, W., . . . Fox, L. (2002). Positive behavior support. Evolution of an applied science. *Journal of Positive Behavior Interventions, 4*, 4–16.

Carr, E.G., & Durand, V.M. (1985). Reducing behavior problems through functional communication training. *Journal of Applied Behavior Analysis, 18*, 111–126.

Carr, E.G., Horner, R.H., Turnbull, A.P., Marquis, J., Magito-Mclaughlin, D., McAtee, M.L., . . . Doolabh, A. (1999). *Positive behavior support for people with developmental disabilities: A research synthesis.* Washington, DC: American Association on Mental Retardation.

Carr, E.G., Levin, L., McConnachie, G., Carlson, J.I., Kemp, D.C., & Smith, C.E. (1994). *Communication-based interventions for problem behavior: A user's guide for producing positive change.* Baltimore, MD: Paul H. Brookes Publishing Co.

Chafouleas, S., Riley-Tillman, T.C., & Sugai, G. (2007). *School-based behavioral assessment: Informing intervention and instruction.* New York, NY: Guilford.

Christie, J.F. (1988). The effects of play period duration on children's play patterns. *Journal of Research in Childhood Education, 3*, 123–131.

Clarke, S., Dunlap, G., Foster-Johnson, L., Childs, K.E., Wilson, D., White, R., & Vera, A. (1995). Improving the conduct of students with behavioral disorders by incorporating student interests into curricular activities. *Behavioral Disorders, 20*, 221–237.

Connell, M.C., Carta, J.J., Lutz, S., & Randall, C. (1993). Building independence during in-class transitions: Teaching in-class transition skills to preschoolers with developmental delays through choral-response-based self-assessment and contingent praise. *Education and Treatment of Children, 16*, 160–174.

Conroy, M.A., Davis, C.A., Fox, J.J., & Brown, W.H. (2002). Functional assessment of behavior and effective supports for young children with challenging behavior. *Assessment for Effective Intervention, 27*, 35–47.

Conroy, M.A., Dunlap, G., Clarke, S., & Alter, P.J. (2005). A descriptive analysis of positive behavioral intervention research with young children with challenging behavior. *Topics in Early Childhood Special Education, 25,* 157–166.

Cooper, J.O., Heron, T.E., & Heward, W.L. (1987). *Applied behavior analysis.* Upper Saddle River, NJ: Merrill.

DePaepe, P., Reichle, R., & Reichle, J. (1993). Applying general case instructional strategies when teaching communicative alternatives to challenging behavior. In J. Reichle & D. Wacker (Eds.), *Communicative approaches to the management of challenging behavior* (pp. 237–262). Baltimore, MD: Paul H. Brookes Publishing Co.

Duda, M.A., Dunlap, G., Fox, L., Lentini, R., & Clarke, S. (2004). An experimental evaluation of positive behavior support in a community preschool program. *Topics in Early Childhood Special Education, 24,* 143–155.

Dunlap, G. (2006). The applied behavior analytic heritage of PBS: A dynamic model of action-oriented research. *Journal of Positive Behavior Interventions, 8,* 58–60.

Dunlap, G., & Carr, E.G. (2007). Positive behavior support and developmental disabilities: A summary and analysis of research. In S.L. Odom, R.H. Horner, M. Snell, & J. Blacher (Eds.), *Handbook of developmental disabilities* (pp. 469–482). New York, NY: Guilford Press.

Dunlap, G., Carr, E.G., Horner, R.H., Zarcone, J., & Schwartz, I. (2008). Positive behavior support and applied behavior analysis: A familial alliance. *Behavior Modification, 32,* 682–698.

Dunlap, G., dePerczel, M., Clarke, S., Wilson, D., Wright, S., White, R., & Gomez, A. (1994). Choice making to promote adaptive behavior for students with emotional and behavioral challenges. *Journal of Applied Behavior Analysis, 27,* 505–518.

Dunlap, L.K., Dunlap, G., Koegel, L.K., & Koegel, R.L. (1991). Using self-monitoring to increase students' success and independence. *Teaching Exceptional Children, 23,* 17–22.

Dunlap, G., Ester, T., Langhans, S., & Fox, L. (2006). Functional communication training with toddlers in home environments. *Journal of Early Intervention, 28,* 81–96.

Dunlap, G., & Fox, L. (1999). A demonstration of behavioral support for young children with autism. *Journal of Positive Behavior Interventions, 1,* 77–87.

Dunlap, G., & Fox, L. (2009). Positive behavior support and early intervention. In W. Sailor, G. Dunlap, G. Sugai, & R.H. Horner (Eds.), *Handbook of positive behavior support* (pp. 49–71). New York, NY: Springer.

Dunlap, G., & Fox, L. (2011). Function-based interventions for children with challenging behavior. *Journal of Early Intervention, 33,* 333–343.

Dunlap, G., Iovannone, R., Kincaid, D., Wilson, K., Christiansen, K., Strain, P.S., & English, C. (2010). *Prevent-Teach-Reinforce: A school-based model of individualized positive behavior support.* Baltimore, MD: Paul H. Brookes Publishing Co.

Dunlap, G., Iovannone, R., Wilson, K., Kincaid, D., & Strain, P. (2010). Prevent-Teach-Reinforce: A standardized model of school-based behavioral intervention. *Journal of Positive Behavior Interventions, 12,* 9–22.

Dunlap, G., & Kern, L. (1996). Modifying instructional activities to promote desirable behavior: A conceptual and practical framework. *School Psychology Quarterly, 11,* 297–312.

Dunlap, G., Kern-Dunlap, L., Clarke, S., & Robbins, F.R. (1991). Functional assessment, curriculum revision, and severe behavior problems. *Journal of Applied Behavior Analysis, 24,* 387–397.

Dunlap, G., & Koegel, R.L. (1980). Motivating autistic children through stimulus variation. *Journal of Applied Behavior Analysis, 13,* 619–627.

Durand, V.M. (1990). *Severe behavior problems: A functional communication training approach.* New York, NY: Guilford Press.

Foster-Johnson, L., Ferro, J., & Dunlap, G. (1994). Preferred curricular activities and reduced problem behaviors in students with intellectual disabilities. *Journal of Applied Behavior Analysis, 27,* 493–504.

Fox, L., Dunlap, G., Hemmeter, M.L., Joseph, G.E., & Strain, P.S. (2003, July). The teaching pyramid: A model for supporting social competence and preventing challenging behavior in young children. *Young Children,* 48–52.

Fox, L., & Hemmeter, M.L. (2009). A program-wide model for supporting social emotional development and addressing challenging behavior in early childhood settings. In W. Sailor, G. Dunlap, G. Sugai, & R. Horner (Eds.), *Handbook of positive behavior support* (pp. 177–202). New York, NY: Springer.

Frea, W.D., & Hepburn, S.L. (1999). Teaching parents of children with autism to perform functional assessments to plan interventions for extremely disruptive behaviors. *Journal of Positive Behavior Interventions, 1,* 112–116.

Halle, J., Bambara, L.M., & Reichle, J. (2005). Teaching alternative skills. In L. Bambara & L. Kern (Eds.), *Individualized supports for students with problem behaviors* (pp. 237–274). New York, NY: Guilford Press.

Harding, J.W., Wacker, D.P., Berg, W.K., Cooper, L., Asmus, J., Mlela, K., & Muller, J. (1999). An analysis of choice making in the assessment of young children with severe behavior problems. *Journal of Applied Behavior Analysis, 32,* 63–82.

Hemmeter, M.L., Ostrosky, M., & Fox, L. (2006). Social and emotional foundations for early learning: A conceptual model for intervention. *School Psychology Review, 35,* 583–601.

Hemmeter, M., Smith, B., Sandall, S., & Askew, L. (2005). *DEC recommended practices workbook.* Missoula, MT: Division for Early Childhood.

Hester, P.P., Baltodano, H.M., Hendrickson, J.M., Tonelson, S.W., Conroy, M.A., & Gable, R.A. (2004). Lessons learned from research on early intervention: What teachers can do to prevent children's behavior problems. *Preventing School Failure, 49,* 5–10.

Iovannone, R., Greenbaum, P., Wang, W., Kincaid, D., & Dunlap, G. (in press). Reliability of an individualized behavior rating scale tool for progress monitoring. *Assessment for Effective Intervention.*

Iovannone, R., Greenbaum, P., Wei, W., Kincaid, D., Dunlap, G., & Strain, P. (2009). Randomized control trial of a tertiary behavior intervention for students with problem behaviors: Preliminary outcomes. *Journal of Emotional and Behavioral Disorders, 17,* 213–225.

Joseph, G.E., & Strain, P.S. (2003). Comprehensive evidence-based social–emotional curricula for young children: An analysis of efficacious adoption potential. *Topics in Early Childhood Special Education, 23,* 65–76.

Kaiser, B., & Rasminsky, J.S. (2003). *Challenging behavior in young children: Understanding, preventing, and responding effectively.* Boston, MA: Allyn & Bacon.

Kern, L. (2005). Responding to problem behavior. In L. Bambara & L. Kern (Eds.), *Individualized supports for students with problem behaviors* (pp. 275–302). New York, NY: Guilford Press.

Kern, L., & Dunlap, G. (1999). Assessment-based interventions for children with emotional and behavioral disorders. In A.C. Repp & R.H. Horner (Eds.), *Functional analysis of problem behavior: From effective assessment to effective support* (pp. 197–218). Belmont, CA: Wadsworth Publishing.

Kern, L., Vorndran, C.M., Hilt, A., Ringdahl, J.E., Adelman, B.E., & Dunlap, G. (1998). Choice as an intervention to improve behavior: A review of the literature. *Journal of Behavioral Education, 8,* 151–169.

Koegel, R.L., & Koegel, L.K. (2012). *The PRT pocket guide: Pivotal response treatment for autism spectrum disorders.* Baltimore, MD: Paul H. Brookes Publishing Co.

Koegel, L.K., Koegel, R.L., Boettcher, M.A., Harrower, J., & Openden, D. (2006). Combining functional assessment and self-management procedures to rapidly reduce disruptive behaviors. In R.L. Koegel & L.K. Koegel (Eds.), *Pivotal response treatments for autism: Communication, social, and academic development* (pp. 245–258). Baltimore, MD: Paul H. Brookes Publishing Co.

Kohler, F.W., & Strain, P.S. (1992). Applied behavior analysis and the movement to restructure schools: Compatibilities and opportunities for collaboration. *Journal of Behavioral Education, 2,* 367–390.

Kohler, F.W., & Strain, P.S. (1999). Maximizing peer-mediated resources within integrated preschool classrooms. *Topics in Early Childhood Special Education, 19,* 92–102.

Kontos, S. (1999). Preschool teachers' talk, roles, and activity settings during free play. *Early Childhood Research Quarterly, 14,* 363–383.

Krantz, P.J., & Risley, T. (1977). Behavioral ecology in the classroom. In K.D. O'Leary & S.G. O'Leary (Eds.), *Classroom management: The successful use of behavior modification* (2nd ed., pp. 349–366). New York, NY: Pergamon Press.

Landy, S. (2009). *Pathways to competence: Encouraging healthy social and emotional development in young children* (2nd ed.). Baltimore, MD: Paul H. Brookes Publishing Co.

Lane, K.L., Wehby, J.H., & Cooley, C (2006). Teacher expectations of student's classroom behavior across grade span. *Exceptional Children, 22,* 153–167.

McCormick, K.M., Jolivette, K., & Ridgley, R. (2003). Choice making as an intervention strategy for young children. *Young Exceptional Children, 6,* 3–10.

Neilsen, S.L., Olive, M.L., Donovan, A., & McEvoy, M. (1998). Challenging behaviors in your classroom? Don't react, teach instead. *Young Exceptional Children, 2,* 2–10.

Nunnelley, J.C. (2002). *Powerful, positive, and practical practices: Behavior guidance strategies.* Little Rock, AR: Southern Early Childhood Association.

Odom, S.L., & Strain, P.S. (1986). Combining teacher antecedents and peer responses for promoting reciprocal social interaction of autistic preschoolers. *Journal of Applied Behavior Analysis, 19,* 59–71.

Pretti-Frontczak, K., & Bricker, D. (2004). *An activity-based approach to early intervention* (3rd ed.). Baltimore, MD: Paul H. Brookes Publishing Co.

Quill, K. (1997). Instructional considerations for young children with autism: The rationale for visually cued instruction. *Journal of Autism and Developmental Disorders, 27,* 697–714.

Ratcliff, N. (2001). Use the environment to prevent discipline problems and support learning. *Young Children, 56,* 84–87.

Reeve, C.E., & Carr, E.G. (2000). Prevention of severe behavior problems in children with developmental disorders. *Journal of Positive Behavior Interventions, 2*, 144–160.

Rosenkoetter, S.E., & Fowler, S.A. (1986). Teaching mainstreamed children to manage daily transitions. *Teaching Exceptional Children, 19*, 20–23.

Sailor, W., Dunlap, G., Sugai, G., & Horner, R. (Eds.). (2009). *Handbook of positive behavior support.* New York, NY: Springer.

Sainato, D.M. (1990). Classroom transitions: Organizing environments to promote independent performance in preschool children with disabilities. *Education and Treatment of Children, 13*, 288–297.

Sainato, D.M., Strain, P.S., Lefebvre, D., & Repp, N. (1990). Effects of self-evaluation on the independent work skills of preschool children with disabilities. *Exceptional Children, 56*, 540–549.

Sandall, S., Hemmeter, M., Smith, B., & McLean, M. (Eds.). (2005). *DEC recommended practices: A comprehensive guide for practical application.* Longmont, CO: Sopris West Educational Services.

Sandall, S.R., & Schwartz, I.S. (2008). *Building blocks for teaching preschoolers with special needs* (2nd ed.). Baltimore, MD: Paul H. Brookes Publishing Co.

Schmit, J., Alpers, S., Raschke, D., & Ryndak, D. (2000). Effects of using a photographic cueing package during routine school transitions with a child who has autism. *Mental Retardation, 38*, 131–137.

Smith, B., & Fox, L. (2003). *Systems of service delivery: A synthesis of evidence relevant to young children at risk of or who have challenging behavior.* Tampa: University of South Florida.

Snyder, P.A., Crowe, C.D., Miller, M.D., Hemmeter, M.L., & Fox, L. (2011). *Evaluating implementation of evidence-based practices in preschool: Psychometric evidence for the Teaching Pyramid Observation Tool.* Paper presented at the annual meeting of the American Educational Research Association, New Orleans, LA.

Strain, P.S. (2001). Empirically-based social skill intervention. *Behavioral Disorders, 27*, 30–36.

Strain, P.S., & Bovey, E.H. (2011). Randomized, controlled trial of the LEAP model of early intervention for young children with autism spectrum disorders. *Topics in Early Childhood Special Education, 31*, 133–154.

Strain, P.S., Bovey, E.H., Wilson, K. & Roybal, R. (2009). Leap preschool: Lessons learned of over 28 years of inclusive services for young children with autism. *Young Exceptional Children, Monograph Series 11*, 49–68.

Strain, P.S., & Danko, C.D. (1995). Caregivers' encouragement of positive interaction between preschoolers with autism and their siblings. *Journal of Emotional and Behavioral Disorders, 3*, 2–12.

Strain, P.S., & Kohler, F.W. (1998). Peer-mediated social intervention for young children with autism. *Seminars in Speech and Language, 19*, 391–405.

Strain, P.S., & Schwartz, I. (2001). Applied behavior analysis and social skills intervention for young children with autism. *Focus on Autism and Other Developmental Disorders, 8*, 12–24.

Strain, P., Wilson, K., & Dunlap, G. (2011). Prevent-Teach-Reinforce: Addressing problem behaviors of students with autism in general education classrooms. *Behavioral Disorders, 36*, 160–171.

Waldron-Soler, K.M., Martella, R.C., Marchand-Martella, N.E., & Ebey, T.L. (2000). Effects of choice of stimuli as reinforcement for task responding in preschoolers with and without developmental disabilities. *Journal of Applied Behavior Analysis, 33*, 93–96.

Walker, H.M., Ramsey, E., & Gresham, F.M. (2004). *Antisocial behavior in school: Evidence-based practices* (2nd ed.). Belmont, CA: Wadsworth.

Wien, C.A. (1996). Time, work, and developmentally appropriate practice. *Early Childhood Research Quarterly, 11*, 377–393.

Winterling, V., Dunlap, G., & O'Neill, R.E. (1987). The influence of task variation on the aberrant behavior of autistic students. *Education and Treatment of Children, 10*, 105–119.

Zanolli, K.M., Saudargas, R.A., & Twardosz, S. (1997). The development of toddlers' responses to affectionate teacher behavior. *Early Childhood Research Quarterly, 12*(1), 99–116.

APPENDIX

Interventions

A

Prevent Interventions

The following are common, evidence-based interventions that can be used in preschool classroom settings as strategies for the prevent component of PTR-YC. They are intended for use with individual children who have challenging behaviors that are not being satisfactorily resolved with high-quality classroom practices. At least one prevent intervention must be selected for behavior intervention plans; however, many behavior intervention plans include more than one prevent intervention. Prevent interventions are strategies that involve antecedent manipulations that should make the challenging behavior less likely to occur, and the effects are usually seen in a short period of time.

PROVIDE CHOICES

Strategy: Provide opportunities to choose between two or more options.

Description of strategy: This strategy involves providing the child with an opportunity to make choices among activities, the order of activities, materials, snacks, play partners, or many other possibilities in which there may be more than one alternative. Although you may already be providing choices to children throughout the day, this strategy for a particular child involves identifying when, where, how, and how often choices will be provided to reduce challenging behaviors. Teams need to create a plan that includes all of these components.

Rationale for using strategy: When provided as a prevent strategy, choice making can be effective because 1) it allows the child to select an option that is preferred (and when children are engaged with preferred activities or stimuli, they tend to exhibit fewer challenging behaviors) and 2) it allows the child to have some control over what happens. As adults, we seek to organize our environment by making choices throughout the day in a variety of ways and in a variety of situations. Providing choices for children teaches them how to manage or have some control in their environment. A great deal of research has shown that choice making can reduce the occurrence of challenging behaviors if the choices are relevant to the context in which challenging behaviors tend to occur. Providing choices prevents challenging behavior by allowing children to express a preference and to engage with that preferred option. This is a valuable process and problem-solving skill, and in some situations, the act of control in and of itself is reinforcing and can thereby reduce challenging behaviors.

Consider using this strategy when the PTR-YC assessment indicates the following.

- Challenging behavior occurs when the child is asked to do something that he or she finds disagreeable.

- Challenging behavior occurs when the child is given a direction.

- Challenging behavior occurs when the child makes the transition from a preferred activity to a nonpreferred activity.

- When a child says "no" to everything.

- When a child refuses to do things on a regular basis.

Steps for Implementation

1. Determine when choices will be offered. This should usually be shortly before the time that challenging behaviors are anticipated to occur (as identified by the functional behavioral assessment). Choices may be offered many times per day or only before especially difficult routines. It depends on the child and the frequency of challenging behaviors.

2. Determine what choice options will be made available. All options should be reasonable from the perspective of the teachers and the child, and it is understood that the child's choice must be honored.

3. Determine how the choices will be presented. Choices are often best offered with both verbal and visual cues. A choice menu in the form of a pictorial array may need to be prepared.

4. When choice-making opportunities are presented, the child's choice should be immediately honored.

Strategy ideas: Listed next is a sample of ideas that can be utilized as choices; there are many more. The list is intended to illustrate some options of how and when to integrate choices. Teams are encouraged to be creative with choices and to ensure these choices fit the function of the behavior and fit within classroom routines and activities.

Arrival/dismissal

- Choose which table activity to start with

- Choose how to put your things in your cubby (e.g., hang up coat, hang book bag)

- Choose which peers to greet

Small group

- Choose materials (e.g., which color marker)
- Choose where to sit
- Choose the order or sequence of activity (e.g., color, cut, glue)

Large group

- Choose a song
- Choose motor actions for counting
- Choose a job for the day

Transition

- Choose an object on which to line up
- Choose peer buddy
- Choose transition movement (e.g., hop on one foot)

Implementation Considerations

- Choices should be offered immediately before an activity that has been associated with challenging behavior.
- Choices should be made among two or three possible selections.
- The child's selection should be immediately honored. Delayed selections do not tend to be effective with young children.
- Choices may need to be presented in a variety of ways (e.g., pictures, talking devices, objects) to ensure children with all abilities can make meaningful choices. Many young children require visual cues in order to make accurate choices.
- Some children may not know how to make choices and will need some careful instruction before the procedure can be effective.
- Choices you offer should be positively stated, acceptable and desirable to the child, and honored by the adults. If something is not an option, is not acceptable, or is not available, then do not offer it as a choice.

Supporting Evidence

Dunlap et al. (1994)
Dunlap & Kern (1996)
Harding et al. (1999)
Kern et al. (1998)
McCormick, Jolivette, & Ridgley (2003)
Waldron-Soler, Martella, Marchand-Martella, & Ebey (2000)

INTERSPERSE DIFFICULT OR
NONPREFERRED TASKS WITH EASY OR PREFERRED TASKS

Strategy: Intersperse difficult or nonpreferred tasks with easy or preferred tasks.

Description of strategy: This strategy involves reducing challenging behaviors that are as-sociated with difficult or unpleasant activities by mixing in (interspersing) tasks that are easy for the child or which the child clearly enjoys. Task interspersal makes the overall context of the activity more pleasant and more successful for the child and thereby serves to reduce challenging behaviors.

Rationale for using strategy: When tasks are difficult, we tend to avoid them or we do not put much effort into doing what we are supposed to do. If something is hard for us to do and we fail at it, then we are likely to not want to do it anymore. Providing multiple opportunities for children to be successful and to be able to demonstrate appropriate skills while interspersing in harder or more difficult tasks provides children with opportunities to persist with activities or tasks that are difficult or not preferred. Interspersing difficult tasks with easy tasks prevents challenging behavior by allowing more opportunities for children to be successful and creates an environment where learning is fun and enjoyable. It can prevent or reduce a variety of emotions (e.g., frustration, anxiety, anger, fear) that can negatively affect children by associating a variety of tasks with negative emotions and negative consequences. Children who do not respond well to failure, have difficulty learning new skills, take a long time to learn new skills, or have limited skills and/or interests may benefit from interspersing difficult or nonpreferred tasks with easy or preferred tasks. For example, children may use problem behavior to avoid tasks that are difficult for them or that they do not want to do. Some children have limited interests in which they choose to play with the same toys all the time or will only engage in a few activities throughout the classroom. This strategy may help children be successful in engaging in a variety of activities and expand on their skills and interests.

Consider using this strategy when the PTR-YC assessment indicates the following.

- Challenging behavior occurs when the child is avoiding a particular task or activity.

- Challenging behavior occurs when the child is refusing a particular task or activity.

- Challenging behavior occurs when the child is corrected or told that something he or she did is wrong.

- Challenging behavior occurs during an instructional activity.

- Challenging behavior occurs when making the transition to a nonpreferred activity.

- Challenging behavior occurs during a nonpreferred activity.

- Challenging behavior occurs when a preferred activity ends.

- Challenging behavior occurs when a new task or activity is introduced.

- Challenging behavior occurs when a task is difficult.

- Challenging behavior occurs when an activity is too long.

Steps for Implementation

1. Identify the activity or routine in which challenging behavior occurs and in which the challenging behavior appears to be related to the difficulty or the unpleasant nature of the activity. This should occur during the process of functional behavioral assessment.

2. Identify activities (or tasks) at which the child is fluent, is successful, and seems to enjoy. These are the tasks that will be interspersed among the difficult expectations, so they should be compatible with the overall context. Sometimes the task can be as simple as, "Give me 5!" or "Show me something that is green."

3. During difficult activity or routine, sprinkle in the easy and preferred activities with a dense enough ratio so that challenging behavior is reduced or eliminated.

Strategy ideas: Listed next is a sample of ideas that can be utilized as ways to intersperse difficult tasks with easy tasks; there are many more. This list is intended to illustrate some options of how and when to integrate this strategy. How your team chooses to implement this strategy will depend on the task itself and what skills the child already has. Teams are encouraged to be creative and ensure these choices fit the function of the behavior and fit within classroom routines and activities.

Arrival/dismissal

- If the child likes to say, "Hi," to everyone but does not know or use anyone's name, then have him or her say, "Hi," to most of the children or adults and work on using the name (nonpreferred task) for one or two of their preferred peers or adults (preferred task).

- If the child has difficulty with the arrival or dismissal routine on a consistent basis, then have a preferred activity ready for the child to do first, such as Bob the Builder matching game (preferred task), followed by the classroom routine (nonpreferred task).

Free play

- Set up a simple turn-taking sequence (your turn, my turn) to expand a child's play skills. Allow the child 5 minutes to independently play blocks (preferred task), then practice turn-taking sequence for 2 minutes (nonpreferred task), then allow the child to independently play again (preferred task). Repeat this sequence twice during free play. The time should be based on the child's ability to be successful with turn taking, and the times will fluctuate.

Large group

- If the child has difficulty with singing along with a song but can easily and readily imitate the motor movements associated with the song, then pause the singing and movement at a key point in the song and have the child say the next word or phrase (nonpreferred task), then continue to sing the rest of the song (preferred task) with the motor movements. This can involve one opportunity to intersperse a nonpreferred task or can include many opportunities.

Special Considerations

Consider the following when interspersing nonpreferred or difficult tasks with preferred or easy tasks for children who may have differing needs or when special circumstances are present.

- When a child has cognitive delays or has difficulty learning new tasks, tasks may need to be broken up into smaller steps and the steps may need to be taught and practiced more often (provide multiple opportunities for instruction).

- The amount of time spent on nonpreferred activities should be relatively short compared with the amount of time spent on preferred activities. These activities need to be arranged so that children can be successful engaging in nonpreferred activities, and children may only be able to initially handle a few seconds.

Implementation Considerations

Make sure of the following when implementing these strategies.

- Requirements for difficult tasks are attainable for the particular child. It is important for the child to be successful.

- Interspersing nonpreferred with preferred tasks are planned in advance and any required materials are prepared and available.

- The expectations for the nonpreferred task are clear and well defined.

- Preferred or easy tasks are positively reinforced on a consistent basis.

Supporting Evidence

Dunlap & Koegel (1980)
Koegel & Koegel (2012)
Winterling, Dunlap, & O'Neill (1987)

USE VISUAL SUPPORTS AND SCHEDULES

Strategy: Use visual supports and schedules.

Description of strategy: This strategy involves the use of visual supports and visual schedules to help children understand what is expected of them and to increase their ability to engage in tasks and independently follow directions. Visual supports can include pictures to demonstrate or represent an item or activity (e.g., photographs, illustrations, clip art, posted signs, magazine cut outs), actual items or objects (e.g., representations of items, miniatures, toy versions of items), and physical gestures (e.g., using sign language, pointing, nodding your head). Visual supports can be extended to include sequences to produce visual schedules.

Rationale for using strategy: Visual supports are a regular part of everyday life and help to serve as reminders for what we need to do or to give nonverbal directions. Road signs, posted reminders to wash your hands in the bathroom, calendars and schedules, or a person pointing you in the right direction are just a few everyday examples of ways that we utilize and provide visual supports to increase understanding and give directions to others in a nonverbal way. Visual supports are a normal way to help us successfully navigate our environments. Visual supports can support children's success throughout their day and may increase their independence in daily routines. Using visual supports prevents challenging behavior by providing nonverbal cues for what you want a child to do (and can also help the child understand what you want him or her to do). Nonverbal cues or visual supports can be one way to help improve the success of children who have difficulty following verbal directions or processing verbal information.

A fundamental classroomwide strategy, described in Chapter 6, involves using schedules that are predictable and comprehensible to every child in the class. This prevent strategy is aligned with classroom practice, but it is developed and applied at the individual level.

Consider using this strategy when the PTR-YC assessment indicates the following.

- Challenging behavior occurs when the child is given a verbal direction.
- Challenging behavior occurs when the child refuses to follow a direction.
- Challenging behavior occurs when there is a change in the child's schedule.
- Challenging behavior occurs when the child and adult engage in power struggles.
- The child has difficulty responding to instructions.
- The child does not seem to understand what he or she is supposed to do.
- The child has difficulty independently following daily routines.
- The child can independently complete parts of routines.
- The child has difficulty engaging in activities.

Steps for Implementation

1. Identify activity or activities during which the child appears to be in need of additional guidance. This information should be available from the functional behavioral assessment.

2. Determine the type of supports needed by the child to more successfully perform the activity or routine.

3. Prepare materials needed to implement the supports.

4. Provide instruction as necessary for child to respond to visual supports or schedules.

Strategy ideas: Listed next is a sample of ideas that can be utilized as ways to use visual supports; there are many more. This list is intended to illustrate some options of how and when to integrate this strategy. How your team chooses to implement this strategy will depend on what types of visual supports the child responds to and how the visual supports are used. Teams are encouraged to be creative and to ensure these choices fit the function of the behavior and fit within classroom routines and activities.

Transitions

-   Classrooms should have a daily schedule for the whole class. For a child who has difficulty with making transitions, one suggestion is to make the activities on the schedule as separate pictures that are removable in order to be able to take it to the next activity. For example, a child could take the picture of the circle activity and when he or she sits down at circle, the child would hand the picture to the teacher and the teacher would reinforce the child for coming to circle.

Centers/learning areas

-   Develop a play sequence.

Special Considerations

Consider the following when using visual supports for children who may have differing needs or when special circumstances are present.

-   Determine what types of visual supports are successful for a particular child (e.g., pictures to demonstrate or represent an item or activity, actual items or objects, physical gestures) before implementing this strategy.

-   Visual supports are a necessary part of intervention strategies when a child has a hearing and/or vision impairment.

-   Visual supports can be effective for any and all children—adapting supports for children with differing abilities should be considered.

Implementation Considerations

Make sure of the following when implementing these strategies.

-   Visual supports are strategically used to help the child become independent in daily routines and activities.

-   The purpose of the strategy needs to be clear. For example, if the schedule is posted for the order of the day, then a stationary schedule is fine. If the purpose of the schedule is transition, then the activities on the schedule need to be removable.

-   The child knows what the visual support means or represents (if the strategy is not successful, then perhaps the visual support needs to be changed or the child needs to be taught what it means).

-   Visual supports are used for as long as the child needs them. Do not remove them too early.

-   Visual supports need to be accessible and useable. They should be readily available in all situations and settings and at the child's level.

Supporting Evidence

Duda, Dunlap, Fox, Lentini, & Clarke (2004)
Sandall & Schwartz (2008)
Schmit, Alpers, Raschke, & Ryndak (2000)

EMBED PREFERENCES INTO ACTIVITIES

Strategy: Embed preferences into activities.

Description of strategy: This strategy involves incorporating a child's likes and preferences into activities to prevent challenging behaviors. Preferences can be incorporated into any aspect of a child's day and can include what is incorporated into activities, who participates, where activities occur, how activities are presented, or when activities occur.

Rationale for using strategy: Most people like to personalize their environments by having pictures of loved ones, scented candles, specific snacks or candy, favorite music, or mementos in their workspace (e.g., at their desk, around their office, in the classroom). Some people personalize their environments with multiple items, whereas others have very few items. Although we may love our work, we bring preferred things to improve and enhance our day. We personalize how our work is done based on our personal preferences. If a teacher loves when kids get messy, then that teacher will provide a lot of opportunities for activities in which children can get messy. If a teacher loves Halloween, then that teacher will have a lot of fun activities around the Halloween theme. Incorporating or embedding the personal preferences of children who struggle with particular activities into activities can increase their interest and engagement in the activities and improve their knowledge in a variety of ways. It is highly unlikely that children will exhibit any challenging behaviors when they are engaging in and enjoying activities. One way to prevent challenging behavior is to incorporate preferences into activities to gain a child's interest and keep a child actively engaged in a variety of activities. Using preferences and items a child likes helps motivate him or her to do a variety of things, and the activities become naturally reinforcing for the child. This strategy can be effective for a child who may have limited interests, has a strong interest in a few things, avoids particular activities or does not participate in activities for very long, or does not like to be told what to do.

Consider using this strategy when the PTR-YC assessment indicates the following.

- Challenging behavior occurs when the child is asked or told to do a nonpreferred activity.

- Challenging behavior occurs during a particular activity.

- Challenging behavior occurs when making a transition to or beginning a particular activity.

- Challenging behavior occurs when an activity is not an option.

- Challenging behavior occurs at a certain time of the day.

- Challenging behavior occurs when a teacher is attending to someone else.

- A child refuses to participate in activities or classroom routines.

Steps for Implementation

1. Identify an activity or routine in which challenging behavior occurs and in which the challenging behavior appears to be related to the difficulty or the unpleasant nature of the activity. This identification should occur during the process of functional behavioral assessment.

2. Identify the child's preferences, such as types of animals (e.g., dinosaurs, horses), vehicles (e.g., trucks, spaceships), characters from movies, and so forth.

3. Determine how preferences can be incorporated into difficult activities or routines. This may require some creativity but can usually be accomplished with materials, pictures, or photographs.

Strategy ideas: A child's preferences can be embedded into activities in many ways. How your team chooses to implement this strategy will depend on the types of preferences the child has, how the preferences are embedded into activities, and when the preferences are used. Teams are encouraged to be creative and to ensure these choices fit the function of the behavior and fit within classroom routines and activities.

Special Considerations

Consider the following when embedding preferences into activities for children who may have differing needs or when special circumstances are present.

- Identifying preferences that can be embedded into activities may be difficult for children with limited interests. It may be necessary to conduct a preference assessment. In our experience, however, it is always possible to find something that inspires a child's interest and pleasure.

- Make sure the identified preferences do not interfere with any classroom policies or conflict with classroom practices.

Supporting Evidence

Clarke et al. (1995)
Dunlap & Kern (1996)
Dunlap, Kern-Dunlap, Clarke, & Robbins (1991)
Foster-Johnson, Ferro, & Dunlap (1994)

ENHANCE PREDICTABILITY WITH SCHEDULES

Strategy: Using schedules and other cues to enable children to understand and follow activity sequences. This strategy may be very useful with transitions.

Description of strategy: This strategy involves purposefully planning a routine to prepare a child for their day (review schedules and routines prior) or a transition (e.g., visual timers, break signal). This strategy is preventative, and materials that are needed should be prepared and readily available. If a visual schedule is used, then a preparation routine would include reviewing the schedule with the child prior to a change or transition and prior to beginning the activity on the schedule. If a timer is used for transition warnings, then the team must also plan for having the timer available and accessible and ensure it is where the child can see it. This strategy is closely related to the classroomwide practices described in Chapter 6, but is designed for individual applications.

Rationale for strategy: Many challenging behaviors can arise when we are not prepared for the day or not prepared for transitions. Think about a time when you may have lost your own schedule, electronic or hand written, and how that made you feel. When we do not know our own schedule or cannot review it, we get anxious and stressed. A child also needs to know the daily schedule, the routine within the activity, and when a transition is coming. We often get a schedule to review when a child begins to resist making a transition. This strategy involves reviewing that schedule to prepare a child for the day, or changes in the day, to prevent challenging behaviors from occurring. Children can be more successful in all activities and routines when they are prepared for the day and know the routines within the schedule.

Consider using this strategy when the PTR-YC assessment indicates the following.

- Challenging behavior occurs when following the daily routine.

- Challenging behavior occurs around transitions.

- Challenging behavior occurs at specific times of the day.

- Challenging behavior occurs when given a direction.

- Challenging behavior occurs when making a transition to a nonpreferred activity.

- Challenging behavior occurs when a preferred activity ends.

- Challenging behavior occurs at the beginning or end of an activity.

- Challenging behavior occurs when there is a change in the schedule.

- General classroom transition supports are not working.

Steps for Implementation

1. Identify activities and routines during which the child has challenging behaviors and the child is unsure of the sequence or timing of activities. This information should be derived from the functional behavioral assessment.

2. Determine the types of schedules, timers, or other cues that will be necessary to help the child understand the sequence of upcoming events and where favored activities will be occurring.

3. Develop or obtain materials needed.

4. Implement procedures to help the child understand the schedules at times during the day when challenging behaviors have been observed to occur.

Strategy ideas: The following are a sample of ideas that can be utilized to prepare children for their day, changes in schedule, and making transitions. The key component with this strategy is to be preventative. Preparing a child for the daily routine, schedule changes, and making transitions requires action prior to the events occurring.

Prepare for arrival routine

- Have a visual sequence or schedule of every step of the transition for arrival available when the child arrives. The first picture may be go to cubby, then hang up coat, take picture to blue table, put together a puzzle. This visual sequence would be reviewed with the child prior to beginning the routine and could be reviewed with the teacher, assistant, or parent.

- This routine could also include the activities for arrival—sign in, choose a table to play at (art or manipulatives table), go to obstacle course, clean up, go to large group or circle. Again, the focus is on reviewing this schedule with the child prior to beginning the activities.

Prepare for the daily routine

- Review the daily schedule with the child individually in addition to the whole-class activity in order to build consistency and predictability. For example, the teacher reviews the daily schedule with the class as a whole, then provides additional support for one child by reviewing the schedule again one to one (during large-group time or immediately after). Modifications in the presentation of the daily schedule can be made (it can be portable so teachers can carry it; it may have objects or pictures). The purpose of this strategy is to prepare a child prior to activities, perhaps by using a visual schedule. The schedule can be reviewed throughout the day, prior to each activity, and to review what has already been done.

Prepare for transitions

- Many classrooms may already use timers to signal the end of playtime. This strategy looks at the purposeful planning and use of a timer to help prevent a targeted challenging behavior. For example, when Johnny hears "Five more minutes, then we are all done," he runs around the room even if he was engaged in the activity. When general classroom transition supports are not working, we need to individualize. Using a timer to prepare Johnny for transitions might involve him getting the timer and letting his friends know they have 5 minutes. The timer would need to be placed in close proximity to Johnny where he could easily see it. In addition, he may need specific steps for the transition and a visual reminder of what is next. The preparation sequence might be Johnny gets the timer and sets it on the top of the shelf of the block area where he is playing. Then, he tells his friends they have 5 minutes to play. Then, it is cleanup. The teacher reviews the steps of cleanup and what is next in pictures with Johnny. The teacher may then remind Johnny after 2 minutes of his transition sequence. Another reminder may also be given for Johnny using the same language and transition sequence (in 1 minute it will be time to pick up our blocks and put them in the bin, then we go to circle).

Special Considerations

Consider the following when preparing a child who may have differing needs or when special circumstances are present for his or her daily schedule and routines, changes in the schedule or routines, and making transitions.

- The steps of the transition may need to be broken up into small steps when a child has cognitive delays or has difficulty with change. For example, "Pick up one block. Pick up another block. Put block bin on the shelf. Sit at circle." Preparation for this transition would involve reviewing each step.

- Daily schedules may need to be mobile and portable especially if the child has difficulty making a transition. The teacher may need to bring the schedule to the where the child is at instead of bringing the child over to a stationary schedule.

Implementation Considerations

Make sure of the following when implementing these strategies.

- Plan time to review schedules prior to activities, routines, transitions, or changes.

- Visual schedules and routines must be prepared and accessible.

- Implement preparation strategies with the whole classroom and individualize further when necessary.

Supporting Evidence

DePaepe, Reichle, & Reichle (1993)
Sandall & Schwartz (2008)

ALTER PHYSICAL ARRANGEMENT OF THE CLASSROOM

Strategy: Alter physical arrangement of the classroom.

Description of strategy: This strategy involves changing or moving elements of the classroom in order to prevent challenging behaviors. This can include changing or removing a center or learning area, changing a child's seating arrangement, altering elements within a center or learning area, moving a center or learning area to a different place in the room, removing or restricting particular items from an area or from the classroom, making items more accessible for the child, increasing the amount of materials available, limiting the number of children who can be in a certain center or learning area, and keeping certain peers and/or adults separate from the child. This can also include arranging the room to indicate the flow of activities. If the classroom has sinks, then snack tables can be set up by them.

Rationale for using strategy: Changing aspects of our physical environment can affect our behavior and prevent us from doing certain things. If we are working on losing weight or eating better, then we might avoid purchasing certain foods that are not part of a healthy diet, preventing the temptation and possibility that we will eat something we should not eat. Although this strategy alone will not prevent us from eating everything we should not, it can help prevent some of our challenging behavior. Creating an environment so children can be successful can prevent challenging behaviors. Altering the physical arrangement of a classroom can prevent challenging behavior by changing parts of the classroom to promote the appropriate behavior that you want. When classrooms are created so that it is clear what an area is for and what you are supposed to do, it reduces the number of directions, commands, and demands that adults have to give to children. This can reduce power struggles, increase children's independence in daily routines, and increase opportunities to make positive comments about children's appropriate behavior.

Consider using this strategy when the PTR-YC assessment indicates the following.

- Challenging behavior occurs in a particular area of the classroom.

- Challenging behavior occurs in the presence of particular materials.

- Challenging behavior occurs during a particular activity.

- Challenging behavior occurs with a particular peer or adult.

- Challenging behavior involves power struggles.

- Challenging behavior occurs when told "no" or given a direction.

- Children require a lot of direction about daily routines and transitions.

Steps for Implementation

1. Identify activities and routines in the classroom that are associated with a child's challenging behaviors. This information should be derived from the functional behavioral assessment. Determine if there are physical elements in the classroom setting associated with those activities that might contribute to the challenging behaviors.

2. If there are physical arrangements that can be modified to facilitate desired behavior change, then make the modifications.

Strategy ideas: There are many possibilities for adjusting the physical arrangement of the classroom. How your team chooses to implement this strategy will depend on your classroom space and what resources you have available. Teams are encouraged to be creative and ensure these choices fit the function of the behavior and fit within classroom routines and activities.

Special Considerations

Consider the following when altering the physical classroom arrangement for children who may have differing needs or when special circumstances are present.

- If the child has any physical impairments or delays in gross motor skills, then the physical arrangement of the classroom will need to be considered based on any needs for the child. If the child uses a wheelchair, a walker, crutches, or any other device to help the child physically move around, then it is crucial to make sure there is enough space for the child to navigate through the classroom as independently as possible.

- If the child has a visual and/or hearing impairment, then it may be necessary to make accommodations based on those specific needs.

Implementation Considerations

Make sure of the following when implementing this strategy.

- The physical arrangement of the classroom does not violate any regulations or licensing requirements.

- Teachers are flexible with their physical classroom arrangements. What works one year with one group of children may not be as effective the next year with a different group of children.

- The room is arranged so that adults can see all areas of the classroom from any part of the room.

Supporting Evidence

Duda, Dunlap, Fox, Lentini, & Clarke (2004)
Krantz & Risley (1977)
Ratcliff (2001)
Rosenkoetter & Fowler (1986)
Sainato (1990)
Sandall & Schwartz (2008)

REMOVE TRIGGERS FOR CHALLENGING BEHAVIORS

Strategy: Remove triggers for challenging behaviors.

Description of strategy: This strategy involves removing or avoiding something or someone that serves as an immediate trigger for a child's challenging behavior to prevent the challenging behavior from occurring. If a specific activity, item, request, or person serves as an immediate trigger to challenging behavior, then the strategy involves removing it so that it no longer serves as a trigger. This is a common and effective strategy, but it depends on an accurate process of functional behavioral assessment in order to identify the specific trigger. Also, removing a trigger is effective as a short-term procedure and must be accompanied by appropriate teach and reinforce strategies to produce long-term benefits and generalization.

Rationale for using strategy: Removing triggers is a well-established procedure that is based on a major principle of learning known as stimulus control. For our purposes, stimulus control means that behavior (including challenging behavior) is influenced by antecedent (and contextual) events. If we change the antecedent stimuli, then we can change the child's behavior.

Also, when we remove triggers, we open up opportunities to help the child learn crucial social and problem-solving skills. Therefore, it is important to remember that the removal of triggers is almost always a temporary measure that can be implemented only when we have enough control to make sure that the trigger does not occur. In most cases, however, it is likely that the trigger will occur in other settings and in the future. Therefore, it is important to be sure that the child has opportunities to learn how to more effectively handle the triggers.

Consider using this strategy when the PTR-YC assessment indicates the following.

- Challenging behavior occurs around specific peers or adults on a consistent basis.

- Challenging behavior occurs when starting or during a particular activity on a consistent basis.

- Challenging behavior occurs when a particular activity ends or is signaled to end.

- Challenging behavior occurs when a particular word or phrase is said to the child (e.g., told "no," asked to do something).

- Challenging behavior occurs when the child makes a transition to a particular activity or area.

- Challenging behavior occurs when given a direction.

Steps for Implementation

1. Identify the triggers for challenging behavior. The triggers should be identified during the process of functional behavioral assessment and by specifically using the PTR-YC Functional Behavioral Assessment Checklist: Prevent and through the discussion during the assessment meeting.

2. Determine whether the trigger can be removed for the focus child. Sometimes the trigger (e.g., a specific activity, the presence of a specific peer) can be removed from the child's curriculum or immediate presence. At other times, however, removal of the trigger could involve too much of an accommodation. If this is the case, then perhaps the impact of the trigger might be ameliorated by using another strategy such as choice making or embedding.

3. Determine exactly when and how the trigger will be removed and what instruction, activity, item, or peer might need to serve as a replacement.

Strategy ideas: Listed next is a sample of ideas that can be utilized as ways to eliminate immediate triggers for challenging behaviors; there are many more. This list is intended to illustrate some options of how and when to integrate this strategy. How your team chooses to implement this strategy will depend on the specific triggers for the child and your ability to eliminate the triggers. Teams are encouraged to be creative and ensure these choices fit the function of the behavior and fit within classroom routines and activities.

Arrival

- Mary, the classroom assistant, typically triggers challenging behavior when she greets Joe. Because the initial transition is difficult for Joe, the team decided the lead teacher would greet Joe and transition him into the classroom. Once Joe has made the transition and is engaged in a preferred activity, Mary can sit with Joe while he is engaged in something he enjoys.

Nap/rest time

- If challenging behavior occurs with particular children when they are near each other at naptime, then strategically place children away from each other during nap.

Toileting/diapering

- If the challenging behavior occurs when the teacher says, "Time for potty" or "Time for diaper change," then the phrase, which is the trigger, can be eliminated by using a picture or object to signal this activity. For example, the teacher may hand a picture of the bathroom to the child to take with him or her to the bathroom. This is most effective when the teacher hands the child the picture without saying anything. Objects can also be used, such as giving a child the wipes when it is time to change his or her diaper.

Special Considerations

Consider the following when eliminating immediate triggers for challenging behavior for children who may have differing needs or when special circumstances are present.

- Triggers may need to be eliminated for a longer time for children with significant needs in order to teach more appropriate behaviors.

- It is always important to use this strategy in conjunction with an effective teaching strategy to teach alternative behaviors.

Implementation Considerations

Make sure of the following when implementing these strategies.

- All adults who interact with the child on a regular basis are agreeable to eliminating the specific triggers that the team identifies for a defined period of time.

- A plan is in place for how to teach appropriate replacement skills when triggers are eliminated.

Supporting Evidence

Dunlap & Kern (1996)
Kern & Dunlap (1999)

Teach Interventions

The following describe common, evidence-based interventions that can be used in preschool classroom settings as strategies for the teach component of PTR-YC. They are intended for use with individual children who have challenging behaviors that are not being satisfactorily resolved with high-quality classroom practices. At least one teach intervention must be selected for behavior intervention plans. Teach interventions are strategies that involve instruction and building new skills for the child. It is expected that the results of teach strategies will be of ongoing benefit for the child. A few things should be noted about teach interventions. First, teaching occurs best in the absence of challenging behaviors. Teach strategies are not responses to challenging behaviors. Rather, they should serve to reduce the need for the child to engage in challenging behaviors because they increase the child's ability to manage his or her environment without having to rely on challenging behaviors. Second, most teach strategies are most effective if they are implemented in the natural context in which the child's new behaviors are to be demonstrated. That is, the instruction should occur in the context of ongoing activities and routines. Finally, practice is a critical part of effective instruction. Therefore, it is important to plan for as many opportunities for instruction (and practice) to occur throughout the day as possible.

TEACH COMMUNICATION SKILLS (FUNCTIONAL COMMUNICATION TRAINING)

Strategy: Teaching communication skills to replace challenging behavior is known as a functional communication training (FCT) strategy.

Description of strategy: This is the most common and most effective of all the teach strategies in PTR-YC. It is supported by a great deal of research, and it is a strategy that can help children in the short term as well as longitudinally. FCT can be extremely effective if it is carefully and consistently used.

FCT involves 1) identifying the function or purpose of a child's challenging behavior and 2) teaching the child a more appropriate, communicative behavior that serves the same purpose or function. The more appropriate communicative behavior is referred to as the replacement behavior. The idea behind FCT is to get the child to use the replacement behavior instead of the challenging behavior. The replacement behavior must be at least as effective for the child as the challenging behavior in terms of getting what the child wants. For example, if a child has been observed to hit other children in order to get access to a desired toy, then we may want to teach the child to use a more desirable communicative method to ask the other children for a turn with the toy.

The method of communication to be selected as a replacement behavior must be something that the child can already use or something that can be taught very easily, and it must be something that will be noticed by anybody who will be expected to respond. The communicative method can be speech, pictures, gestures, sign language, technology-aided communication output, or a combination of these methods. Remember that the goal of FCT is not necessarily to teach a child a new method of communication; instead, it is to teach the child to use a more appropriate method of communication as a replacement for challenging behavior.

Rationale for using strategy: When children engage in challenging behavior instead of using appropriate communication skills, it is usually because children do not know how and, therefore, they need to be directly taught how to use a more appropriate method of communication. These children have learned that challenging behavior works for them. So, to get rid of the challenging behavior, they need to learn that appropriate communication works and, in fact, that it works better. Therefore, a vital part of this teaching strategy is to allow the child opportunities to either get what he or she wants or to avoid something that the child does not want when using the replacement behavior. If a child's communication is not honored (listened to), then the child will stop doing it.

Consider using this strategy when the PTR-YC assessment indicates the following.

- Challenging behavior occurs when the child is avoiding a particular task or activity.

- Challenging behavior occurs when the child is refusing a particular task or activity.

- Challenging behavior occurs during a particular activity.

- Challenging behavior occurs when making a transition to a nonpreferred activity.

- Challenging behavior occurs during a nonpreferred activity.

- Challenging behavior occurs when a preferred activity ends.

- Challenging behavior occurs when interacting with other children.

FCT should be considered for use whenever the functional behavioral assessment (FBA) has identified a clear function for the behavior and whenever the team can identify a communicative behavior that can serve as a replacement.

Steps for Implementation

1. Identify the function of the challenging behavior through the FBA process. What is the child trying to communicate? Remember that the function is usually to get something (e.g., a toy) or to get rid of something (e.g., a difficult request, too many demands, a required transition).

2. Identify an appropriate and desirable way for the child to communicate the same message in a more appropriate manner. Choose a skill that the child already has or that would be easy and quick for the child to learn, and make sure the skill (the replacement behavior) is one that will be conspicuous enough to be noticed when the child uses it.

3. Identify situations that typically result in the child using challenging behavior to communicate. These situations will be the context in which instruction will take place. Be sure and arrange for many of these situations to occur per day because the child will only learn through many good opportunities to practice. Be sure to have any materials ready that you may need.

4. Do your best to anticipate when the challenging behavior might occur, and then prompt the child to use the new communicative (replacement) behavior. When the child uses the replacement behavior, be sure to honor the child's request.

5. Create and plan for multiple opportunities to practice this new skill throughout the day, and be sure that every time the child uses the new skill that the new skill "works" for the child.

6. If the communication skill is with a peer, then it is important for an adult to facilitate these interactions and communications until the child can do it independently on a regular basis.

7. As the child learns to use the replacement behavior instead of challenging behavior, gradually remove the amount of assistance (prompting) so that the child uses the behavior on his or her own. But be careful not to remove the assistance too rapidly.

Strategy examples: The following are some examples of ways that FCT can be used.

Outside: Zoe at the water table

Zoe was observed to engage in challenging behaviors, and the FBA revealed that the problems often occurred at the water table. The water table was popular with the children, so it was often crowded. Zoe would typically run up to the table and push children out of the way, sometimes hitting the other children so she could play with the water. The function was clearly to gain access to the water table. The team decided to teach Zoe to ask, "Can I play?" or to say, "My turn." Because the teachers were implementing a behavior intervention plan for Zoe, they were willing to take extra measures to have the water table available and to teach Zoe how to more effectively communicate to play with the water. Part of the planning was to prepare the other children to cooperate with Zoe's instruction. During the FCT intervention, when Zoe approached the table, the teacher would tell Zoe, "If you want to play in the water, say 'My turn.'" The teacher was ready to use more than one prompt, if necessary. Zoe was allowed to enter the table area at an open spot when she used the replacement behavior. She was praised for saying "My turn" and encouraged to play. The teacher stayed at the table to continue to facilitate appropriate communication and to ensure that the interactions during this activity were positive and successful. The idea was to get Zoe to use the replacement behavior before she engaged in challenging behavior. As Zoe became successful with the use of "my turn," she was gradually taught other ways to communicate her wants and also how to be respectful of other children's play activities.

Inside: Kai in Small Group

Kai was a boy who typically moved around from activity to activity and did not spend much time engaged in any activity. His teachers tried to get him to stay longer by redirecting him back to the materials after he left. Kai would scream, drop to the floor while continuing to scream, and kick his legs and flail his arms around (tantrum). It eventually became too difficult to try to get him to get up off the ground, so the teacher would walk away and Kai would eventually calm down, get up, and move on to another activity. The function of Kai's tantrums was determined to be escape from the activity that he completed. Although a long-term goal was to get Kai engaged in small-group activities for longer periods of time, the immediate objective was to reduce the tantrums and get Kai to use sign language to say ALL DONE when he is finished with an activity. The teachers in the classroom learned the sign for ALL DONE and prepared to work with Kai during small-group time to teach this new skill. While this skill was being taught, a teacher was always within arm's reach of Kai during small-group activities. When it was apparent that Kai was ready to leave or as he was actually beginning to leave, the teacher prompted Kai to sign ALL DONE by modeling it, saying "all done," and using hand-over-hand prompting for him to sign ALL DONE. He was permitted to move on to the next activity once he signed (either on his own or with prompts), and there was another teacher (or aide) near him at the next activity, ready to follow the same procedure. This was done throughout the small-group time until Kai was able to independently sign ALL DONE.

Special Considerations

Consider the following when teaching communication skills to children who may have differing needs or when special circumstances are present.

- Find a method of communication that is easy for the child who has limited or restricted verbal skills.

- Find a method of communication that is feasible and practical for the child who has physical limitations.

- A child with cognitive delays or who has difficulty learning new skills may need many opportunities to practice the skill before progress is demonstrated, and he or she may need individual opportunities to practice the skill.

Implementation Considerations

Make sure of the following when implementing these strategies.

- The communication method chosen is simple and easy for the child to use.

- The child is only required to say what is necessary to communicate the message. When first teaching this skill, do not require appropriate grammar, full sentences, or pleasantries (e.g., please, thank you). Allow the child the easiest way to communicate his or her message when first teaching communication skills.

- The communication (replacement behavior) must work for the child every time (the child gets what he or she wants or avoids something he or she does not want).

- If materials are needed (e.g., pictures, devices), then they need to always be available and accessible to the child and everyone needs to know how to appropriately respond.

- If using sign language or gestures, then everyone who interacts with the child (e.g., peers, adults) needs to know what the sign language or gesture looks like for the child and how to respond to it.

- Create multiple opportunities for the child to practice the new communication and plan for times when the child will work on that skill.

Supporting Evidence

Carr & Durand (1985)
Carr et al. (1994)
Dunlap, Ester, Langhans, & Fox (2006)
Dunlap & Fox (1999)
Durand (1990)
Neilsen, Olive, Donovan, & McEvoy (1998)
Reeve & Carr (2000)

EMBED MULTIPLE INSTRUCTIONAL OPPORTUNITIES

Strategy: Embed multiple instructional opportunities throughout or across routines or activities.

Description of strategy: This teaching strategy involves creating multiple planned instructional opportunities throughout the day that are embedded within a variety of routines or activities or multiple planned instructional opportunities embedded throughout a particular routine or activity. For example, if you are targeting a communication skill of asking for a turn, then instead of targeting one routine or time of day to work on teaching that skill (e.g., during center time at the block center that is typically problematic), you would plan for and create ways to work on asking for a turn within large-group time, small-group time, the art center, outside, and so forth. In other words, you would plan for and create as many opportunities to target that skill during established classroom routines and activities in order to provide multiple functional and practical opportunities for the child to demonstrate asking for a turn. Multiple instructional opportunities can also be embedded throughout one routine or activity.

Note: This is a strategy that should be used in conjunction with other teaching strategies and, in general, as an approach for effective instruction of any key skill the child needs to learn. By embedding instruction throughout the day in activities in which the skill should be practiced, there is a greater likelihood that the behavior will become a generalized skill that the child will use in multiple circumstances.

Rationale for using strategy: If we want to become fluent or extremely skilled at anything, such as learning a new sport, language, or hobby, we typically spend many hours and targeted learning opportunities in order to obtain the necessary skills. Once we learn the skills and become confident and competent with those skills, we engage in targeted practice in order for those skills to become routine or automatic. Children also need targeted learning opportunities to obtain the necessary skills. When children are provided with many targeted learning opportunities in a variety of contexts, and they have opportunities to engage in this targeted practice multiple times each day, there is a higher likelihood that the child will become competent with that skill much sooner.

Consider using this strategy when the PTR-YC assessment indicates the following.

- Challenging behavior occurs across multiple activities.

- Challenging behavior occurs with multiple children/adults.

- Challenging behavior occurs during multiple circumstances.

Steps for Implementation

1. Identify the skill that you want to teach during goal setting.

2. Identify the steps in order to teach the skill. Include enough necessary steps and detail so that anyone who implements the strategy can easily do so.

3. Identify what natural routines or activities can be used to target that skill.

4. Identify how the skill will be embedded into each routine or activity (you may want to use a behavior matrix to organize this information).

Strategy examples: The following are examples that can be utilized as ways to embed multiple instructional opportunities throughout or across routines or activities.

Embed multiple instructional opportunities throughout a routine/activity

Carson is a boy with limited verbal skills, and the team wants to target having him ask for things by putting his hand out, palm up, when he wants something instead of grabbing items out of others' hands. Carson really enjoys art, so the teacher has all of the materials needed for the activity at the art table. Carson is prompted to put his hand out to ask for materials that he needs, and he has multiple opportunities to ask for materials because the activity includes the use of scissors, glue, markers, crayons, and other items. When a peer has something that Carson wants, the teacher is able to prompt Carson to put his hand out to his peer, and the teacher also makes sure the peer understands what Carson is saying and prompts the peer to give the item to Carson. The teacher also facilitates having the peer put her hand out to Carson to ask him for items as well, and Carson is able to practice asking for items appropriately with adults and peers multiple times during an activity that he enjoys.

Embed multiple instructional opportunities across routines/activities

Taylor is a girl who has difficulty taking turns and will often push, scratch, scream, and hit others when she wants a turn and has to wait. Taylor's team wants her to be able to wait her turn without getting so upset and hurting others. The team wrote out the steps for how they were going to teach Taylor how to wait her turn and decided on which routines and activities they could use to target this skill. They decided that they could target turn-taking during arrival, large group, center/free play, snack, and lunch. The team created a behavior matrix and a simple progress monitoring sheet. The teachers decided who would take the lead to facilitate turn-taking during each of the activities each day and made sure that they were prepared for each of these instructional opportunities.

Special Considerations

Consider the following when embedding multiple instructional opportunities for children who may have differing needs or when special circumstances are present.

*   A child who has intellectual disabilities or delays or has difficulty learning new skills may require a lot of prompting for a longer period of time in order to be successful.

Implementation Considerations

Make sure of the following when implementing these strategies.

*   The plan for how this strategy will be implemented includes who will work with the child and when that will occur, as well as appropriate training and coaching.

*   If materials are needed, then they need to be ready and available for any and all areas in which the instruction will be targeted

Supporting Evidence

Pretti-Frontczak & Bricker (2004)
Sandall & Schwartz (2008)

PEER-RELATED SOCIAL SKILLS

Strategy: Directly teaching skills that help a child effectively interact with peers, including sharing, following another's lead, and entering play.

Description of strategy: This strategy involves purposefully teaching children skills for effectively and positively interacting with peers. The strategy is related to the classroom practice (see Chapter 6) of directly teaching social skills, but here we are referring to instruction that is focused on the child who exhibits challenging behaviors. It is understood that teaching social skills is an endeavor that requires the involvement of more than one child, so this individualized strategy is basically an extension of the classroom practice previously described. We recommend that peer-related social skills instruction be provided for the full class and, if the team decides, additional emphasis and instructional precision can be provided for the child with challenging behavior.

The FBA should be used for identifying the context in which challenging behaviors occur. If the context involves peer interaction, then social skill instruction is usually recommended. The team can determine what specific social skills are to be targeted, including sharing, requesting, sustaining an interaction, initiating an interaction, and tolerating a peer's misbehavior.

Rationale for strategy: All children must learn to interact with peers. Peer social interactions are an important basis for virtually all development, and they are crucial in determining the success that a child will experience throughout the child's childhood, adolescence, and adulthood. They are the essential foundation for the establishment of friendships and all other types of relationships. In addition, social skills are key to the presence or absence of challenging behaviors. Social skills are instrumental for children in getting their needs met, and if a child can meet his or her needs through the use of good social skills, then there may be little need for challenging behaviors.

Steps for Implementation

Teaching a social skill in the context of a group setting is highly recommended. It is important to teach how to respond to peers and how to initiate. The specific social skill being targeted needs to be specified. It often is necessary to include individualized instruction and assistance for a child who may need extra support (the child with challenging behaviors).

Instruction can be provided in many ways as long as the process is systematic and well planned. A teaching process or methodology could look like the following.

1. Explain the skill and rationale—tell why this skill is important.

2. Have a visual that demonstrates and labels the skill (e.g., have the word *sharing* with a picture of children sharing a toy).

3. Demonstrate the right way—model how the skill is supposed to look.

4. Practice the skill—teacher and child, peer to peer.

5. Demonstrate the wrong way—let children tell you what you did wrong and what you are supposed to do.

6. Review the skill and the right way.

7. Set up opportunities for all children to practice.

8. Set up specific structured opportunities for the child who needs more practice and more assistance to be successful.

Then, in this context, provide additional assistance (e.g., verbal, gestural, or physical prompts) for the child with challenging behaviors.

Consider using this strategy when the PTR-YC assessment indicates the following.

- Challenging behavior occurs when sharing is necessary.

- Challenging behavior occurs when taking turns.

- Challenging behavior occurs when beginning interactions with peers/adults.

- Challenging behavior occurs when responding to or answering peers/adults.

- Challenging behavior occurs when engaging in interactions.

- Challenging behavior occurs when playing with toys and materials with peers.

- Child has difficulty establishing and maintaining relationships with peers/adults.

Strategy ideas: The following are a sample of ideas that can be utilized as ways to teach social skills and embed opportunities to practice these skills.

Large group
Plan to teach social skills as part of your daily routine during circle time. Have a visual to support the social skill (e.g., have the word *sharing* with a picture of children sharing a toy). Practice the skill through role-playing; the use of puppets is a great tool for teaching social skills. If the child with challenging behaviors is having a hard time attending to the lesson, then you may use puppets that are particularly interesting to him or her. You may also practice sharing materials that are motivating for him or her (e.g., trains, dolls). It is also helpful to involve the child in modeling and practicing the new skill during large group.

Free play
Teaching a social skill during free play involves planning. You should have visuals posted that show the skill being targeted where children can see them. Pick one area of free play and set up an activity that will require children to share. The teacher needs to be able to facilitate this activity, so start small with a planned and targeted activity. Teach children how to follow the steps involved in the skill and practice those steps in that activity. For example, a game table can be set up as a center during free play. Children would need to practice turn-taking to participate in this activity. If the teacher wanted a child to practice turn-taking, then he or she might put the game "Don't Break the Ice" in the game center because the teacher knows the child loves that game. Practice turn-taking using visual supports when the focus child comes to play. This strategy needs to be intentionally created and planned.

Small group
Directly teach a social skill lesson at small-group time. Prepare a lesson plan and set up the small-group activity to support the lesson and provide opportunities for practice. For example, if the social skill lesson is sharing, then the small-group activity would involve planning to ensure the children need to share. If a child needs extra assistance with sharing, then the activity will be set up using materials that are especially motivating. If the child likes outer space, then make spaceships and use materials he or she likes that need to be shared. Teachers need to be ready to provide support and visuals that remind all children how to share.

Special Considerations

Consider the following when teaching peer-related social skills such as sharing, taking turns, entering play, and following another's lead for children who may have differing needs or when special circumstances are present.

- Steps may need to be broken up into smaller pieces for a child who has cognitive delays or difficulty learning new skills, and the steps may need to be taught and practiced more often (provide multiple opportunities for instruction). For example, getting your friend's attention may start with responding instead of initiating, with many more planned opportunities for practice.

- Set up opportunities to practice the skill that are more likely to be successful. Marcus may be more willing to begin sharing when it involves a marker rather than his favorite truck.

- Social skills may need to be taught on a one-to-one basis in brief teaching episodes when a child has a vision or hearing impairment, processing delays, or other developmental delays, with opportunities to practice this skill in the classroom or setting. Visuals and gestures may be needed to prompt the use of a new social skill.

- Extra reinforcement may be needed for a specific child when teaching a new social skill, especially if the child is not initially motivated to use the new skill. For example, when Sophie grabs a toy from a peer, she typically gets the toy. Therefore, to ask for a toy and wait for a response may require extra reinforcement for this child, such as verbal praise, a high-five, or tangibles.

- Teaching social skills to the entire class and modifying this lesson for individual students who need extra supports and extra practice has a greater success than just simply teaching a new social skill to one child in isolation from the rest of the classroom or setting. Whenever possible, teachers should consider group instruction with specific modifications for individual children.

- Do not attempt to provide social skills training when the child is engaging in challenging behavior. Redirection can be used, but effective instruction occurs when challenging behavior is absent.

Implementation Considerations

Make sure of the following when implementing these strategies.

- Many opportunities are planned for children to practice the skill, and extra practice times are planned for the child who needs more support.

- The new skill is directly taught and modeled by all adults in the classroom or setting.

- Children are recognized for using their new skill (e.g., "Wow. Sarah shared her blocks with Tim. What a nice friend"). You can also comment about Tim's responding (e.g., "And Tim, you answered Sarah when she said your name. Look at her smile").

- More attention is given to children who are using their new skill.

- Children who need to learn this skill and do not yet have mastery need to have many opportunities for practice and success.

Supporting Evidence

Brown, McEvoy, & Bishop (1991)
Brown & Odom (1995)

Kohler & Strain (1999)
Strain (2001)
Strain & Danko (1995)
Strain & Kohler (1998)
Strain & Schwartz (2001)

SELF-MONITORING

Strategy: Teaching children to self-monitor their behavior.

Description of strategy: Self-monitoring is a strategy involving teaching the child to observe his or her own behavior. It may also involve having the child record the behavior using a checklist or counter. Self-monitoring is established by teaching the child to make indications about when the behavior occurs and then having adults provide rewards for changes in the designated behavior as well as for successful self-monitoring. Research has shown that when children observe their own behavior, the behavior tends to improve. The strategy is usually most effective with and most appropriate for young children who are 4 or 5 years of age; although some self-monitoring procedures have been used with younger children. The procedures have also been used with children with moderate and severe disabilities; however, applying self-monitoring strategies with these children usually requires considerable care and precision.

Rationale for strategy: Children show awareness of their behavior when they are able to observe it, talk about it, and record whether it occurs. This awareness can be an important step toward behavior change and self-control. The more self-control a child demonstrates, the greater the likelihood of maintenance and generalization of the behavior change. Research has shown that self-monitoring can lead to improvements in speech, on-task responding, and academic and preacademic performance.

Consider using this strategy when the PTR-YC assessment indicates the following.

- There is a need to increase specific desirable behaviors.

- The child is capable of demonstrating awareness of his or her behaviors.

- Self-control is an important objective.

Steps for Implementation

The best methods for teaching a child to use self-monitoring will vary, depending on the child's level of functioning and the nature of the behavior. Behaviors that are easier to observe will generally be easier to monitor. The recommended steps for teaching a child to use self-monitoring are as follows.

1. Carefully define the target behavior. The target behavior can be almost any behavior that is important for the child and that is clearly observable. The behavior should always be a desirable behavior that you want to increase. For example, self-monitoring has been used to increase behaviors such as wearing glasses, staying in a chair, and using an indoor voice. It is important to define the behavior in terms that cause no misunderstandings for the teachers or for the child.

2. Identify effective rewards. The child will have to receive effective rewards for engaging in accurate self-monitoring and for desired changes in the target behavior in order for self-monitoring to work. Rewards can be almost anything that the child desires (e.g., praise, stickers, special snacks), but they must be effective for the individual child. Reinforcement will need to frequently occur in the initial stages, but can be reduced as the child gains fluency with the procedures and as the behavior demonstrates improvement.

3. Determine the period during which the child will use the self-monitoring strategy. This will depend on the target behavior and when the target behavior is expected to occur. For instance, wearing glasses is a target behavior that may be important for the full day, but staying in the child's seat may be important for only 5 or 10 minutes at a time.

4. Determine how the child will observe and monitor the behavior. Consider how the child will indicate whether the behavior occurred. At first, this indication may be as a response to a teacher's question such as, "Are you wearing your glasses?" or "Are you sitting in your seat?" But then, when the child can respond accurately, the child should record the correct answer with a simple device such as a yes/no checklist or a counter or sticker chart. This will depend on the child's level and preference.

5. Teach the child to self-monitor and to use the self-monitoring device. Instruction will require a good amount of teacher involvement in the beginning. The child will need to be prompted to correctly answer, and it may be important to demonstrate examples and nonexamples of the target behavior. When the child correctly answers almost all of the time, then it is time to introduce the recording device and teach the child to record his or her answers on the device. The child should be enthusiastically rewarded for doing this successfully.

6. Gradually reduce the amount of teacher assistance. The goal is for the child to successfully and independently use the self-monitoring device so that the amount of teacher assistance is reduced (faded). But this should not occur too rapidly. Also, it is important to continue to provide reinforcement for both accurate self-monitoring and for desired improvements in the target behavior.

Special Considerations

Consider the following when teaching self-management skills for children who may have differing needs or when special circumstances are present.

*   Self-monitoring instruction may need to be broken into smaller steps, practiced more often, and reinforced more frequently when a child has cognitive delays or has difficulty learning new skills.

*   Teaching periods should be as frequent as possible (and reasonable).

*   Materials should be customized to the child's level and to incorporate the child's abilities and interests.

*   Celebrate all efforts the child makes toward success at self-monitoring.

Implementation Considerations

Make sure of the following when implementing these strategies.

*   All materials that will be needed are complete and accessible.

*   There is short, direct teaching time planned.

*   The child is recognized and rewarded for efforts and progress related to self-monitoring and improvement in the target behavior.

Supporting Evidence

Connell, Carta, Lutz, & Randall (1993)
Dunlap, Dunlap, Koegel, & Koegel (1991)

Koegel, Koegel, Boettcher, Harrower, & Openden (2006)
Sainato, Strain, Lefebvre, & Repp (1990)

TOLERATE DELAY OF REINFORCEMENT

Strategy: Directly teaching skills that help a child to wait by handling delays in reinforcement.

Description of strategy: This strategy involves purposefully teaching a child how to wait for reinforcement or gratification. Timers and other methods of counting down wait time are often used to assist in teaching how to wait for reinforcement. Initial wait times may be rather short and are then gradually extended as the child becomes more successful with waiting.

Teaching a child how to wait and tolerate delay will require knowledge of the child's current ability to wait. For example, a child who exhibits no current ability to wait may need to start with a wait time of less than 1 minute or even just a few seconds. This strategy needs to be specific to meet the child's current abilities. Refer back to the PTR-YC assessment to determine specific wait times with which to begin. If you feel you do not have enough information to decide, then plan for another observation to gather this specific information.

Rationale for strategy: Waiting and tolerating delay are embedded parts of everyone's day; everyone must learn how to tolerate waiting. Although waiting can be difficult for all of us from time to time, some children consistently exhibit challenging behavior when waiting and delayed gratification is necessary. Direct teaching of how to successfully wait can help children increase their ability to participate in activities, make and sustain friendships, follow schedules and routines, and control anger and impulses.

Consider using this strategy when the PTR-YC assessment indicates the following.

- Being told to wait is a trigger to challenging behavior.

- Child has difficulty waiting for a turn.

- Anger and impulse control are difficult for the child.

- Challenging behavior occurs when teacher is giving attention to others.

- Challenging behavior occurs when the child needs to wait.

Steps for Implementation

Teaching children to tolerate waiting or delays can be taught in large-group instruction. However, for individual children who exhibit challenging behavior related to waiting and delays, additional individual support is often needed. Effectively teaching a child to wait involves systematically planning opportunities and directly teaching waiting when the child can be supported; adults need to be ready and available to assist.

There are multiple ways to provide instruction. The most important teaching components with this strategy are beginning with a wait time that is achievable for the child, structuring the wait time to allow a visual countdown of the wait time remaining, positive praise, and immediate access when the wait time has ended. A teaching process or methodology could look like the following.

1. Discuss with the child that waiting can be difficult and yet sometimes we need to wait. Use specific situations that relate to the child's experience (e.g., sometimes we need to wait for our turn in blocks, and that can be hard).

2. Develop a planned visual sequence for waiting. Use a timer or sand timer to display how much wait time is left.

3. Directly teach the child about the timer to help him or her wait by showing how the timer works (e.g., it will be your turn when all the sand runs out, it will be your turn when all the red disappears from the timer).

4. Practice waiting and using the timer with the child.

5. Set up specific structured opportunities for the child to practice using the timer and waiting.

6. Be sure to comment and give specific praise when the child is patiently waiting.

7. The duration of the wait time should be gradually extended when the child has learned how to be successful waiting with the initial wait time.

Strategy ideas: The following are examples that illustrate situations in which teaching a child to wait or delay gratification is beneficial.

Free play/taking turns

Set up a center that is designed for taking turns (e.g., a game table). The game at this table should be one that the child is interested in (you will need to know the child's interests). For example, José is a boy who enjoys activities that involve physical activity. His teacher decided to incorporate the game "Don't Break the Ice" in which children get to take turns hammering out one chunk of ice at a time as a center at free play. José was excited about this game and would choose a peer to take turns with at this center. A visual turn-taking schedule was created with the children's pictures in a sequential order with a moveable arrow. The teacher initially moved this arrow so that it pointed at the child's picture when it was his or her turn. José soon requested to move the arrow himself so he could keep track of everyone's turn.

Small group/art activity

Small-group activities may naturally include wait time or delayed gratification, which can be great times to practice waiting or delay. However, with this teaching strategy, we want to be purposeful and systematic in specifically planning teaching opportunities. It is simple to limit the amount of markers in art activities so children need to ask, wait, and share. If Kara is not interested in markers, however, then this teaching opportunity will be less successful. Instead, the teacher may limit the glitter (which Kara is very interested in) and only place one container of glitter at the table and help Kara use a timer to wait for her turn with the glitter.

Individual

Seth was taught with FCT to raise his hand when he wanted his teacher's attention. The teacher initially responded immediately whenever Seth raised his hand and, as a result, the tantrums he used to throw when he wanted attention declined to zero. Seth's teacher, however, realized after a week or so that she could not continue to immediately respond to Seth raising his hand because she had other ongoing responsibilities. She devoted three individual sessions to teach Seth how to watch a kitchen timer to know when he would get what he wanted. She started with small treats that she would give to Seth when the bell dinged. She initially used durations of 5 seconds and then 10 seconds until he was able to wait nicely for 2 and then 5 minutes. When Seth had learned the purpose of the timer, she began to use it when Seth raised his hand for her attention. She initially used short intervals of 1 minute and then was able to extend it to 5 and then 10 minutes. When the bell sounded, Seth's teacher would always hustle to make sure that Seth received the attention he had been waiting for. His new ability to tolerate the delay helped him control his behavior in a more mature manner, and it helped his teacher be able to manage her classroom without having to drop everything whenever Seth raised his hand.

Special Considerations

Consider the following when teaching to wait for reinforcement or delay gratification for children who may have differing needs or when special circumstances are present.

- Initial wait times may be very short and more encouragement and praise may be necessary when a child has cognitive delays or has difficulty learning new skills.

- Consider setting up opportunities to practice the skill that are more likely to be successful with a clear end to the wait time, such as using timers and counting down remaining wait time.

- The team must be sure to use a countdown method that will fit the child's learning needs when he or she has a vision or hearing impairment, processing delays, or other developmental delays.

- Extra reinforcement may be needed for a specific child when teaching waiting that would be specific to what the child really likes.

- Wait times need to be structured so the child can see a clear beginning and end to the delay.

- Children should be set up to be successful, and wait times may be short at first.

Implementation Considerations

Make sure of the following when implementing these strategies.

- Opportunities to teach this skill need to be planned and systematic. Although opportunities to wait may be naturally occurring, this strategy requires planned wait times.

- Adults need to be sure they are available to assist the child with wait time when teaching this skill. Plan opportunities when the additional support is available.

- Be sure to comment and praise on all attempts to patiently wait, giving greater attention to the child when he or she is waiting.

- Children who need to learn this skill and do not yet have mastery need to have success and many successful opportunities.

Supporting Evidence

Carr et al. (1994)
Halle, Bambara, & Reichle (2005)

TEACH INDEPENDENCE WITH VISUAL SCHEDULES

Strategy: Directly teaching the child to use schedules to increase independence.

Description of strategy: This strategy involves building on the classroom system to assist individual children in learning how to follow and use schedules. For example, a specific child may exhibit challenging behavior during the circle routine. Helping this child follow a visual schedule through that routine could involve defining each step of the activity (task analyze each step of the routine), creating a visual schedule that pictorially shows each step, and teaching the child how to remove each step as he or she progresses through the routine. This teach strategy focuses on teaching the child how to use visuals to follow schedules in either brief episodes (e.g., circle routine) or for extended periods. The visual schedules provide extra guidance for children who need additional support to understand and predict the sequence of events. Before implementing this strategy, review classroom practices and make sure general classroom practices are in place. Note that this strategy is similar to the prevent strategy of using visual supports, but this teach strategy involves instruction and a goal of producing independent responding.

Rationale for strategy: Directly teaching children how to follow schedules can help them to be more successful throughout their day. Some children will need to be taught how to follow and manage their daily schedule and may also need direct instruction regarding following a routine or sequence. Sometimes children learn this skill quickly, and other times we need to provide visuals, smaller steps, direct instruction, and additional support.

Steps for Implementation

Methods for teaching a child independence with visual schedules should vary depending on what skills the child currently has, what the next reasonable steps should be, and the child's individual strengths and learning styles. Most of this information can be gathered from the data already collected (e.g., goal sheet, assessment). If you feel as a team, however, that you do not know exactly where the child is at regarding current skills and strengths, we advise you to spend more time observing and gathering that specific information. This will be necessary in guiding the teaching process. A teaching process or methodology could look like the following.

1. Identify the child's current level of skill and learning style. It is helpful to have some knowledge of the child's interests as well.

   - For example, Liam consistently exhibits challenging behavior during circle time. Liam will sit for the first 2 minutes, during opening song that usually involves song props. Then he will get up and run to the blocks and begin playing with toys in that area. Current skill level: Liam sits for 2 minutes; learning style: visual and kinesthetic (hands on); interests: blocks.

2. Identify the skill that will be taught to help the child self-manage.

   - The team decided to teach Liam the routine of circle time using a visual schedule that had a picture of each circle activity attached by Velcro.

3. Introduce the strategy to the child and communicate the purpose of the strategy and how it will be used.

   - The teacher sat down with Liam 5 minutes before circle time and showed him the circle schedule. The teacher explained the purpose of the routine schedule and showed Liam how to remove each activity as it is completed. The teacher and Liam practiced using the schedule, taking off each activity and placing it in the "all done" pocket.

4. Facilitate use of the schedule initially, giving instructions related to how to use it.

   - Pull off the activity and put it in the "all done" pocket.

5. Be conscious to fade back support as soon as the child begins to demonstrate the skill.

   - Liam began to pull off the activities without being prompted, leading to independence in next the circle time routine.

6. Reinforce and celebrate each success.

   - The teacher would praise Liam for taking off every activity and being at circle time. That faded to Liam receiving attention and reinforcement after every other activity. That also faded to attention and reinforcement when Liam independently removed activities, and eventually attention and reinforcement for Liam being able to be independently present throughout the circle time routine.

Consider using this strategy when the PTR-YC assessment indicates the following.

- Challenging behavior occurs when making a transition between activities.
- Challenging behavior occurs during daily routines.
- Challenging behavior occurs when required to follow directions.
- Challenging behavior occurs when following daily schedule.
- Challenging behavior occurs around staying engaged in activities.
- Challenging behavior occurs when getting engaged in an activity.

Strategy ideas: The following are a sample of ideas that illustrate how to teach children to follow schedules, routines, and directions. Keep in mind these teaching strategies need to be set up to meet the child's current skill level and learning styles and should incorporate his or her interests whenever possible.

Arrival time
Jonas would cry and lay on the floor for up to 20 minutes at arrival time. Miss Krissy and the preschool team developed a picture routine schedule for arrival to help Jonas make a successful and independent transition. Miss Krissy showed the picture schedule to Jonas on Monday and talked with him about how to use the schedule. They practiced together, removing the pictures while explaining how to use it. Miss Krissy and Jonas discussed that they will begin using this schedule in the morning. The next morning, Miss Krissy greeted Jonas with the schedule they had practiced and began helping Jonas follow each piece of the routine. Every time Jonas made an effort to use the pictures, Miss Krissy gave behavior specific praise such as, "Jonas, you are doing so well using your pictures." Miss Krissy also reminded Jonas of what was next and when he will be done. As Jonas began to use the pictures, Miss Krissy backed off her assistance but continued to provide a lot of positive feedback. Miss Krissy knew Jonas loved insects and stickers from a previous assessment. Miss Krissy gave Jonas an insect sticker when he completed the arrival routine.

Free play
The teachers at Wagon Wheel preschool noticed that Terrance wandered throughout free play without appropriately engaging in any play activities. The teachers created a picture schedule to help structure free play for Terrance to improve engagement and develop independence. The team knew that Terrance liked to play at the water table. The picture schedule had a picture of the block area first, then a picture of the water table. The teacher reviewed this schedule with Terrance twice during the day prior to free play. The teacher showed Terrance that first he would play at blocks for 2 minutes; then he could play at the water table. The teacher also showed Terrance the sand timer and explained how it worked. The teacher reminded Terrance that they would be using the schedule at free play. When free play began, the teacher assisted Terrance in following the schedule and helped him engage in play at blocks for 2 minutes. Terrance used his schedule to make a transition to the water table after 2 minutes. The teacher provided feedback and positive praise when Terrance was on task and following his schedule.

Small group
Every art activity at small-group time had a visual support for all children that displayed the beginning, middle, and end of the steps for the art activity (i.e., color, cut, paste). Even with this general classroom support, Oliver still had consistently challenging behavior during these small-group activities and needed adult assistance the entire time. The team developed an individual schedule for Oliver with the steps to the art activity attached with Velcro on a file folder. The teacher practiced how to remove each step with Oliver and put it in the "all done"

folder when the step was complete. Oliver loved teacher attention, which he received a lot of when he exhibited challenging behavior. Therefore, the teacher purposefully gave Oliver a lot of attention, high fives, praise, commenting, and was enthusiastic when Oliver completed each step of the art project. The teacher would also redirect Oliver back to his visual schedule when he was off task and provide enthusiastic attention when Oliver was back on task.

Special Considerations

Consider the following when teaching independence with visual schedules for children who may have differing needs or when special circumstances are present.

- Steps may need to be broken up into smaller pieces, taught and practiced more often, and reinforced more frequently when a child has cognitive delays or has difficulty learning new skills.

- Teaching episodes should be short and positive experiences. Building on the child's interests can be important in creating positive experiences.

- Materials may need to be made and customized to incorporate the child's abilities and interests when he or she has a vision or hearing impairment, processing delays, is primarily a visual learner, or has other developmental delays.

- Celebrate all efforts the child makes toward the goal of self-management; every step is important.

- Remember to fade back assistance when the child is beginning to manage him- or herself, and have a fade back plan that involves continued support for the child yet allows for independent mastery of the skill.

Implementation Considerations

Make sure of the following when implementing these strategies.

- All materials that will be needed are complete and accessible.

- There is short, direct teaching time planned for teaching the new self-management skill.

- The new skill is directly taught and modeled by all adults in the classroom or setting.

- The child is recognized for efforts and progress related to the new self-management skill.

Supporting Evidence

Duda, Dunlap, Fox, Lentini, & Clarke (2004)
Quill (1997)
Sandall & Schwartz (2008)
Schmit, Alpers, Raschke, & Ryndak (2000)

Reinforce Interventions

The following describe common, evidence-based interventions that can be used in preschool classroom settings as strategies for the reinforce component of PTR-YC. They are intended for use with individual children who have challenging behaviors that are not being satisfactorily resolved with high-quality classroom practices. At least one reinforce intervention must be selected for behavior intervention plans; however, many behavior intervention plans include more than one reinforce intervention.

There are a few things that need to be emphasized about the use of reinforce interventions. First, we often use the term *reward* to mean positive reinforcer, and rewards (or positive reinforcers) are the consequences that produce the effect known as positive reinforcement. We use the term *reward* to mean the same thing as positive reinforcer or just reinforcer. Reinforcers are also referred to as maintaining consequences for both challenging and desirable behavior. Second, the definition of *positive reinforcement* means that the act of following a behavior with a reinforcer results in an increase in the behavior. The definition is based on its effect on behavior. So, sometimes what we think of as a reward (or reinforcer) might not actually be a reward for that particular child and that particular behavior. For example, sometimes attention serves as a reward, but sometimes it does not. It depends on the child, the behavior, and the circumstance. Sometimes an item that served as a reinforcer on one day (e.g., a graham cracker) will not serve as a reinforcer on the next day. A general and important rule is to make sure that what is being used as a reinforcer actually works to increase the behavior. If it does not work, then you should find a more effective item (or activity) to use as a reinforcer.

Third, it is a good idea for reinforcers to be as natural as possible. Praise is natural. Smiles and high fives are also natural, and if these are effective as reinforcers, that is great. But sometimes we need something extra, such as stickers, snack items, or a special activity. We need to use what works, even if it might seem a little artificial or going overboard. If the behavior is important to change, then a more powerful reinforcer might need to be used for a while—at least until the behavior starts to change. Then, when the change is well established, we can (and should!) gradually reduce the amount and type of reinforcers used. The behavior should become a natural part of what the child does, and the consequences should also become natural.

Finally, we want to emphasize that reinforcers should always be a major part of the classroom environment. As discussed in Chapter 6, one of the most important elements of a high-quality classroom environment is the use of a high ratio of positive to negative interactions. We strongly recommend a ratio of 5 positives to 1 negative for all children in the classroom, including (and especially) the child with challenging behaviors.

REINFORCE DESIRABLE BEHAVIOR

Strategy: Reinforce desirable behavior.

Description of strategy: This reinforce strategy involves specifically identifying a desirable behavior and using positive reinforcement to increase the behavior. The desirable behavior is almost always a social behavior in PTR-YC, which might include communication. The strategy is related to the teach strategy of teaching communication skills, but it is broader in the sense that the desirable behavior can be almost anything that the team decides is an important target and need not be a behavior that is functionally related to the child's challenging behavior.

Rationale for using strategy: It is important to increase behaviors that are considered to be desirable, and the use of positive reinforcement is the most direct and efficient approach.

Steps for Implementation

1. Carefully define the desirable behavior to be reinforced in such a way that it is measurable and that everybody does not question whether the behavior is present.

2. Identify effective reinforcers. It is essential that the reinforcers used will serve to increase the behavior if they are provided immediately following the desirable behavior. Reinforcers might be positive acknowledgment (e.g., praise) or they might need to be more powerful and tangible (e.g., special snacks, stickers).

3. Determine exactly how the reinforcers will be provided when the child engages in the desirable behavior. This might require planning to determine who will be available to deliver the reinforcers.

4. Be sure that a reinforcer immediately follows the desirable behavior every time the behavior occurs, at least initially. The team may decide to reduce the amount of reinforcement provided when the desirable behavior is increased to a satisfactory level, and they may decide to change the reinforcer so that it is as natural as possible. However, if the desirable behavior decreases again, then the previous amounts and type of reinforcement should be reinstated.

Supporting Evidence

Cooper, Heron, & Heward (1987)
Hester et al. (2004)
Kaiser & Rasminsky (2003)
Kern (2005)
Landy (2009)
Nunnelley (2002)

REINFORCE PHYSICALLY INCOMPATIBLE BEHAVIOR

Strategy: Reinforce physically incompatible behavior.

Description of strategy: This reinforce strategy involves specifically identifying a desirable behavior that is physically incompatible with the challenging behavior and then using positive reinforcement to increase the physically incompatible behavior. By *physically incompatible*, we simply mean a behavior that cannot be exhibited at the same time as the identified challenging behavior. For example, if a child's challenging behavior involves running around the classroom, then sitting quietly in a chair or on a designated carpet square is a physically incompatible behavior. If a child's challenging behavior is hitting peers, then using "quiet hands" and keeping hands to oneself would be a physically incompatible behavior. In all other respects, this strategy is the same as reinforce desirable behavior.

Rationale for using strategy: It is important to increase behaviors that are considered to be desirable, and using positive reinforcement is the most direct and efficient approach.

Steps for Implementation

1. Carefully define the desirable behavior to be reinforced in such a way that it is measurable and that everybody does not question whether the behavior is present.

2. Identify effective reinforcers. It is essential that the reinforcers will serve to increase the behavior if they are provided to the child immediately following the desirable behavior. Reinforcers might be positive acknowledgment (e.g., praise) or they might need to be more powerful and tangible (e.g., special snacks, stickers).

3. Determine exactly how the reinforcers will be provided when the child engages in the desirable behavior. This might require planning to determine who will be available to deliver the reinforcers.

4. Be sure that a reinforcer immediately follows the physically incompatible behavior every time the behavior occurs, at least initially. When the incompatible behavior is increased to a satisfactory level, and when the challenging behavior has decreased correspondingly, then the team may decide to reduce the amount of reinforcement provided, and they may decide to change the reinforcer so that it is as natural as possible. However, if the desirable behavior decreases again, then the previous amounts and type of reinforcement should be reinstated.

Supporting Evidence

Cooper, Heron, & Heward (1987)
Kern (2005)

REMOVE REINFORCEMENT FOR CHALLENGING BEHAVIOR

Strategy: Remove reinforcement for challenging behavior.

Description of strategy: This reinforce strategy involves identifying the maintaining consequence(s) (reinforcers) for a challenging behavior and then making adjustments so that the reinforcing consequences no longer follow the challenging behavior. This means discontinuing the connection between the challenging behavior and its consequence so that the challenging behavior no longer works for the child. This operation is technically known as extinction.

The effectiveness of this strategy generally depends on three factors: 1) the ability to accurately identify the maintaining consequences for challenging behavior, 2) the ability to prevent the maintaining consequences from following the challenging behavior during intervention, and 3) the ability to provide the child with a reasonable alternative way to obtain the consequence that had previously followed the challenging behavior.

Rationale for using strategy: The reason that a challenging behavior occurs is that it works for the child because it produces a reinforcing consequence. If the challenging behavior no longer works to produce the consequence, then the behavior should decrease. This is a well-known and well-established principle of behavior. In practice, however, it can sometimes be tricky to implement, especially if the maintaining consequence is difficult to control, such as when the maintaining consequence is attention from peers. If teams are creative and diligent, however, then the strategy can almost always be effective, particularly when the strategy is combined with other intervention practices.

Steps for Implementation

1. Identify the maintaining consequences (reinforcers) for the challenging behavior during the functional behavioral assessment process. Sometimes the maintaining consequences

have to be identified on a routine-by-routine or situation-by-situation basis because the same behavior can have different functions in different circumstances.

2. Determine how the maintaining consequences for the challenging behaviors can be removed or discontinued. This can be relatively straightforward if the reinforcers are under the direct control of the teacher (e.g., when the reinforcer is teacher attention, when the maintaining consequence is removal of a request), but it can also be complicated (e.g., when the reinforcer is peer attention or a toy relinquished by a peer). In those cases in which there might be complications, the team needs to figure out how to arrange things so that the challenging behavior no longer works to obtain the maintaining consequences. The teacher might need to intervene when peers are involved or enlist the peer to cooperate by not attending to the challenging behavior.

3. Determine how the child can gain access to the reinforcer (maintaining consequence) in an appropriate manner rather than via challenging behaviors. This can be arranged as simply as by providing the reinforcer to the child at times when the child is not exhibiting the challenging behavior, or providing the reinforcer for desirable behavior. The point is that when a child can obtain the desired reinforcer when he or she is not engaging in challenging behavior, then the child's motivation to engage in challenging behavior is reduced.

Important Considerations

- A common consideration when using this strategy is that the behavior may get worse before it gets better. Implementers are therefore often advised to be prepared for an initial burst of higher intensity challenging behavior. This temporary escalation need not occur, however, if the behavior intervention plan includes effective prevent strategies and a clear way for the child to use desirable behavior to gain access to the same reinforcer. With these additional strategies in place, the temporary burst should not take place.

- This strategy should always be used in combination with other PTR-YC strategies. Because this strategy involves removing reinforcers that had previously been available, it is especially important that the child have access to ample reinforcers for desirable behavior.

- In order to be effective, it is necessary to know exactly what item or event has been the reinforcer (reward) for the challenging behavior. Remember that the maintaining consequence could be that the child receives something when challenging behavior occurs (e.g., attention, physical contact, a toy) or it could be that the child avoids or gets rid of something (e.g., a demand, a transition, the presence of a disliked classmate). In other words, this strategy is especially dependent on a good functional behavioral assessment.

Supporting Evidence

Cooper, Heron, & Heward (1987)
Kern (2005)

EMERGENCY INTERVENTION PLAN

Strategy: Emergency intervention plan

Description of strategy: This strategy is included only for those very rare circumstances in which a child is known to have a history of behavior that is so violent that it presents real danger to the child or to the child's peers. The strategy consists of clear plans for ensuring the safety of all children and adults and for calming the situation to the point that the classroom routine can resume.

An emergency intervention plan is outside the scope of the PTR-YC approach, and it should not be considered to be part of a behavior change effort. In the rare situations in which dramatically out-of-control behavior might be anticipated, however, it is important for the team to be fully prepared. The preparation should involve plans for ensuring safety and deescalating the behavior.

We refer teams to "Preventing the Use of Restraint and Seclusion with Young Children," a brief produced by the Technical Assistance Center on Social Emotional Intervention (http://www.challengingbehavior.org). It provides further information about positive strategies for addressing explosive behavior and avoiding the use of restraint and seclusion.

Index

Page numbers followed by *f* indicate figures; those followed by *t* indicate tables.

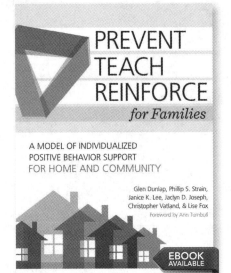

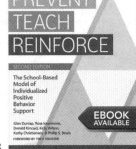